Islam Beyond Borders

Assuming a central place in Muslim life, the Qur'an speaks of one community of the faith, the *umma*. This unity of the faithful is recognised as the default aspiration of the believer, and in the modern era, intellectuals and political leaders have often vied both to define and to lead it.

Based on case studies of actors such as Saudi Arabia, Iran, and ISIS, James Piscatori and Amin Saikal consider how some appeals to pan-Islam prove useful, yet other attempts at cross-border institutionalisation including the Sunni Caliphate or the modern Shi'i-inspired Islamic Revolution, founder on political self-interest and sectarian affiliations. Accompanied by a range of scriptural references to examine different interpretations of the *umma*, Piscatori and Saikal explore why, despite it meaning such widely different things, and its failure to be realised as a concrete project, neither the *umma*'s popular symbolic appeal nor its influence on a politics of identity has diminished.

JAMES PISCATORI is Professor and Deputy Director of the Centre for Arab and Islamic Studies at the Australian National University. A recipient of research grants, including those awarded by the Ford Foundation, British Academy, and the Economic and Social Research Council (UK), he is a member of the Society of Fellows at The Johns Hopkins University. He is the author of *Islam in a World of Nation-States* (1986) and co-author of *Muslim Politics* (2004) with Dale F. Eickelman.

AMIN SAIKAL is Distinguished Professor and Director of the Centre for Arab and Islamic Studies at the Australian National University. A recipient of the Order of Australia (AM) and elected Fellow of the Academy of Social Sciences in Australia (FASSA), he is the author of *Zone of Crisis: Afghanistan, Pakistan, Iran and Iraq* (2014), *Iran at the Crossroads* (2016), and *Iran Rising: the Survival and Future of the Islamic Republic* (2019).

Islam Beyond Borders

The *Umma* in World Politics

JAMES PISCATORI
Australian National University, Canberra

AMIN SAIKAL
Australian National University, Canberra

CAMBRIDGE
UNIVERSITY PRESS

CAMBRIDGE
UNIVERSITY PRESS

University Printing House, Cambridge CB2 8BS, United Kingdom

One Liberty Plaza, 20th Floor, New York, NY 10006, USA

477 Williamstown Road, Port Melbourne, VIC 3207, Australia

314–321, 3rd Floor, Plot 3, Splendor Forum, Jasola District Centre,
New Delhi – 110025, India

79 Anson Road, #06–04/06, Singapore 079906

Cambridge University Press is part of the University of Cambridge.

It furthers the University's mission by disseminating knowledge in the pursuit of
education, learning, and research at the highest international levels of excellence.

www.cambridge.org
Information on this title: www.cambridge.org/9781108481250
DOI: 10.1017/9781108666589

First published 2019

Printed in the United Kingdom by TJ International Ltd, Padstow Cornwall

A catalogue record for this publication is available from the British Library.

Library of Congress Cataloging-in-Publication Data
Names: Piscatori, James P., author. | Saikal, Amin, 1950- author.
Title: Islam beyond borders : the umma in world politics / James Piscatori, Amin Saikal.
Description: Cambridge, United Kingdom : Cambridge University Press, 2019. | Includes
   bibliographical references and index.
Identifiers: LCCN 2019015907 | ISBN 9781108481250 (hardback : alk. paper) |
   ISBN 9781108740555 (pbk. : alk. paper)
Subjects: LCSH: Ummah (Islam) | Islam and politics. | IS (Organization)
Classification: LCC BP163 .P497 2019 | DDC 320.55/7–dc23
LC record available at https://lccn.loc.gov/2019015907

ISBN 978-1-108-48125-0 Hardback
ISBN 978-1-108-74055-5 Paperback

Contents

Preface

The prospect of a united Muslim world has long inspired both dreams and fears. Many Muslims regard the pan-Islamic community, the *umma*, as the embodiment of the spiritual kinship of the faith, but it has also often been assumed to be inherently antagonistic to adherents of other faiths. Questions over relations with the Other are mirrored by debates over what constitutes the acceptable contours of Islamic doctrine itself. Indeed, the *umma* has had variant and contested meanings over time, and divergent perspectives on its inclusiveness or exclusiveness and whether it must have concrete or institutional form have become acute. The rise of jihadist movements has especially brought these related issues to the fore, with the targeting of external and internal 'enemies' presented as part of a purifying and defensive mission to rescue the *umma* from its current degradation. The anthem of the Islamic State of Iraq and Syria (ISIS), 'My *Umma*, Dawn Has Appeared', extols Muslims to give up this life in order to revive the *umma* and assure victory for Islam. The idea of the *umma*, so central and yet so elusive, has taken on a talismanic quality.

It is not surprising, therefore, that, when Muslims are asked about self-identification, their rapport with fellow Muslims across the world ranks high. The sense of belonging to a wider community is often tied to issues that appear to confirm Muslim vulnerabilities, even victimisation, and evocative terms such as 'Jerusalem', 'Srebrenica', or 'Rohingyas' become signifiers of an embattled *umma*. While such sentiments are widespread and forms of solidarity and transnational linkages have evolved, Islamic unity has seemed impossible, particularly as Muslim elites have accommodated themselves to the realities of the world order. The territorial nation-state has been not only accepted by default, but also validated through the intermixture of nationalist and Islamic symbolism – in effect, an Islamo-nationalism.

The penetration of the Westphalian model is even deeper, with Muslim states competing with each other for leadership of the *umma*, to which they all theoretically belong as equal members. Manipulation of this paramount, socially resonant concept has been markedly useful for a kind of one-upmanship in Muslim politics today. Such is the persuasive instrumentality of the *umma* that even non-state actors – Islamist and jihadist groups, for instance – seek to appropriate the idea to advance their claims to the moral and political guardianship of Muslims. But these attempts also have built-in limitations. Sectarian differences, political heavy-handedness, and failures to live up to expectations may undermine the pursuit of legitimisation.

The purpose of this book is to explore the dynamics by which the concept of the *umma* affects, and is affected by, Muslim politics. The contestation over what the central symbol means and who controls it lies at the heart of the matter. Our aim is not to provide universal coverage, but through selected cases – Saudi Arabia, Iran, and ISIS – to illuminate the ways in which a contested but core concept is shaped, 'owned', and at times repudiated by political actors. While elite pathways are thus privileged in this study, the competitive claims to vanguard status in the *umma* and ideological positioning they represent would not have been possible without underlying sentiments of common belonging and, to a degree, shared normative understandings.

Throughout this volume, 'Muslim world' is deployed as a shorthand description for Muslims across the world, in majority and minority situations. We recognise the manifold diversity among them, and there is no intention to suggest by the term anything more than the expansive demographic distribution of Muslims beyond one locality. As will be clear in this volume, we recognise that the 'Muslim world' displays neither uniformity of action nor unity of purpose.

A modified transliteration scheme has been adopted for Arabic words: the *'ayn* is represented, but the *ta marbuta* is not transliterated, except when followed by a vowel when it becomes *t*. For Persian words, the standard Iranian version is used. Proper names in common usage, such as Ruhollah Khomeini and Saddam Hussein are rendered as they have appeared in English-language media.

We use 'Salafi' to refer to a strict theological interpretation of Sunni Islam and to its proponents, who advocate a return to what is believed to be 'true' Islam. 'Salafist', where it appears, refers to an ideological-political orientation and to its proponents, such as ISIS.

We are grateful to several individuals and institutions. Our editor at Cambridge University Press, Maria Marsh, has been supportive and cooperative from the start. Catherine Waldby, Director of the Research School of Social Sciences at the Australian National University (ANU), generously provided funds that enabled research trips to Iran and Saudi Arabia. Our colleague Stephanie Wright provided valuable editing assistance with a couple of chapters, Andrew Feng proved instrumental as a research assistant, and Anita Mack enriched us with her research skills. We are, above all, very thankful to Elisabeth Yarbakhsh for having read the final version of the manuscript with admirable editing precision and care. We are also indebted to the Australian National University where we both are employed. Throughout this project and others, Mary-Lou Hickey has provided both consistent encouragement and unfailing good cheer.

James Piscatori and Amin Saikal
Canberra, November 2018

1 | Introduction

We are living in a period when globalisation is criticised from various quarters for its social and economic imbalances, cultural imperialism, and political distortions.[1] The interconnections among Muslims across the world are often presented as a kind of sub-globalisation that has equally come under attack for its divisiveness and negative impacts. Often in the West the prospect of a united Muslim world, or at least pan-Islamic solidarity, has been exaggerated and viewed as threatening; among Muslims, its political utility in enhancing state or regime interests has been enticing. Yet, for a majority of Muslims worldwide, the sense of communal affiliation is pre-eminently spiritual – a kind of fraternity of the faith.

At issue is one of the central concepts of Islam, the *umma*, which this volume seeks to explore from several perspectives. The concept has Qur'anic roots with variant interpretations. The bedrock tenet of belief, *tawhid* (oneness), endorses the ultimate goal of 'one community' of the faith (*umma wahida*). Whether this scripturally endorsed community is a statement of fact or aspiration has troubled Islamic thought for centuries. Some perceive of the *umma* in non-territorial terms; others see it as in competition with the nation-state or other parochial forms of community. Many millions of Muslims who are living as minorities in predominantly non-Muslim societies routinely affirm their connections with a wider and common religious enterprise but are often suspected of disloyalty to it. A cosmopolitan sense of identity has at times taken the form of an explicit ideology – pan-Islamism – which itself has often been viewed in the West as hostile and aggressive. In short, the idea of the *umma* has been idealised and is frequently invoked, but its precise meaning has remained vague. Nor should it be confused with the convenient and now often used shorthand, 'Muslim world', which, as Cemil Aydin insightfully shows, is a contrivance of late nineteenth-century 'imperial globalization and its concomitant ordering of humanity by race'.[2]

While the term '*umma*' is thus of universal appeal today, it has been invested with both political and sectarian understandings. The Caliphate (*khilafa*) in Sunni circles has become virtually synonymous with the *umma* and, in the non-Muslim world, with pan-Islam. Medieval thinkers such as Taqi al-Din Ahmad ibn Taymiyya argued that leadership was an essential ingredient for the unity of the community. It is not surprising, therefore, that the Caliphate's abolition in 1924 inspired extensive introspection among Muslims and speculation among Orientalists, as to what the future held for Islam. While T. W. Arnold argued that it was a temporal institution, lacking a 'pre-vision', bound by history, and subject to evolution,[3] H. A. R. Gibb held out hope for a 'spiritual Caliphate' embodying the 'religious conscience of the people as a whole'.[4] Muslim thinkers in a succession of international meetings and in various publications debated not only the doctrinal justifications of the Caliphate but also who should occupy the position of Caliph.

While the Shi'a also link leadership to the preservation of the *umma*, they invest authority in the theologically distinctive Imamate. The inerrant Imams are morally exemplary and serve as the religious and symbolic pole around which communal order ought to be organised. The centuries-long absence of the Imams did not deprive *de facto* dynastic rulers in Iran of appropriating a proximate form of legitimacy, especially when affirming broader relevance for Muslims elsewhere. The clerical leadership that took power following the 1978/79 revolution has taken extra-territorial ambitions to a higher level, committing itself to 'export' an ideology that is meant to be inherently cosmopolitan but is Shi'i forged and largely self-limiting.

Complex Muslim Geography

Fragmentation

Although the notion of the *umma* has nearly universal appeal, pan-Islamic, trans-sectarian unity is patently elusive. Following Qur'anic disapproval (6:159), Sunnis and Shi'a alike have decried those who 'divide their religion and break into sects' (*faraqu dinahum wa-kanu shi'an*). In the latter part of the twentieth century, the Egyptian Shaykh Muhammad al-Ghazali, went so far as to lament a lacerated and immobile *umma*, 'half dead or frozen'.[5] There are today multiple lines of division among Muslims, seen mainly, but not only, in nation-state terms. There are also mobile communities that escape easy categorisation, now especially seen in Muslim minorities of the West, who render a strict divide between an Islamic 'here' and a non-Islamic 'there' nonsensical. Muslim transnational networks are well-financed organised additions to the scene, but they could not exist without underlying – and variably defining – strata of affiliation and support, however unformulated and inarticulate they may at times be.[6] Moreover, there is also a more sharply delineated sense of inclusion and exclusion among Muslims themselves – one that aspires to redraw the internal borders of Islam on sectarian, doctrinal, or national-territorial lines: Sunni–Shi'a; Salafi–Sufi; Wahhabi–Shi'a; and Saudi–Iranian–Turkish rivalries are all firmly entrenched, undermining ambitions to Islamic unity and belying a simple dichotomous presumption of a monolithic Islamic–Western antagonism.

The idea of a Muslim international organisation, in lieu of real unity, has been around since at least the Turkish abolition of the Caliphate in 1924. The Caliphate's history over the centuries had been chequered, it represented political theory in its Sunni orthodox form, and even for Sunnis it was very rarely the undisputed heart of Muslim societies. Nevertheless, it acquired for the majority of Muslims a central symbolic significance,[7] and emotional attachment occurred even in areas distant from the Middle East. The Muslims of South and Southeast Asia, in particular, became vocal defenders of the institution, perhaps finding in it the means to connect their perceived 'periphery' with the 'centre'.

Yet when it was abolished, many assumed that Islam's demographic and geographical strength could be harnessed in some form of common enterprise. In the event, this very same strength produced failure, with the diverse viewpoints and experiences of Muslims, and competing dynastic claims to the Caliphate, rendering impossible any agreement on what should be done. Muhammad Rashid Rida called for the restoration of a traditional Caliphate, whereas 'Ali 'Abd al-Raziq argued that it was a political institution that was not integral to the faith. 'Abd al-Razzaq al-Sanhuri advocated a Caliphate that would be subject to periodic election at the *hajj* pilgrimage, with the Caliph presiding over a loose grouping of Oriental nations akin to, and in association with, the League of Nations – a general argument that has been endorsed as a 'confederation' of Muslim countries in a variety of circles.[8] The Organisation of Islamic Cooperation (OIC) is the current manifestation of this inter-state project, but, like similar organisations, it is based above all on preservation of the territorial sovereignty of its members and, as we shall see, constrained by the competition of states to be its – and, by extension, the *umma*'s – leading light.

Although we have witnessed the creation of a supposed 'Islamic state' in Iraq and Syria around a reconstituted Caliphate, unity has not followed. Indeed, Muslims, including even al-Qa'ida, have argued against the so-called Islamic State of Iraq and Syria (ISIS), on the grounds that a Caliphate cannot be imposed but must result from general consensus; it must occur gradually over time and not by instant proclamation; and it must be for the good of the entire community and not work to the advantage of a particular group. Simply put, the reality of the current Muslim world is of structural fragmentation, and the very idea of the *umma* appears chimerical.

Interconnections

Yet Muslims themselves see it as a definable, perhaps even palpable, presence. It clearly forms an integral part of rhetorical claims to legitimacy, invoked by states, regimes, sub-state actors, religious officials, individual preachers, and missionaries, but the movements across borders themselves have also had reinforcing effects on the sense of interconnectedness. The *hajj* is the great convocation of Muslims, indistinguishable in principle by national or sectarian identity; early and medieval Islamic history is replete with examples of networks of traders who significantly helped to advance the word of Islam; travelling elites such as students, scholars, judges, and political officials routinely sought knowledge (*rihla*) far from their home societies or went on minor pilgrimages (*ziyarat*); Sufi orders rapidly spread from their spiritual centres and created expansive 'brotherhoods'; and the various Muslim empires constituted multi-ethnic, far-flung political organisations.

Pilgrimage, educational travel, trading networks, and mystical brotherhoods persist today, and are complemented by globalised communications, transnational Islamist movements, such as the Muslim Brotherhood or Hizb al-Tahrir al-Islami (the Islamic Liberation Party), and near-constant and large-scale migration.[9] Some argue that these patterns are so pronounced that a kind of spatial detachment or deracination has occurred – or, at least, that concepts of space and distance have been redefined. Through the Internet, and through broadcast and social media, images of political and religious authority, as well as community, are daily projected into domestic space; and 'cyber-Islam' takes Muslims into some ethereal neighbourhood that understates the physical, and even perhaps to some extent the cultural, distances. To the extent that these developments are in fact occurring, optimists celebrate them as 'virtual Islam', whereas pessimists fear a 'de-culturation' that paves the way for reactionary radicalism.

The pan-Islamic dimension is an important part of the logic of today's evolving jurisprudence, since, it is argued, minority Muslims, no matter where they reside, are still members of the larger *umma* and feel obligations as its members. This permanent presence of Muslims outside majority Muslim countries runs counter to the expectation that believers should live in the *dar al-Islam* (abode of Islam), but modern guidance on issues such as participation in elections, contracting home mortgages, and military service has been felt to be necessary. This incrementally articulated 'jurisprudence of the minorities' (*fiqh al-aqalliyat*) makes clear that minority Muslims, regardless of their transnational religious bonds, are expected to obey the laws of the land in which they reside, unless, naturally, those contravene God's universal law. Although some view this pragmatic development as dividing the *umma* between a minority and majority Islam, its proponents see it as reconnecting disparate communities under the common moral umbrella of 'Islamic law'.

Even attempts at doctrinal ecumenism have occurred. Scholars, especially since the twentieth century, have attempted a kind of rapprochement between different doctrinal and legal pathways – a *taqrib* or 'bringing closer'. Advocates of this approach argue for a dialogue across the traditions based on a fundamental premise: all share the common roots of the faith (*usul*) but constitute different 'branches' (*furu'*). In eighteenth-century Persia, Nader Shah had tried to induce the Ottoman Sultan to recognise Twelver Shi'ism, representing the majority of Shi'a, as a valid school of law. Greater effect was attained when post-colonial state formation and modernisation in the Middle East facilitated cross-border travel and education and encouraged the new loyalty of nationalism over traditional sectarianism. Shi'i luminaries such as Muhammad Husayn Kashif al-Ghita' (1877–1954) in Iraq and 'Abd al-Husayn Sharaf al-Din al-Musawi (1872–1957) in Lebanon urged Muslims to rise above their divisions and unite in a common enterprise.[10] In Egypt, the pre-eminent Egyptian Sunni religious leader, Mahmud Shaltut (1893–1963), issued a *fatwa* (religious opinion) in 1959 authorising Shi'i instruction at al-Azhar – considered the premier Sunni educational institution in the world – for the first time in nine hundred years. The Society for Reconciliation (Jama'at al-Taqrib), unusually initiated by an Iranian but with broad support in Sunni intellectual circles, had paved the way in Egypt from the late 1940s, and today Yusuf al-Qaradawi, associated with the Egyptian Muslim Brotherhood, has proposed 'Principles for Sunni– Shi'i Dialogue'.

In Iran in 1990, the newly installed Supreme Leader, 'Ali Khamenei, created the Society for Reconciliation of the Islamic Schools (Majma' al-Taqrib Bayna al-Madhahib al-Islamiyya), which convenes international conferences to this end and publishes the journal *Risalat al-Taqrib* (Message of Reconciliation). Perhaps the most ambitious attempt has been the 'Amman Message'. King 'Abdullah of Jordan convened an international conference in July 2005 in order to counter the rise of intolerant versions of Islam. It delineated eight doctrinal groups as acceptable: four Sunni and two Shi'i schools of law, the Ibadi school based mainly in Oman, and the Zahiri school that privileges textual authority over other legal sources. According to this manifesto, signed by 552 religious scholars and intellectuals from eighty-four countries, no one was entitled to delegitimise the others as non-Muslim.

The Moroccan regime has also launched religious reformist initiatives that espouse jurisprudential reconciliation. The religious establishment argues that, while differences have been exploited for personal and political reasons and undermined the unity of the *umma*, difference as to the 'sub-details and details' (*al-umur al-far'iyya wa-al-tafsiliyya*) is 'normal'.[11] The moderate form of Islam that is encouraged, *al-wasatiyya*, is a conflation of the locally predominant Sunni Maliki school, Sunni Sufi movements, and Sunni Ash'arite theology, and is proselytised via the Mohammed VI Institute for the Training of Imams, Morchidins, and Morchidates.[12] Building on the credentials of the King (b. 1963, r. 1999–) as 'Commander of the Faithful' (*amir al-mu'minin*), it was established in 2015 ostensibly to combat extremist trends and, implicitly, as a counter to Sunni Wahhabism. It principally trains religious officials from throughout Africa and, in the process, has become a valuable instrument of Morocco's continental diplomacy.[13] But, in spite of the reformist and pluralist agenda, its wider, pan-Islamic attractiveness is limited, given the embedded Sunni orientations of its ideological approach.

The modern geography of Islam is thus complex. A new communal idea that emerged out of seventh-century Arabian social structures – an 'Arab commonwealth', in Marshall Hodgson's phrase[14] – defined membership by common religious affiliation. Dynastic and imperial expansion took the faith into further reaches of the globe, and in the late medieval period – roughly from 1250 until 1500 – political boundaries among Muslims were largely insignificant. The crystallisation of the Ottoman, Safavid, and Mughal empires from the sixteenth century solidified what might be called the internal frontiers of Islam, and the Western imperial assault and resultant post-colonial struggles only intensified the divisions. But doctrinal and sectarian disputes have complicated the search for unity as well. The permeability of borders, the mobility of individuals, groups, and social movements, and new emphases on ethnicity, sect, and faith have all helped to define and reorient Muslim communalism today.

Two Registers

Muslim communalism operates on two interlinked levels: identity and instrumentality. With regard to *identity*, competing ideas and self-ascribed labels, such as Wahhabi, Salafi, or Shi'a, which have historically existed across and within Muslim societies, are being reified anew today and complicate the pan-Islamic project. But, simultaneously, the sense of belonging to a greater enterprise has helped to foster an alternative, if aspirational, form of affiliation. The rhetorical trope is family-centred: Muslims constitute one 'brotherhood'; they are all 'children' or 'grandchildren' of the *umma*; at times, even, to convey the sense of despair at disunity, they are 'orphans of the *umma*'.

But identity is rarely, if ever, homogeneous and is shaped by several attachments. The perpetrators of the London underground bombing in 2005 and the murderer of a British soldier on a London street in 2013, referred explicitly to British action against Muslim brothers in Iraq and Afghanistan as motivating factors, and the attackers in Paris in November 2015 purportedly shouted, 'c'est pour la Syrie' (this is for Syria). Events perceived to be anti-Islamic, whether external aggressiveness or Islamophobic attacks, often stimulate identification with co-religionists.[15] Yet, at the same time as Islamic solidarity can be

galvanising, Muslims everywhere must contend with competing loyalties – national, ethnic, and local. When specifically asked in surveys,
most Muslims affirm *umma*-loyalty over national or ethnic ties,[16] but
the commingling of *umma* and other bonds is common and accepted as
a fact of life.[17]

With regard to *instrumentality*, appeals to the *umma* are also often
used to validate a regime's or movement's general *bona fides* or bolster
support for a particular policy. The Saudi, Pakistani, Iranian, and
Malaysian governments and groups like al-Qaʻida and ISIS, among
others, invoke their declarative defence of the *umma* as self-validating.
In some quarters there is a calculated effort to project – through
publications, think-tank work, official speeches, sponsored conferences, and student exchanges – a sense of dedication to a larger
mission, and so to enhance legitimacy.

In both the identity and instrumental aspects, while it is understood
that Muslims across the globe may be bound together, the manifest-
ations of the *umma* are not merely 'virtual', as has been argued, or
restricted to an abstract ether. Olivier Roy's work on global Islam is
characteristically insightful, but the 'de-territorialisation' that he identifies as integral to the 'new *ummah*' appears overstated.[18] If more than
narrowly territorial, the *umma* is not disconnected from territory. The
worldwide concern about ISIS was precisely centred on its capture of
territory, and ISIS itself acknowledged the imperative for control over
Islamic lands (*dar al-Islam*) to which Muslims must migrate (*hijra*).
While the idea of the *umma* has gained some social weight, it is not
disconnected from the political realities of states and other communities: it is a modern 'personality', but also a tool; an idealised end, but
also a manipulable means.

Focus of the Volume

The central focus of this book is to elucidate the degree to which the
affective symbol of the *umma* shapes Muslim identities today and
inspires social and political action. It explores the 'pull' of the *umma*
on Muslims, noting, for instance, the publicly expressed concern for
fellow Muslims who are thought to be victimised or endangered. The
latent sense of attachment to a great enterprise of the faith is omnipres-
ent, but, like other affiliations, seems more pronounced when facing
opposition. A kind of societal pan-Islam – grassroots empathy with

Muslims worldwide – has undergirded identification with the Palestinians or Rohingyas, for example. Even when this popular sentiment is expressed, however, Muslim states may find economic and political interests more important than support for Muslim victims, as the inaction of Saudi Arabia, Iran, Pakistan, Turkey, Malaysia, and Indonesia, among others, suggests when it comes to China's suppression of its Muslim Uighur population.[19] In practice, the *umma* is understood differently, with its nature and meaning subject to theological (particularly sectarian) and political contestation. The identity that the *umma* provides must thus be contextualised and seen as open to widely divergent interpretations and self-interested political concerns.

This book also investigates the effects of the 'push' of the *umma* on Muslims. It demonstrates that states, such as Iran and Saudi Arabia, seek to foster a sense of the *umma* and its importance through various means. Through institutions, conferences, publications, and rhetoric, they affect to work for Islamic solidarity while hoping to enhance their presumption to worldwide Islamic leadership. So, too, collective non-state actors, such as ISIS, attempt to harness the symbolic power of the *umma* in order to pressure individuals and groups into taking action. Manipulating the idea of the *umma* forms part of the pursuit of authentication and influence in today's Muslim world – and is a particularly potent instrument to address any legitimacy deficit.

While we do not presume to offer a comprehensive treatment of dogma, issue areas, or regional coverage, our focus on the larger debates of Sunni and Shiʻi scholars as well as the activities of two states and a jihadist movement provides a pathway into making sense of a critical but understudied phenomenon. This volume, therefore, takes appeals to Islamic solidarity and brotherhood seriously – more so than has generally been done in academic and policy analyses – but it also recognises the countervailing forces of Islamic fragmentation, such as sectarianism, and alternative identities.

The Volume's Structure

Following this Introduction, Chapter 2 discusses the contested meanings of the *umma*, specifically in Sunni thought. It reviews the ways the concept is understood as having a classical reference point in the era of the Prophet and his immediate successors, and follows its development through medieval and modern scholars. A consistent theme has been that the community of the faith must be tied to proper leadership, but the declining and then dismissed Caliphate in the second decade of the twentieth century stirred intellectual and political agitation. Today calls for unity, or at least solidarity, contend with debates over how extensive the *umma* is and how much difference is allowable within it. The aspiration to both comprehensiveness and internal tolerance is commonly reaffirmed; yet challenged by normative ambivalence within the concept itself.

Chapter 3 provides a complementary discussion of the *umma* in Shiʻi thought and practice. While religious authority is central, as with the Sunni conception, the Shiʻi conceptualisation of the Imams elevates genealogical descent and theological erudition to essential ingredients of leadership. It follows that their absence from this world created a dilemma with religious and political significance: who would guide the community until the return of the redeeming Imam Mahdi (Guided One)? From the medieval centuries to the modern period, a rough consensus emerged that the clerical class would fill the void of religious guidance. The minority view that they should also have a political role found its full articulation, in the last quarter of the twentieth century, in Ayatullah Ruhollah Khomeini's theory of clerical rule and its institutionalisation in the Islamic Republic. The Khomeinist-revolutionary Iranian appeal to lead the universal *umma* has, however, been undermined by an assertive sectarian interpretation and geopolitical rivalries.

Much the same can be said of Saudi Arabia, as Chapter 4 details. The Saudi state's evolution is tied to a Sunni-Wahhabist ideology underpinning the interconnected political and religious establishments. Control of the Holy Places of Mecca and Medina and of the annual pilgrimage – one of the core pillars of the faith – have inflated the regime's claim to speak for universal Islam, but the hostility of the religious authorities to the Shiʻa and 'unbelievers' has diminished its credibility to do so. The institutions that have been developed and supported ostensibly to encourage *umma*-wide solidarity have seemed more adept at advancing Saudi interests than pan-Islamic ones. Islamic sentiment from below, stimulated, for example, by the Palestinian, Afghan, Iraqi, and Syrian conflicts, has influenced Saudi policy positions. Yet, both the promotion of Wahhabi ideas – although not univocal or unchanging – and the competition with Iran, and even Sunni Egypt and Turkey, have constrained the realisation of the Kingdom's sense of *umma* entitlement.

It is an ironic development of the contemporary world that the Saudi-Wahhabi legacy has indeed had a powerful transnational effect, but one which some would say is antithetical to Saudi state interests: the creation of ISIS. As discussed in Chapter 5, its literalist and expressly politicised interpretations of doctrine have led it to espouse exclusionary and aggressive notions of the *umma*. The community of the faith becomes identifiable with a revived Caliphate, based on territorial dimensions and purist standards of community membership. The brutality against the Shi'a and others, subverts its avowed expansionist aim, as many within the Muslim world as well as non-Muslim powers have sought to destroy it. But military defeat and territorial retrenchment are unlikely to exorcise the allure, in receptive quarters, of a purportedly 'authentic' but highly romanticised *umma*.

Drawing on the discussion of prior chapters, the Conclusion highlights the simultaneity of forces – the transnational and local, the pan-Islamic and national – in keeping with much of the theoretical literature on transnationalism and globalisation. It affirms that pan-Islam has an enduring appeal that has resonance at the popular level and thereby serves as an influence on Muslim identities. We acknowledge the extensive work that has been done to document an intermediate realm of Muslim solidarity[20] – neither an institutionalised *umma* nor merely a nationalised Islam – but focus on the effects these transborder self-understandings and affective attachments can have. They prompt governments and Islamist groups to fulfil what is deemed to be an Islamic mission. Political actors instrumentalise the pan-Islamic sentiment as well, serving as self-appointed patrons of the *umma* and hoping thereby for legitimacy, especially at home, and the extension of influence abroad. These factors reveal a built-in territorial dimension that, without denying the emergence of cosmopolitan discourses and networks, suggests that, to find the *umma* today, we need to take into account rooted contestations.

Notes

1 Lui Hebron and John F. Stack, Jr. present an acute analysis of the critiques of globalisation: *Globalization: Debunking the Myths*, 3rd edn. (London: Rowman & Littlefield, 2017), especially pp. 6–15, 125–35.
2 Cemil Aydin, *The Idea of the Muslim World: A Global Intellectual History* (Cambridge, MA: Harvard University Press, 2017), p. 3. As an encompassing and resonant descriptor in common parlance, the term

'Muslim world' will be periodically used in this volume, but it is not meant to be synonymous with the *umma*.

3 Thomas W. Arnold, *The Caliphate* (Oxford: Clarendon Press, 1924), p. 10.

4 H. A. R. Gibb, *Modern Trends in Islam* (University of Chicago Press, 1947), pp. 113–14.

5 Muhammad al-Ghazali, *Qadha'if al-haq* [Bombshells of Truth], 2nd edn. (Damascus: Dar al-Qalam, 1418 A.H./1997), p. 5.

6 For an insightful study that demonstrates how transnational Shi'i clerical networks are shaped and sustained by religious, educational, and family affiliations, see Elvire Corboz, *Guardians of Shi'ism: Sacred Authority and Transnational Family Networks* (Edinburgh University Press, 2015).

7 A 2007 poll of Moroccans, Egyptians, Pakistanis, and Indonesians showed that 65.2 per cent agreed – 'strongly and somewhat' – with what was identified as al-Qa'ida's goal 'to unify all Islamic countries into a single Islamic state or Caliphate'. Seventy-four per cent personally agreed with this goal in Pakistan, 71 per cent in Morocco, 67 per cent in Egypt, and 49 per cent in Indonesia. Steven Kull, 'Muslim Public Opinion on US Policy, Attacks on Civilians and al Qaeda' (report, WorldPublicOpinion. org, University of Maryland, College Park, 24 April 2007), pp. 15–16.

8 One strand of the Muslim Brotherhood has argued this – for example, Muhammad Abu Zahra and Muhammad 'Abdullah al-'Arabi wrote, respectively, of a 'league' and 'confederation' of Muslim countries in the Brotherhood publication *al-Muslimun* in 1953. In 2011, the Kuwaiti Muslim Brother Tariq Suwaydan endorsed the idea of an 'Islamic Confederation'. Noha Mellor, *Voice of the Muslim Brotherhood: Da'wa, Discourse, and Political Communication* (Abingdon: Routledge, 2018), pp. 202–3, 205–6, 275. The British Muslim leader Inayat Bunglawala aspired to a European Union-style confederation of 'democratic' Muslim states. Inayat Bunglawala, 'Bringing Back the Caliphate', *The Guardian*, 16 July 2007, www.theguardian.com/commentisfree/2007/jul/16/bring ingbackthecaliphate?CMP=Share_iOSApp_Other, accessed 3 November 2018.

9 Peter Mandaville introduces a very useful typology of the various forms of Muslim transnationalism: Muslim people flows; globalising Muslim social and political movements; the global Muslim public sphere; and discourse and practice of *ummah*-oriented solidarity: 'Muslim Transnational Identity and State Responses in Europe and the UK after 9/11: Political Community, Ideology and Authority', *Journal of Ethnic and Migration Studies* 35, 3 (March 1990): 491–506.

10 For a learned study of Shi'i sectarian and ecumenical trends in the twentieth century, see Elisheva Machlis, *Shi'i Sectarianism in the Middle*

East: Modernisation and the Quest for Islamic Universalism (London: I. B. Tauris, 2014), on al-Ghita': pp. 47–8, 165–6, 179–82, 187–9; on al-Musawi: pp. 61–4, 69–71, 74–6, 142–3.

11 'Abd al-Qadir al-Kittani, 'al-Ikhtilaf al-fuqaha' fi ijtihadathum wa turuq al-astifada minhu' [The Difference among the Jurists on Their Interpretations and Ways to Benefit from It], lesson 4, al-Durus al-Hasaniyya [The Hasanid Lessons], Kingdom of Morocco, Wizarat al-Awqaf wa-al-Shu'un al-Islamiyya [Ministry of Endowments and Islamic Affairs], 14 Ramadan 1439 A.H./30 May 2018, www.habous .gov.ma/dourouss/-القادر-عبد-الحسنية-الدروس-1527/الحسنية-الدروس-2018/11140 منه-الاستفادة-وطرق-اجتهاداتهم-في-الفقهاء-اختلاف-الكتاني.html, accessed 4 November 2018.

12 'Morchidins' are male Islamic preachers charged with low-level religious training; 'morchidates' are the female equivalents.

13 Cédric Baylocq and Aziz Hlaoua, 'Diffuser un "Islam du juste milieu"?' [Spread of 'a Middle-Ground Islam'?] , *Afrique contemporaine* 257 (2016): 113–28. For other Moroccan religious initiatives, see Mohammed Masbah, 'The Limits of Morocco's Attempt to Comprehensively Counter Violent Extremism' (briefing paper *Middle East Brief* 118, Crown Center for Middle East Studies, Brandeis University, Waltham, Massachusetts, May 2018).

14 Marshall G. S. Hodgson, *The Venture of Islam*, vol. 1, *The Classical Age of Islam* (University of Chicago Press, 1974), p. 187.

15 In response to the attacks of 11 September 2001, many young Muslims identified more with the faith than they had previously. In the words of a young Bangladeshi teacher in Britain: 'you have that link, you have that link with that person who, wherever they are in the world because they follow your faith, they are part of your faith'. Orla Lynch, 'British Muslim Youth: Radicalisation, Terrorism and the Construction of the "Other"', *Critical Studies on Terrorism* 6, 2 (2013): 241–61 (p. 255). In addition, a study of young second-generation Muslims in five cities of Belgium, Netherlands, and Sweden showed that discrimination led to linking personal identity with a 'contested collective identity'. Fenella Fleischmann, Karen Phalet, and Olivier Klein, 'Religious Identification and Politicization in the Face of Discrimination', *British Journal of Social Psychology* 50, 4 (2011): 628–48 (p. 629).

16 A 2005 Pew Foundation poll, for example, showed that 79 per cent of Pakistanis identified as Muslim first, whereas only 7 per cent identified as Pakistani first. For Turkey, it was 43 per cent Muslim first and 29 per cent Turkish first; and for Indonesia, it was 39 per cent Muslim first and 35 per cent Indonesian first. Pew Research Center, 'Support for Terror Wanes Among Muslim Publics/Islamic Extremism: Common Concern

for Muslim and Western Publics' (report, The Pew Global Attitudes Project , Washington, DC, 14 July 2005), p. 21. A 2015 poll by the Merdeka Centre in Malaysia showed that 60 per cent of Malay Muslims identified as Muslim first, while 27 per cent identified as Malaysian first. Teo Cheng Wee, 'More Malays Say They Are Muslim First: Malaysian Poll', *Straits Times,* 12 August 2015, www.straitstimes.com/asia/se-asia/ more-malays-say-they-are-muslim-first-malaysian-poll, accessed 3 November 2018.

17 For example, among British Muslims in 2010–11, 'three-quarters (74%) said their religion is *very important,* 55% their ethnic or racial background, and 55% their national identity'. Kully Kaur-Ballagan, Roger Mortimer, and Glenn Gottfried, 'A Review of Survey Research on Muslims in Britain' (report, Social Research Institute of Ipsos MORI, London, February 2018), p. 37, emphasis added; moreover, this aggregation of surveys says that 95 per cent of British Muslims, in a 2015 opinion poll, said they feel loyal to Britain (p. 36). In 2016, 93 per cent felt they 'belonged' to Britain – 55 per cent 'very strongly' and 38 per cent 'fairly strongly' (p. 34). Even among foreign-born British Muslims, the sense of belonging to Britain, on the one hand, and to the home country, on the other, was roughly the same (48 per cent 'very strongly' for both; 36 per cent and 31 per cent, respectively, 'fairly strongly') (pp. 33–4).

18 Olivier Roy, 'La communauté virtuelle: L'internet et la déterritorialisation de l'islam' [The Virtual Community: The Internet and the Deterritorialisation of Islam], *Réseaux: Communication, Technologie, Société* 18, 99 (2000): 219–37 (pp. 226–31); Olivier Roy, *Globalised Islam: The Search for a New Ummah* (New York: Columbia University Press, 2004).

19 Alexandra Ma, 'Why the Muslim World Isn't Saying Anything about China's Repression and "Cultural Cleansing" of Its Downtrodden Muslim Minority', *Business Insider Australia,* 27 August 2018, www.businessinsider.com.au/why-muslim-countries-arent-criticizing-china-uighur-repression-2018-8?r=US&IR=T, accessed 5 September 2018. Also: Nithin Coca, 'Islamic Leaders Have Nothing to Say about China's Internment Camps for Muslims', *Foreign Policy,* 24 July 2018, https://foreignpolicy.com/2018/07/24/islamic-leaders-have-nothing-to-say-about-chinas-internment-camps-for-muslims/, accessed 18 December 2018.

20 In Peter Mandaville's evocative phrase, 'an intermediate space of affiliation and socio-political mobilisation that exists alongside and in an ambivalent relationship with the nation-state': 'Transnational Muslim Solidarities and Everyday Life', *Nations and Nationalism* 17, 1 (2011): 7–24 (p. 7). Also see his *Transnational Muslim Politics: Reimagining the*

Umma, rev. edn. (Abingdon: Routledge, 2003). To cite but two of many other examples of the important work that has been done on the evolving transnationalism of modern Islam: on transnational media: Dale F. Eickelman and Jon W. Anderson, *New Media in the Muslim World: The Emerging Public Sphere*, 2nd edn. (Bloomington: Indiana University Press, 2003); and, on Muslim migrants: Ousmane Kane, *The Homeland is the Arena: Religion, Transnationalism, and the Integration of Senegalese in America* (Oxford University Press, 2011).

2 | *Sunni Constructions of the* Umma

The abolition of the Caliphate by the Turkish Grand National Assembly in March 1924 was a landmark event in modern Muslim history. Muslims worldwide expressed outrage, colonial offices feared the agitation would destabilise Western rule or political influence, and intellectuals debated whether the institution should be revived in the modern era. The Caliphate became the tangible symbol of pan-Islamic unity, the concrete representation of the *umma*.

The *umma* had long assumed a central place in Muslim life, however. Unity of the faithful has universally been recognised as the default aspiration of the believer, and in the modern era intellectuals and political leaders have vied to define, shape, and even lead it. In some circles, it has taken on talismanic qualities, serving as the 'gold standard' of Islamic achievement. That it means widely different things and has failed to be realised as an institutional project, has diminished neither its appeal nor its influence. In every sense, it is an 'essentially contested concept'.[1]

This chapter outlines the various levels of meaning attached to the *umma* idea among Sunnis. It begins by showing that, even with scriptural reference points, there are ambiguities. In addition to several different usages in the Qur'an, conventions that date to the first Islamic century – the Constitution of Medina and the Caliphate – are thought to be exemplary. But, as we will then see, from the medieval period to the collapse of the Ottoman imperial order theologians and statesmen debated whether institutions flow from or, alternatively, create the *umma*. The chapter argues, finally, that, especially in the modern era, it has consistently been promoted as a political and social community, as well as a doctrinal and spiritual one, with universal relevance. But its universality and unity have proven elusive as debates have swirled over who is a 'believer' and what level of difference within the faith is accepted. In short, the chapter lays out the permutations in Sunni thinking over the centuries and points to later discussions in this volume of why and how the *umma* has persistent political appeal.

Roots of the Concept

The concept is ambiguous lexically as well as semantically. Many scholars trace the roots of the word *umma* to the Arabic word for 'mother' (*umm*),[2] but the lexicographer Edward William Lane said it derived from 'way', 'course', or 'mode' of conduct.[3] Still others suggest it is connected to the Hebrew word for 'tribe' or 'people'.[4] The derivative genealogy aside, modern Arab scholars allow for similarities with other Semitic languages, but insist the word has specific religious meaning in Arabic.[5] To add further ambiguity, the term *umma* intersects with, and in modern interpretations diverges from, the Arabic word for *qawm* or 'people'.[6] The Meccans, who were initially hostile to the Prophet's message, were referred to in the Qur'an as a *qawm* (52:32), but a Muslim could belong to a *qawm*, even of non-believers, with whom he had a treaty (4:92). If these references appear to imply that a *qawm* was somewhat of lower moral worth,[7] an *umma* could be transgressive as well: '*umma*s of jinns and people' (7:38) could be consigned to Hell. Simply in terms of terminology, therefore, both the *umma* and *qawm* seem to have been thought of as cohesive communities arising from the tribal society of seventh-century Arabia.[8]

The presentation of the communal *umma*, however, also took on a religious and trans-tribal character. There are sixty-four Qur'anic references to *umma*,[9] of which the most commonly invoked endorse 'one community' (*ummatan wahidatan*) as the original condition and final objective of mankind (2:213; 21:92). While the community of Muslims acquires normative preferment – it is 'the best community among the people' (3:110: *khayr ummatin ukhrijat li-nasi*) – other scriptural verses suggest the term does not exclusively apply to Muslims. There is Qur'anic justification for believing that every faith group has its own *umma*; each was sent its own Messenger and will be judged with justice (10:47; 16:36). Moses had his own community (7:159), and Ibrahim (Abraham) was himself an *umma* (16:120). The broad textual sense suggests that, although mankind had been one community, it had deviated and so was in need of prophetic correction, the final being that of Muhammad.

Scriptural references make clear that unity is enjoined on all members of the *umma*. The Qur'an commands (3:103), for example, to hold fast to the rope of Allah, 'all of you (*jami'an*), and do not break into factions (*wa la tafarraqu*)', and it enjoins believers 'not to fall into disputes (*la tanaza'u*, 8:46)' or break into 'sects' (*shiya'an*, 6:159). It also disapproves of 'rivalries' (*baghyan*, 42:14) among the believers, and in fact proclaims them 'brothers' (*ikhwatun*, 49:10) or, at times, 'friends' or 'allies' of each other (*awliya'u*, 9:71). Prophetic traditions are also invoked to endorse the collectivising impulse of Islam. The contrast with the pre-Islamic Arabian condition, known as the 'era of ignorance' (*al-jahiliyya*), is clear and is the state to which adherents of tribal loyalty are consigned.[10] An often-cited *hadith* denounces those who advocate, practise, or die in the way of tribalism or kin partisanship (*'asabiyya*); 'they are not of us' (*laysa minnan*).[11] One of the most prominent traditions states that the *umma* is 'like one person's body' (*ka-rajulin wahidin*) and, if one part aches, the whole body aches.[12] Another, presenting the verbal image of the Prophet interlocking his hands, says the relationship of believer to believer is like a reinforced 'structure' or wall (*al-bunyan*).[13]

A comforting *hadith* or saying of the Prophet, as recorded by al-Tirmidhi (824–92 CE), one of the most reputable transmitters of *hadith*, says: 'Allah does not gather (*la yajma'u*) his *umma* or Muhammad's *umma* on error (or misguidance, *dalalatin*)'.[14] A variation renders it as, 'My *umma* will not agree on error'.[15] Like al-Tirmidhi's account, some consider this a weak *hadith*, however, and the second part, which is often ignored, is subject to contention: 'and so if there is disagreement (*ra'aytum al-ikhtilaf*), follow the great majority (*bi'l-sawad al-a'zm*)'. The saying is considered to validate a basic principle of jurisprudence, *ijma'* or consensus, and with the formulation of the legal schools by the medieval period, the *umma* was seen as infallible and a 'socio-religious reality with legal and political import'.[16] But debate has swirled throughout the centuries as to whose consensus and how extensive it must be. Interpretation is complicated by another often-heard saying that seems to validate difference: 'difference of opinion in my *umma* is a mercy (*ikhtilafu ummati rahma*)'.[17] Scholars of *hadith* tend to view this as invalid, but the point it raises, the validation of permissible difference, is fundamental to continuing conversations about communal unity.

If the *umma* is to have solidarity among the believers, what are the implications for non-believers? Debate has unfolded over time as to how extensive the *umma* is – that is, if it is to be broadly encompassing, who among the non-believers is to be included? Toshihiko Izutzu says that 'the establishment of this new concept of religious community caused naturally a great disturbance in the structure of the semantic field of "society"'.[18] In simple terms, it set up a sharp contradistinction: local society now attained what the philosopher Eric Voegelin called a 'transcendental irruption',[19] and the believing community was juxtaposed with the unbelieving one (*kuffar*). But this broad category masks differences: are the unbelievers those who deliberately reject the new revelation, or the people without a revealed religion, the *ummayin* as mentioned in the Qur'an (3:20)?

Like any scripture, the Qur'an has conflicting statements about the non-believers. It is clear, however, that the line of illegitimacy is drawn at the polytheists (*al-mushrikun*), those who breach the fundamental commitment of revelation to monotheism; ascribing divinity to other gods is directly denounced as a 'great sin' (*ithman 'azim*, 4:48). The so-called Sword Verse (9:5) is often invoked as an indication of innate Islamic aggressiveness. It calls for polytheists to be captured or killed 'wherever you find them', but, in an often overlooked second part, allows them to be spared if they repent, pray, and pay *zakat* (an Islamic tithing). The greater ethos of the Qur'an is of self-defence: 'God does not love aggressors' (*al-mu'atadina*, 2:190). If defensive action to protect God's word was not taken when necessary, 'monasteries, churches, synagogues, and mosques' would surely have been destroyed (22:40). But references to fighting against 'oppressors' (*al-zalimina*, 2:193) and 'until there is no more disorder' (*hatta la takuna fitnatun*, 2:193; 8:39) remain vague and variously interpreted.

But the Qu'ran also contains more inclusive passages for others of faith. It accepts, in fact, that a Messenger has been sent to every *umma* with the clear injunction to serve God and avoid evil (16:36). The basic religious message (*al-din*) given to the Prophet Muhammad is the same as that given to Noah, Ibrahim, Moses, and Jesus (42:13), and all the prophets had similarly submitted to God (5:44). God gave the Torah to the Jews and the Gospel to Christians, with their 'guidance and light' (*hudan wa nurun*, 5:44; 5:46), but they must live by God's revelation or become among the iniquitous (*al-fasiquna*, 5:47). Moreover, every *umma* has been given different rites and ceremonies (*mansakan hum nasikuhu*) that should be upheld (22:67).

Ibrahim is presented as a symbol of inclusiveness: the Qur'an says that he was neither a Jew nor a Christian (3:67). He was among those of 'certain faith' (*al-muqinin*) (6:75), an 'upright servant of God' (*hanifan musliman*), suggesting that whoever submits to the one God is a believer and therefore belongs in the *umma*. This appears to be the sense of the affirmation that the religion before God (*al-dina 'inda Allahi*) is *al-islam* or submission, and if there is a problem with other monotheists, it is that they lost or corrupted their original revelation and this fundamental commitment.

A defined interpretation over the centuries has been to endorse forms of monotheistic inclusivism. In his medieval exegesis of the Qur'an, Isma'il ibn Kathir (1301–73) explained that the ascription of *umma* to Ibrahim was because he was *hanif* (true believer) – that is, fully accepting of *tawhid* and rejecting of polytheism (*shirk*). He saw, in the textual explanation that prophets had been sent to every *umma* (16:36), the validation of kinship with those who accepted the perennial message of submission to the one God and unmitigated hostility to those who worshipped any other divinity.[20] The idea of the *umma* applied, therefore, to both believers and scripturalist non-believers, but not to the polytheists whose antithesis was embodied in Abrahamic monotheism.

More recently, the modernist intellectual Muhammad Asad (1900–92) formulated the 'Islamic Commonwealth' as standing above Islamic governance. Inspired by the example of the Companions of the Prophet, but not doomed to follow them blindly, Muslims today must work for the 'righteous community' in line with the Qur'anic avowal that they are the 'best community' (3:110). This means internal unity – 'a brotherhood of people bound together by nothing but their consciousness of a common faith and a common moral outlook'. But it also means justice for non-Muslims: 'a truly Islamic community' must never be 'unjust to the non-Muslims living in its midst'.[21]

A former Mufti of Egypt, 'Ali Juma'a (b. 1952; Mufti 2003–13), seemingly goes further and advances a universal sense of the *umma*: it includes all humanity. He affirms 'equality' (*musawa*) for all people within the *umma* since, according to the Qur'an, Muhammad is the Messenger to 'mankind' (*ayyahu al-nasu*, 7:158) and a mercy 'to the worlds' (*li-al-'alamina*, 21:107). Everyone has one origin as a descendant of Adam, one fate in death, and one 'divine discourse' (*al-khitab al-ilhi*). This ostensible universalism is, however, vitiated by two qualifications inherent in his approach – conceptual and practical. The first distinguishes between two kinds of *umma*: the *umma* of the 'call' (*ummat al-da'wa*) and the *umma* of the 'response' (*ummat al-ijaba*). The former incorporates all humanity since all are called to serve God. The latter refers, however, to Muslims who have accepted the call – a categorisation that is, therefore, tantamount to conventional Muslim views of the faithful community. The second qualification is the concession to lived experience. Juma'a is saddened by 'our reality and problems', but the disappointment has more to do with lack of unity among the Arab states than the unlikelihood of creating a truly cosmopolitan *umma*.[22]

Following Juma'a's lead, the official religious bureaucracy of Egypt, Dar al-Ifta' al-Misriyya, seems also mindful of contextual realities. It is no doubt intent on reassuring the Christian Copts of Muslim Egypt when it argues for an inclusivist conceptualisation. In addition to reaffirming the dominant Muslim view that the *umma* ties all believers together in bonds of faith, rather than ethnicity or other affiliations, it argues that there is a place for non-Muslims in the Islamic realm (*dar al-Islam*). However self-congratulatory, the logic is convoluted. Although ostensibly validating the idea of inclusivism, the *umma* seems less important than conflating a medieval juridical and territorial category with a flattering image of a modern 'Muslim' – and presumed, tolerant – nation-state, such as Egypt. An American Muslim feminist, Tamara Gray, is more straightforward. Noting that others, such as Egyptian Shaykh Mutawalli al-Sha'rawi (1911–98), had included even non-practising Muslims in the fideistic community, she went further and extended membership in the *umma* to those of other faiths as well.[23]

But, as we will see in Chapters 4 and 5, other interpretations can be more judgemental, stimulated by a basic debate over whether Muslims can be 'friends' with non-Muslims (3:38; 5:51) and whether believers, in line with Qur'anic injunction, need to be 'firm' (*ashidda'*) against the unbelievers (48:29).

One point on which both modernists and liberals agree is that the seventh-century community established by the Prophet in Medina constituted the primordial *umma*. Conservatives and liberals, Islamists and modernists, all routinely invoke the 'Constitution of Medina'[24] as its foundational document. Not only is it believed to have established the prototype of political order,[25] but it is also thought to have created the model of Islamic cosmopolitanism. W. Montgomery Watt and Said Arjomand note that while faith in the one God displaced kinship as the ultimate bond of identity, it was built on such tribal ideas as blood money and in-group solidarity.[26] The followers of Muhammad, who were comprised of those who migrated with him from Mecca to Medina (the *Muhajirun*, the 'Migrants') and those tribal elements in Medina who helped him there (the *Ansar*, the 'Helpers'), formed the core. At the textual outset, these are said to constitute 'one *umma*', but one which was to the exclusion of 'other people'.[27] Nevertheless, consistent with tribal tradition, they also had non-Muslim clients who were deserving of protection, though not preferential treatment. The *umma* was meant to be unified, a community, but it was not universal and there were also internal distinctions. One stipulation captures this ambivalence: 'the Jews of Bani Awf are one *umma* with the believers, [but] they have their religion (*din*) and Muslims have theirs'.[28] Most observers agree that the Jews were to be protected, but whether they were intrinsically part of the community[29] – as of right, as it were – or a separate sub-grouping[30] dependent on alliance and conduct – included by sufferance, in effect – is open to different interpretations. In some radical quarters today, the debate is less on whether the different sub-groups are equal, but on an even more basic question: can Muslims and non-Muslims form one community?

Whatever the intended meanings of this seventh-century document, it was soon overtaken by two fundamental changes that have affected the further development of the *umma*. First, its geographical spread, reaching within the first century of Islam from the Atlantic to Central Asia, rendered the community of the faith multicultural; second, it transformed leadership of the *umma* from religio-political authority to dynastic rule. The *umma* became bound up with implicit notions of empire and with narrowly-based – some would say, secular – power.

In Sunni circles at least, the institution of the Caliphate became the embodiment of the *umma*. *Khilafa* became central to Muslim political thought, but in an idealised version. Abu al-Hasan al-Mawardi's formulation, *al-Ahkam al-Sultaniyya* (Ordinances of Governance) in the tenth century, is often invoked as presenting the standard justification for the Caliphate – 'defence of the faith and administration of the world'. It built on scripturally encouraged notions of deference to rightful authority and culturally embedded assumptions that authority was linked to Prophetic lineage. While sometimes regarded as the 'high theory' of the Caliphate, reflecting an expansive view of its power and roles, *al-Ahkam* was in fact a defensive reaction to the weaknesses of the institution. It was more empirical than prescriptive, explaining the need for a more articulated scheme of governance, as had evolved in practice, than simply an Islamised version of kingly rule; and it was more polemical than aspirational, legitimising the rule of the current Caliph. By the mid-tenth century, the Sunni 'Abbasid Caliphate in Baghdad was challenged by petty rulers and controlled by the Buyids who fashioned Ithna 'Ashari or Twelver Shi'ism as distinct from both Sunnism and other forms of Shi'ism. While it was thus a commentary on existing political conditions, it also had wider implications. Its emphasis on the divine nature of the institution distanced it from the Mu'tazilite rationalism that had dominated much of the prior century and was now in disfavour, from the messy reality of local political competition, and from Buyid sectarianism. Al-Mawardi's preferred term, *imama* (Imamate) – a term common to both Sunnis and Shi'a – spoke to a trans-sectarian purpose and framed the institution of central authority in what we would now call pan-Islamic terms.

Despite insistence on the divine nature of Caliphate, one could argue that the acknowledgement of the political limitations of caliphal rule moved Islamic political thought to a more secular basis. This was certainly apparent three centuries later when Ibn Taymiyya (1263–1328) distinguished between those who govern in practice and the idea of an Imamate or Caliphate in principle.[31] Writing after the fall of Baghdad (1258) and the transfer of the by then nominal Caliphate to Egypt, he placed greater emphasis on *wali al-amr*, the Sultan or *de facto* ruler, rather than an idealised caliphal figure. This approach simultaneously allowed for multiple centres of authority and transferred the Islamic justification for political rule from an *a priori* normative position, to the rationalist criterion of human will and the functionalist criterion of communal stability. Since human nature is divinely endowed, the believers are fully capable of apprehending what is revelation; they, rather than an institution, become the arbiter of Islamic community. It is in their common interest to promote good and suppress evil (*al-'amr bi-al ma'ruf wa-al- nahy 'an al-munkar*) as well as to apply the *shari'a*, while political authority, in turn, is needed to protect that interest. In short, Ibn Taymiyya took the position that

'Governing the affairs of the people is the greatest obligation of religion; indeed, religion (*din*) cannot be established except by it (*la qiyam illa biha*).[32] Different Sultanates take on legitimacy as they fulfil the Islamic obligation to uphold the law and guard against chaos: Sultans have a duty to rule to defend Muslim societies against the possibility of *fitna* (disorder) and, in return, subjects are obligated to obey, unless commanded to commit a sinful act. The unrest that followed the assassination of the third Caliph, 'Uthman, and the accession of the fourth, 'Ali, was more than a dispute over caliphal succession; it highlighted the costs that disorder can exact. The 'Ali-Mu'awiyya dispute unleashed *fitna*, but, even worse, was the revolt (*baghy*) of the radical dissenters, the Khawarij, against 'Ali.

Preferring not to criticise any of the Companions of the Prophet, Ibn Taymiyya moved the discussion from inherent legitimacy to pragmatism. His invocation of a Prophetic saying, with its powerfully negative allusion to the 'ignorant' pre-Islamic period of *jahiliyya*, makes clear that what was uppermost in his view was group cohesion: 'Whoever sees something from his ruler that he dislikes, let him be patient, for whoever splits away from the *jama'a* [main body of Muslims] by a handspan and dies, that is a death of *jahiliyya*.'[33] For Ibn Taymiyya, then, the cohesion of the community of believers took precedence over a universal Caliphate or, as Rosenthal puts it, 'the centre of gravity . . . shifted from the *khilafa* and the *khalifa* to the community, whose life must be regulated by the divine law'.[34] Whether this amounted to a rejection of the Caliphate[35] or a continuation of Sunni orthodoxy,[36] it was the Caliphate that was in the service of the *umma*, not the other way around. As Ovamir Anjum persuasively argues, 'It is not the Community that owes unqualified obedience and service to the Islamic state, but the state that derives its *raison d'être* from its fulfilment of the Community's mission.'[37]

'Abd al-Rahman ibn Khaldun (1332–1406) further developed the realist strand of thinking. While he famously emphasised group solidarity (*'asabiyya*), he distinguished it from the type of cohesiveness found in the cities. *'Asabiyya* held Bedouin society together by self-reliance, mutual support, sheer courage, and even violence, but in the urban environment people passively looked to rulers to protect them. Kingship (*mulk*) was established by force and abetted by charismatic leadership, as shown with the Seljuks and Mongols. But religion could serve to enhance social and political order, and *shari'a*-guided rule was preferable to one grounded in self-interest alone. While acknowledging the inherent worth of Islamic-based governance (*siyasa shari'iyya*), as did Ibn Taymiyya, Ibn Khaldun argued that the alternation of power depended ultimately on the vitality of group solidarity. 'Ali lost his contest with Mu'awiyya and the 'Abbasid Caliphate declined because of a stronger opposing *'asabiyya*.[38]

The rise and fall of dynastic regimes is tantamount to a law of nature, and the Caliphate should not be considered as pre-ordained, nor its decline exceptional. Ibn Khaldun argued that the Prophet's tribe, the Quraysh, provided the social cohesion necessary to establish Islamic rule at the outset. But since that weakened, the *umma* must look to others with strong *'asabiyya*, regardless of where they come from. Religious law cannot be at odds with the practical exigency of strong leadership and, more broadly, the public interest.[39] Although this argument undercuts both a standard interpretation of a reliable *hadith*, as had earlier writers,[40] and the Mawardian caliphal formula, it opened up the possible claimants to Islamic rule. The effect was both to de-centre the *umma* from its original Arab roots, and, as Khaldunian ideas became popular, to reinforce the Ottoman Turkish title to the Caliphate that had been asserted since the fourteenth century.[41]

Linking Imperialism and Decline

Modern thinking has inevitably been influenced by two historical trends that were interconnected but also endowed with their own distinctive logics: the overweening influence of Western imperialism and the steady decline of the Caliphate as a political institution. Pan-Islamism evolved in response to these twin challenges: a united Muslim world would be in a position to compete with the West; and a revived Caliphate would provide the unifying energy. But the animus was different: the former inspired reformist impulses, whereas the latter stimulated a putative return to Sunni traditionalism.

The idea had been around since the eighteenth century when Ottoman Sultans, for patently political purposes, sought recognition as the Caliph of all Muslims. The famous Küçuk Kaynarca treaty of 1774 ratified the Ottoman loss of territory to the Russians, but it also affirmed that the autonomous Tartars would recognise the Sultan as 'Grand Caliph of Mahometanism' (Article III) – that is, a recognition that extended beyond the borders of the Ottoman Empire itself. To

shore up their claims, the Sultans deployed religious circles to dissemin-
ate the idea of *ittihad-i Islam* (pan-Islamic union) in Central Asia and
elsewhere from the 1780s. In the nineteenth century, sultanic and
imperial interests overlapped, with the British encouraging broader
allegiance in India and elsewhere to the Ottoman Sultans, in order to
counter Russian designs. But, at various times, the Russians, French,
and Germans also self-interestedly encouraged pan-Islamism. In addition to external encouragement, the print capitalism that Benedict
Anderson identified as central to the development of nationalism[42]
was also critical to the construction of a pan-Islamic identity. News-
papers such as *Ibret* (Admonition) and *Besiret* (Insight)[43] helped to
shape the notion of Islamic unity, and Esad Efendi's *Ittihad-i Islam*
(1873) was widely distributed as the Ottomans seemed headed again
for war with Russia. When war came in 1877, sentiment was mobilised, in large part in areas such as India, by the vernacular press whose
loyalties were firmly in favour of the Turks. Coterminous with this
were literary works such as the epic poem of Altaf Husain Hali
(1837–1914), *Madd-o Jazr-i Islam* (The Ebb and Flow of Islam,
1879), which 'took Muslim India by storm and created a widespread
pan-Islamic sentiment'.[44] In the aftermath of the 1905 revolution in
Russia, publications in Shi'i Azerbaijan called for respecting Ottoman
Turks as 'brothers in Islam', in the name of *ittihad-i Islam*, rather than
sectarian rivals.[45]

Jamal al-Din al-Afghani (1838–97) brought together in his personal
biography both the promise and contradictions of pan-Islamic unity.
He was born in Asadabad, but this could have been in what is now
Afghanistan or Iran; 'Afghani' suggests Sunni background, but he
might have been Shi'i; drawn at first to Shah Nasir ud-Din's Tehran,
he ended in the service of Sultan Abdülhamid II in Istanbul; he railed
against Western imperialism, but published most successfully in Paris
and earned the admiration of English Orientalists such as Wilfrid
Scawen Blunt. His level of commitment to the faith has been questioned, at times regarded as no more than expediential, but, if Islam
was an instrument in his view, it was for a morally charged purpose: to
make the collectivity of Muslims stronger.

Al-Afghani built his argument on a theme that continues to have
resonance today: the weakness of the *umma* allowed imperialist intrusions; unity would provide strength and allow a righting of the power
imbalance. While his loyalties and his political endorsements might

have been flexible – at times, tolerating British control (as in Egypt), but more often opposing it – his consistent intent was to free Muslims from imperial domination. But, outlining a theme that is a common feature of modernist self-criticisms today, the weakness that the imperialists exploited was abetted by calcified thinking among Muslims themselves. In his view, Islam needed reform, much as occurred in the Protestant Reformation, so that its transcendental qualities could outshine its historical failings.

Al-Afghani's newspaper, *al-'Urwa al-Wuthqa* (The Indissoluble Link), drew its title from a celebrated Qur'anic verse that adroitly appeals to both liberal and conservative sentiments; it speaks to respectful wider relations as well as to solidarity among Muslims. It is frequently invoked by liberal commentators because it affirms that there is no compulsion in religion. But it also clearly divides believers from unbelievers and suggests that the former share a common positive fate: those who reject the devil and believe in God will hold fast to a bond that is unbreakable (Qur'an 2:256). But that can only occur when harmful bonds are superseded: al-Afghani's hope was that 'Muhammadan society will succeed some day in breaking its bonds and marching resolutely in the direction of civilisation after the manner of Western society'.[46] This reform demands that nationalism and any affiliations based on race or ethnicity should be eschewed in favour of religious solidarity.[47] With a political animus inspiring his life's work, al-Afghani concretised pan-Islamic views and, in the process, prepared the ideological groundwork for a view of unity directed against Western power and divisive nationalisms, but also drew on the appealing ideas of a progressive West.

While polemicists such as al-Afghani, Western apologists such as Blunt, and the Sultan, each had vested interests in advancing the pan-Islamic programme, their long-term impact was to reaffirm that Muslim politics reached beyond territorial borders. In a similar way, the Young Turks doubtless advanced an instrumental view, understanding that a pan-Islamic policy might help to disguise steady losses of territory, such as Libya, and appeal to broader support around the world. The Treaty of Lausanne (1912) confirmed Italian sovereignty over Libya, for instance, but it also reaffirmed larger linkages: the treaty provided for the Sultan's name to be recited as Caliph in the Friday sermon and for the chief judge to be appointed from Istanbul.[48] These vicissitudes of declining imperial power and symbolic transnational authority were followed closely in the local press beyond the Middle East, making an appearance in Abu Kalam Azad's *al-Hilal* (The Crescent) and Zafar Ali Khan's *Zamindar* (Landowner), in South Asia, for instance.[49] Over time, Islamic authority would be de-linked from the Caliphate itself.

Indeed, late Ottoman pan-Islamism as a political project designed to rescue simultaneously the Caliphate and the empire, was to be short-lived. As the Turkish revolutionaries gained ground and the demise of, first, the Sultanate, and second, the Caliphate became a political inevitability, debate swirled over the latter's place in Muslim political thought.[50] The stage for its abolition in early spring 1924 was set by various intellectual and political figures who argued that *ittihad-i Islam* was an ideal that could not be realised when Muslims were so diverse and geographically diffuse.[51] The negative case was made that righteous rule had, throughout Muslim history, swiftly degenerated into *mulk* and, in any event, a Prophetic *hadith* had predicted that the Caliphate would last only thirty years after the Prophet. The affirmative case centred on an analysis that would soon meet with general outrage and only limited endorsement elsewhere. Islam was thought to prescribe political order to ensure justice and stability but not its particular form. In the modern age, the *shari‘a* was best upheld on a national basis, and it fell to the new Kemalist dispensation to accomplish this; 'Caliphate' thus became synonymous with 'government'. According to the intellectual and politician Mehmet Seyyed Bey (1873–1925), the Prophet left it to the *ümmet* to decide what form the Caliphate should take – precisely what the Turkish Grand National Assembly in fact did: 'The task to make someone Caliph, in principle, belongs properly to the nation, a task that belongs to the whole nation.'[52] Since the nation was regarded as having chosen a republican parliament, the parliament became, in effect, the functional equivalent of the Caliphate and the Ottoman version ceased to be valid. Parallel to, but critically deviating from, Ibn Taymiyya's logic, the community gave rise to government, but it was now the nation (*millet*), not the *umma*, which was determining.

What to Do?

As if in validation of this endorsement of alternative identities, the Muslim world failed to agree on what should be done in the wake of the Caliphate's abolition. A series of international conferences between 1926 and 1931 signally failed to reach agreement, while inadvertently publicising rival dynastic and other political ambitions. The caliphal claim of Egyptian King Fu'ad (1868–1936) was behind the Cairo congress in May 1926; in the Mecca conference of June–July 1926, the Sa'udis sought to legitimise their claim to control of the Holy Places of Mecca and Medina; and the Mufti of Jerusalem, Hajj Amin al-Husayni (1895–1974), used the 1931 Jerusalem conference to endorse Arab-Muslim claims against a growing Zionist presence in Palestine. Writing of the 1926 Mecca meeting, George Antonius, a celebrated proponent of Arab nationalism as well as a British mandatory civil servant, reported back to London: 'I am inclined to believe that for the first time in many years, perhaps in the whole course of history, H[is] M[ajesty's] G[overnment] find themselves faced with the problem of a, if not united, then at any rate uniting, Islam.'[53] He could not have been more wrong.

Intellectual ferment accompanied this political agitation and, despite what was thought to be a common religious sentiment, the diversity of ideas reflected these underlying differences. The spectrum of opinion ranged from those wishing to re-establish a purified religio-political institution, almost as if the late Ottoman experience had not occurred, to those who were concerned about the dangers of fusing religious and political authority, and to accommodationists, who saw the need to adapt to the realities of an emerging post-war international order.

Muhammad Rashid Rida (1865–1935), editor of the influential Egyptian periodical *al-Manar* (Lighthouse), framed much of the conservative debate over the Caliphate with his important writings in which he criticised the Turkish decision to abolish the institution.[54] He criticised Ibn Khaldun for valuing the integrating power of kinship over that of faith, but understood that religious leadership had not lived up to the ideal of the Rightly Guided Caliphs, which was based on *shura* or consultation among the learned elite, those who 'loose and bind' (*ahl al-hall wa-al-'aqd*). The Ottomans, however flawed, provided a Caliphate of necessity (*imamat al-darura*), and the institution needed to be revived as best it could, though whether he meant spiritually, temporally, or both, remained vague.[55] He saw British imperialism as inherently opposed to the threat of pan-Islam, but also identified internal recalcitrants – both members of the religious class who could not rise above their own narrow legal school (*madhhab*) and the new

Europeanised educated – who extolled the virtues of nationalism. The tragedy that had befallen the Muslims was that unity had been replaced by fragmentation into separate and weak nation-states and the resultant domination of Western power. Indeed, in his famous 1908 *fatwa*, opposing the translation of the Qur'an, he specifically decried those fellow Muslims who were 'destroying what remains of Islamic bonds' (*taqti'baqiyya al-rawabit al-islamiyya*) and so strengthening racial or national bonds (*al-'asabiyyat al-jinsiyya*).[56] Following the broad Taymiyyan line, he argued that Muslims required strong *shari'a*-centred governance and that, if the Caliphate was to be revived in the modern age and to provide that governance, it had to stem from the legitimising unity of the *umma*.[57]

But it was to be an Arab-dominated Caliphate. As the traditional view held, it was to be based on descent from the Prophet's clan and ideally located in the Arabian peninsula. Rida recognised the kind of political competition that ultimately rendered that revival impossible and eventually backed the aspirations of 'Abd al-'Aziz ibn Sa'ud. This Najdi ruler's alliance with Wahhabi forces testified to a righteous purpose, in clear contradistinction to the Sharifian Hashimites who had sold out to the imperialists, and he was the only leader capable of defending the Holy Cities of Mecca and Medina from imperialist control and Muslim 'enslavement'. Sharif Husayn had alienated much Muslim opinion when in an international gathering in 1924, ostensibly to discuss the pilgrimage but intended to legitimise his pan-Islamic aspirations, he sought to build on his special relationship with the British. Meeting in July, the conference participants argued that pan-Arab solidarity was the core of Islamic unity, but crucially failed to endorse the Sharifian claim to the Caliphate that had been unilaterally asserted on 5 March – two days after the action of the Turkish Grand National Assembly. Sa'udi forces were soon, in any event, to lay siege to the Hijaz, and Mecca was conquered in October.

For Rida, the Hijaz – Mecca and Medina – was the focal point of Islam and, in effect, the Sa'udi *amir* was the protector of Islam itself, conceived of as both a sovereign power (*din sayyadatu wa sultan*) and religious creed (*din 'aqidatu wa iman*).[58] This argument is often criticised for its inherent contradictions – pan-Islam imagined through an Arabist prism; opposition to stagnation and fanaticism through support for an arch-traditionalist movement – but it solidified a line of thought that has had wider appeal: the somewhat begrudging narrowing of focus from caliphal union to Arab-driven Islamic unity. However, the conflation of the 'Islamic and Arab people' (*sha'b*) or – ostensibly, the same thing – the 'Islamic *umma*' and 'Arab *umma*', controversially also worked in favour of the Sa'udi claim to political legitimacy as the natural guardians of the Holy Places.

As attractive as the conventional view of the Caliphate was, not all Muslims who wrote on the subject in the 1920s advocated its reinstatement. In 1925, 'Ali 'Abd al-Raziq (1888–1966), a professor at the venerable al-Azhar university in Cairo, published *Islam wa usul al-hukum* (Islam and the Foundations of Government). He insisted on the need to distinguish between spiritual and temporal power in Islam and was emphatic that the Prophet had established neither a 'kingdom' nor a 'state'. Indeed, the claims and privileges of prophethood over the *umma* were distinct from those of temporal rule.[59]

His disapproval of the Caliphate in particular took two interrelated forms: historical and theoretical. Muslim history was replete with instances of power-seeking rulers, and the collective good – the 'interest of Muslims' (*maslahat al-muslimin*)[60] – was not served by Caliphs who were ineffective, corrupt or both. He endorsed the Khaldunian view that the Caliphate was a worldly and social institution and, hence, subject to decline, as was in fact shown to be the case.

A conventional Muslim view is that with the establishment of the Umayyad dynasty in the seventh century, the righteous Caliphate passed to unacceptable hereditary leadership – a censorious view that later Ayatullah Khomeini was to invoke in order to delegitimise both the Shah and Arab kings. But 'Abd al-Raziq's radicalism lay in identifying the Caliphate per se – any Caliphate – as synonymous with kingship. Unsurprisingly, there was a political subtext to his analysis: supporting the nationalist Umma and later the Liberal Constitutionalist parties in Egypt, in part through family association, he opposed King Faruq's aspirations to a restored Caliphate.

'Abd al-Raziq went to the heart of the matter, however, when engaged with theoretical issues of proper authority. As in Western political thought, which he mirrored, the source could conceivably be either divine right or human will. No one could dispute that government was necessary or that the *shari'a* obligated some form of obedience, but neither it nor reason dictated the particular form that government should take. Moreover, caliphal rule was not mandated by the Qur'an, *sunna* or consensus (*ijma'*). What he thought of as the

Lockean view of communal assent to rule was far preferable to the Hobbesian emphasis on the divine right of kings.[61] Indeed, he argued that Islam constitutes a 'religious union' (*wahda diniyya*) over which the Prophet presided and, as a consequence, Muslims form 'one collectivity' (*jama'a wahda*).[62] But neither the *umma* nor the Prophet's mission was tantamount to a political system, or could be incorporated in a temporal institution such as the Caliphate. Implicitly contesting the common argument built on the Constitution of Medina, he declared that the early Muslim community in Arabia was not a state but, rather, a 'unified faith and religious doctrine' (*wahdat al-iman wa-al-madhhab al-dini*).[63]

If 'Abd al-Raziq rejected the notion that Islam required a caliphal political institution, the distinguished Egyptian jurist 'Abd al-Razzaq al-Sanhuri (1895–1971) argued that Muslims would benefit from it in contemporary international relations. Publishing in 1926 and no doubt influenced by the advent of the League of Nations mandate system, he detailed the historical weakness of the caliphal institution and provided (often unreliable) information on the parlous state of Muslim societies. He argued that the union of the Muslim world could not be achieved within the parameters of a centralised empire such as that of the Ottomans, but that the spirit of pan-Islam was nonetheless tangible and required institutionalised expression. If religious unity was perhaps a distant ambition, political solidarity could be attained and would contribute to broader international cooperation and eventual Muslim unity; these were needed for the liberation from imperialist intrusions.[64]

But the proper basis for the Caliphate was contractual, requiring the assent of Muslims. Al-Sanhuri advocated a Caliphate that would be subject to periodic election at the *hajj*, with the Caliph presiding over a loose grouping of Muslim nations as well as representatives of Muslim minorities.[65] This, in turn, would form part of an Oriental grouping linked to the League of Nations. This wider association would not be exclusively Muslim and would include Christians and Jews. Just as Muslims and Coptic Christians were living harmoniously together in Egypt, so too could this new version of the Caliphate preside over communal cooperation. While insisting on the Caliphate for eventual unity, al-Sanhuri thus advanced two ideas that were steadily emerging in Islamic political thought: unity had at least an implicit, and very often an explicit, political dimension; and whatever institutional form it would take depended on communal assent. As such, the idea of the *umma* and the discourse of modern politics and international relations began to converge.

Hasan al-Banna (1906–49), the founder of the Muslim Brotherhood in Egypt in 1928, made his mark on this critical debate of the 1920s. Starting from the opposite presumption of 'Abd al-Raziq and assuming, rather, that Islam is intrinsically both religious and political, he argued for broad Muslim unity while deferring to obvious political realities. He presented maximal and minimal positions, seemingly without obvious contradiction in his mind. Islam is one *umma* and does not recognise territorial borders or racial and ethnic differences. Unity is the undisputed goal; it is a 'religious holiness' (*al-qadasa al-diniyya*), no less.[66] But there are external and internal impediments: imperialism on the one hand, and Muslim divisiveness on the other. His and his movement's opposition to the Anglo-Egyptian Treaty of 1936 made clear this fundamental opposition to foreign control. With a growing political confidence, he lectured the King and ruling elite on the need to avoid Western ways.[67] Narrow, one-state nationalisms are an imperialist contrivance, but there is also a fragmentation of authority within. The latter takes several forms – al-Azhar, mystical brotherhoods, and 'practical' (*al-'amaliyya*) Islamic associations; although referring naturally to the specific circumstances of Egypt, one could extrapolate to what today we would refer to as the religious establishment, Sufi orders, and Islamist movements. If the power of each authority could be harnessed in a cooperative venture, the *umma* would be 'matchless' (*la nazir*) – guiding, not being guided.[68] Moreover, if a renaissance is to occur, the *umma* required the pillars of 'hope, patriotism (*wataniyya*), science, strength, health, and economy'.[69]

This view elided into a realistic minimalism. Nationalisms are deleterious, especially when put in the European context of parallel secularisation. But if group solidarity takes the form of 'patriotism' within its 'limits', rather than exaggerated and self-serving clannishness, it could be positive.[70] In the Muslim world, it might serve as an interim step towards scripturally ordained unity; the Arab nation and the Egyptian nation are tolerable, even useful, preliminary forms of solidarity. Any revival of the Caliphate would take considerable groundwork – a view no doubt encouraged by an increasing hostility towards the King. Although the pressing reality is that '400 million hearts believe in Islam', there is, in fact, not one united *umma*, but several (*al-umam al-islamiyya wa-al-duwal al-islamiyya*).[71] They should participate in an association of Muslim nations (Hay'at al-Umam al-Islamiyya) or 'Islamic league'[72] – a begrudging acceptance that the Caliphate was not likely to be revived and that territorial differences had imprinted themselves on modern Muslim consciousness. This has become the pragmatic Islamist position: eventual unity, interim international Muslim cooperation, ongoing Islamisation within separate states.

Between Nation and the *Umma*

Sayyid Qutb (1906–66) has become a by-word for radical Islamist, but his thinking on the *umma* was richer than his reputation as an exponent of militant action would suggest. He deepened the Brotherhood line of analysis and re-centred the discussion. He endorsed a form of Arab nationalism as consistent with aspirations for broader unity and specifically Arabic as the language of Islam, as did the Brotherhood, but his larger focus was on the 'supranational idea' (*fikrat al-qawmiyya al-'ulya*) of the *umma*. The fundamental problem of the situation was that Muslims had lost their way and lived in a state of moral 'ignorance' (*jahiliyya*). The default position of all mankind was oneness, but the *umma*, to whom the Qur'an was revealed as a defining gift, ceased to exist once divine sovereignty was compromised by political, national, ethnic, and racial allegiances and God's law suspended. Muslims were egregiously adrift. They persisted in referring to themselves collectively as the 'Islamic world' (*al-'alam al-Islami*), but the *umma* was not territorially or historically defined; rather, it was a group of people whose values, ideas, and rules all came from the 'Islamic programme' (*al-minhaj al-Islami*) or divinely inspired methodology.[73]

In a way that is not entirely lucid, however, Qutb alluded to competing collective identities, such as the 'Party of God' (*hizb Allah*, based on Qur'an 58:22),[74] 'Muslim state' (*al-dawla al-muslima*), and *dar al-Islam*,[75] a territorial concept that jurists developed over the centuries and refers to where the *shari'a* is applied. The larger thrust of his thinking advocated creed (*'aqida*) as the fundamental building block of community. The community could not be held together by race, nationalism, political and economic interests, or geography, but by the bonds of common belief.[76] When this fideistic community was present, Muslims would constitute an *umma* that, while unbounded as an idea, was represented in a realm programmatically and legally guided by Islam[77] – *dar al-Islam*. It would appear, in this way, that some degree of territoriality was reluctantly acknowledged. What is more note-worthy, however, was the consistent emphasis on creed, systematic programme, and law, rather than leadership or Caliphate. Although the *umma* was thus, above all, something more basic than political rule, the consciousness of common religious bonds that was at the heart of the *umma* could, and should, be used as a moral judgement on quotidian political and social arrangements.

Roughly coterminous with the development of Bannist and Qutbist thought was Abu A'la Mawdudi (1903–79). The jumping off point for him were two interconnected principles: the absolute oneness of God and His authority (*tawhid*); and the universality and timelessness of the Prophetic mission. Qur'an 7:158, combines the two elements:[78] for 'all of you' (*ilaykum jami'an*), the Prophet is the Messenger of Allah 'to whom belongs the dominion of the heavens and earth' since 'there is no God but Him'. No doubt in response to a key concept of the modern age, 'dominion' (*mulk*) elided into 'sovereignty' (*hakimiyya*) and, in his formulation and the related interpretation of Sayyid Qutb, it was solely a divine prerogative. Sadly, Muslims laboured under a 'mental slavery', imposed by the Western colonisers and taking the modern form of nationalism. Xenophobia, racism, and exclusion generally were the hallmarks of this new demeaning era of 'ignorance'. Christianity could not supplant it, because it lacked a viable political theory; Hinduism espoused caste divisions; Buddhism was too aloof; Marxism, too bloody. Islam, privileging piety as the only distinguishing characteris-tic, was the answer. Even history, in Mawdudi's idealised perspective, bore out that Muslims had been able, until the advent of imperialism in the nineteenth century, to travel freely as common citizens of a kind of Muslim commonwealth.

The self-justifying claim of modern national rulers was thus pre-sumptuous at best; leadership was of course a necessity but it properly belonged to the *umma* as the successor to the Prophet's mission. *Khilafa*, or viceregency, was devolved to people who accepted God's absolute sovereignty, including his law, and was expressed through the collective enterprise of the *umma*. Mawdudi's exegetical commentary on Qur'an 2:143, pointed to a built-in equivocation about the *umma*, however. On the one hand, the scriptural reference to it as a 'commu-nity of the middle way' (*ummatan wasatan*) suggested, in his view, a morally instructive – balanced – coexistence 'among the nations of the world'. On the other, the *umma*'s obligation to 'bear witness' in line with the Qur'anic injunction (*litakuni shuhada'a*) implied not just universality but also ascendancy: 'This position of standing witness before all mankind on behalf of God, which has been conferred on this community, amounts to its being invested with the leadership of all mankind.'[79]

This ambivalence was borne out by Mawdudi's political experience in South Asia. Although he remained committed to the ideal of Muslim unity, he also founded Jama'at-i-Islami in 1941, as a force for top-down Islamisation and, when British machinations and eventual partition forced his hand, he reluctantly accepted the reality of a separate Muslim nation-state, Pakistan. The ideal of a universal community met the reality of national divisions and, like al-Sanhuri and others, he came to endorse the ostensibly transitional stage of Muslim internationalism – a Muslim 'bloc' of separate states and a Muslim International Court of Justice.[80] But the *umma*'s ability to fulfil its promise of 'bearing witness' to the world was undermined now from within. In chastising the rulers of the Muslim world, he was saying that they were letting the *umma* down: 'Verbally you call each other Muslim brothers but in reality you observe all those distinctions which were prevalent before Islam. These distinctions have prevented you from becoming a strong wall. Each and every brick of yours is disjointed. You can neither rise together nor face a calamity together.'[81]

Yusuf al-Qaradawi (b. 1926) is a contemporary thinker with a vast following, in part owing to his broadcast and social media presence.[82] His philosophical worldview is based on a multi-layered concept, *al-wasatiyya*. The central ethical point is balance, moderation, or opposition to excess (*tashdid*) in its several forms.[83] Muslims ought to constitute one community, in line with Qur'anic prescription, but it is also, as Mawdudi argued, a moderate community – peaceful and unaggressive. However, surveying the world scene, he finds the same interconnected problems that have troubled Muslim thinkers from al-Afghani onwards: external interventionism and debilitating internal disharmony. The United States in particular has been arrogant and hegemonic, whereas Muslims have allowed rivalries and differences to derail them from true missions, such as the liberation of Jerusalem from Israeli control.[84]

The world faces two systemic alternatives: globalisation (*'awlama*) or Islamic universalism (*'alamiyyat al-Islam*). The former is tantamount to American colonialism, the imposition of US military, economic, and cultural power on the rest of the world; the latter, in line with Qur'anic injunction (21:107), is the projection of 'mercy to the worlds' (*rahmatan li-al-'alamin*).[85] Yet, when attention is turned from system- to unit-level analysis, it is clear that universalism is not equivalent to uniformity or, even perhaps, unity. Muslim failures were mainly due to loss of, or inadequate devotion to, faith, which in part accounted for partisan divisions as secularism and other pernicious ideologies proved attractive. In espousing a return to belief, he identified the *umma* with a particular theological interpretation, Asha'rism, which some Salafis oppose. Using this name for one of the standard schools of orthodox Sunnism, he aligned the *umma* with such famous institutions as al-Azhar in Egypt, Zaytuna in Tunisia, Deoband and Nadwatul Ulama in India, and Pakistani *madrasas*, all teaching Ash'arism.[86] Although ostensibly designed to affirm unity across the faith, this formulation highlighted, however, a particular interpretation of the *umma*: Sunni – none of the groups he mentioned are Shi'i – and anti-Salafi – he has been staunchly critical of Wahhabi versions of Salafism.

A Muslim liberal intellectual and leader of Tunisia's Ennahda Party, Rashid al-Ghannushi (b. 1941), has largely been preoccupied with promoting the compatibility of Islam and democracy. In a demonstration of the evolution of thought over the centuries, the *khalifa*, or viceregent of God, is no longer one individual or institution. Rather, it is the *umma*, which is best understood as a faith embodied in a community of people. It flows from the fundamental principle of Islam, oneness or monotheism (*tawhid*), and in fact Muslims constitute *ummat tawhid*.[87] Moreover, it is based on the 'text' (*nass*) of the Qur'an and Sunna. Because its task is to serve as guardian of the *shari'a*, it establishes an Islamic state that will implement the law. The sovereign responsibility to promote the good and suppress evil, lies with the *umma* and, as Rida ideally argued, its virtuous representatives, those who 'loose and bind', not the state. Just as Islam distinguishes between devotional (*'ibadat*) and transactional (*mu'amalat*) matters, so too the *umma* ensures the constancy of revelation and righteousness, whereas the political state presides over evolving rules and regulations. The *umma* is prior to, but constitutive of, the Islamic state, which itself is a religious necessity.

Like many of al-Ghannushi's intellectual predecessors, the Constitution of Medina figures prominently in his thinking, but its meaning
is broadened and becomes, in effect, a blueprint for democracy.
Whereas some of his usage of the term *umma* refers exclusively to
Islam, he also uses it, much as Mawdudi did, to extend to other faith
communities and even to a trans-faith cosmopolitanism. Muslims and
Jews each had their own faith-based *umma*, but they were also bound
together in a larger political community. While Muslims shared communal religious ties with other Muslims, there were citizenship links to
non-Muslims.[88] On the basis of this precedent, what might be called
the political *umma* protects religious pluralism: Muslims cannot
coerce in matters of religion, as enjoined by the Qur'an (2:256), and
non-Muslims should not impose on Muslims.[89] The *umma*, in its
larger meaning, is therefore tantamount to a kind of Rousseauian,
but religiously-inspired, General Will.

According to al-Ghannushi, the reality is, however, different: as
others have argued, the *umma* is both divided internally and dependent
on outside power and capital. The state in the Arab world has been
particularly deformed, authoritarian and subservient to Western interests. Trouble settled in early, even as far back as the latter two of the
four Rightly Guided Caliphs in the seventh century. Certainly by the
time of dynastic rule and geographical expansion, the state, rather than
the *umma*, became the focal point of political loyalty.[90] Added to this,
over time, were the Western-imposed project of modernisation, the
ideology of nationalism, and the philosophy of modernity that have
left only confusion – the 'garbage of our decline' (*mazabil inhitatina*).[91]
The modern state needs, in effect, to be Islamised: the parochialism and
despotism of the modern nation-state can only be tamed through
loyalty to a cosmopolitan and democratic *umma*.

Conclusion

The concept of the *umma* is clearly central to Muslim consciousness,
but is also ambiguous. It has been used in different ways with different
aims. Four themes emerge from our review of these varying interpretations. First, the community incorporating all Muslims – the standard
understanding of *umma* – must be cohesive and, preferably, united.
The aspiration for unity is enduring through the centuries in line with
scriptural authority, with many proponents finding in the theological

principle of oneness (*tawhid*) the paradigmatic inspiration for unity of the believers. The contrasting reality of difference has, however, intruded, and explanations, such as those put forward by al-Afghani or Qutb, have linked Muslim waywardness with imperialism and nationalism. As we will see, the failure to live up to the demands for unity has implications for the international relations of modern Muslim states.

Second, the key to cohesion has been understood as leadership of the community. From al-Mawardi to modern writers, across the centuries and sects, allegiance to the righteous ruler has been viewed as unifying. This point of view may be summed up as 'no *umma* without leadership'. Sunni intellectuals, such as Rida, found in the Caliphate this focal authority but, even when it was not seen as pragmatically possible, Islamic governance in various forms has been deemed necessary. Proper government has varied from the Islamised state regime of al-Mawdudi and al-Banna, to the 'moderate' order of al-Qaradawi and the pluralist system of Asad and al-Ghannushi. Yet this general emphasis on making the realisation of the *umma* dependent on leadership has, ironically, undermined the prospects for attaining solidarity, let alone unity. Debates over the nature of the leadership have echoed throughout history and generated discord. The abolition of the Caliphate in 1924 spurred intense controversy over what leadership was then required, and even Ibn Khaldun's and 'Abd al-Raziq's realistic view of the Caliphate as a temporal institution made provision for *shari'a*-minded governance. Moreover, encompassing rhetoric apart, views of the *umma* and its leadership have been embedded in particular theological understandings, as will also be seen in the next chapter on Shi'i interpretations, which have inhibited universal agreement.

Third, as this suggests, the *umma* has been seen as intrinsically political. While the concept has scriptural and spiritual roots, its meaning has been associated with some form of social and political community. Hamidian pan-Islamism was an obvious attempt to harness Islamic universalism in the service of a declining Caliphate, and its final abolition unleashed bitter dynastic rivalries. For al-Sanhuri and even al-Banna and Juma'a, the modern world required, but was unlikely to achieve, cooperation among Muslim or at least Arab states. All helped to idealise a transnational Islam as the natural position of Muslim politics.

Whereas this kind of politicisation is historically contingent, inherent in the very concept of the *umma* is its political instrumentality. In an inverse of the formulation above, the point may be summarised as 'no leadership without *umma*'. The *umma*, in the words of the legal theorist Hans Kelsen, is the *Grundnorm* – the fundamental order that provides the basis for all political and legal obligations; it imparts the 'reason for the validity' of the order and, as a 'transcendental-logical' presupposition, it does not actually need to exist.[92] Accorded normative priority in this way, the concept of the *umma* inevitably acquires utilitarian value. It is what validates claims to leadership, and to speak in its name is to seek precedence over others.

For Ibn Taymiyya, political governance was subservient to its originating and legitimising source – the community of believers; governance was necessary but it had to serve, and be seen as serving, the *umma*, not the other way around. For modern writers such as Asad and al-Ghannushi, the *umma* precedes and authorises political authority: in the former, a kind of multicultural constitutionalism; in the latter, democracy. To appropriate the *umma* – or to *presume* to do so – is, therefore, to engage in a political act. As we will see, attempts to do so today form a critical part of the contemporary competition among Muslim powers. But this competition will also reveal an ironic tension: the *umma* legitimises the 'correct' political system, but it is then represented by that political system, thereby likely subverting the intended goal of unity.

Fourth, the comprehensiveness of the *umma* is routinely asserted, but it has not necessarily been considered encompassing in breadth or accepting of internal pluralism; the former relates to its universalism and the latter to unity. Several dimensions have complicated the search for clarity. One deals with the question of who are members of the *umma*. The Constitution of Medina is conventionally invoked to represent a broad community, incorporating Muslims and non-Muslims, but whether the latter are merely tolerated or considered integral is a matter of debate. There is a spectrum of viewpoints, ranging from Muslim exclusivity as Qutb espoused, to inclusion of non-Muslim monotheists as Asad and al-Ghannushi proposed, to equating the *umma* with all humanity as in the thinking of Juma'a or, at least, to seeing it as a moral guide for all mankind, as Mawdudi argued. Another dimension has to do with the means by which non-Muslims, if they are considered members, are to be incorporated within the *umma*: is it through the 'call' or by compulsion? We will see that, while most Muslims advocate the former – a reasoned and willing acceptance of Islam – some, such as the so-called Islamic State of Iraq and Syria (ISIS), advocate an imposed and enforced submission.

A final dimension of this fourth theme regarding comprehensiveness of the *umma* centres on the extent of Muslim inclusivity or, simply put, internal Muslim unity. Muslims are all brothers before God, but not necessarily equal in doctrinal soundness. There have been extensive canonical discussions on the permissible limits of legal difference (*ikhtilaf*), and consensus over time has endorsed four Sunni schools of law and one Shi'i school, with the Amman Message, noted in Chapter 1, including additional schools.[93] But all these and other legal, philosophical, and theological interpretations have been subject at times to controversy and criticism. For example, the twelfth-century jurist Ibn al-Jawzi (1126–1200) denounced what he believed to be several deviant schools of thought, including the Mu'tazilites and Sufism, in his *Talbis Iblis* (The Devil's Deception). *Umma*-centred rhetoric notwithstanding, sectarianism has of course become an intensely polarised fact of life today. Moreover, although a great many modern intellectuals, from at least al-Afghani onwards, have called for renewal and reform in Islam, the very subjectivity of the terms has done little to erase internal boundaries within the community of believers. As Henri Lauzière argues, there has often been a tension between unity and purity,[94] and considerations of purity – who is the true believer and who the deviant; who is the enlightened reformer and who is in need of reform – have undermined unity.

The discourse on the *umma* has invariably been universalist and inclusivist. But whether a consensus on the meaning of universality and inclusiveness is achievable remains an open question, while contestation over promotion and control of the concept is an ineluctable part of today's Muslim politics and international relations.

Notes

1 W. B. Gallie, 'Essentially Contested Concepts', *Proceedings of the Aristotelian Society*, New Series 56 (1955–6): 167–98.
2 For example, Louis Massignon, 'L'Umma et ses synonymes: Notion de "communauté sociale" en Islam' [The Umma and its Synonyms: Notion of 'Social Community' in Islam], *Revue des études islamiques 1941–46* (1947): 151–6 (p. 152).

3 Edward William Lane, *An Arabic–English Lexicon*, part 1, vol. 1 (Beirut: Librairie du Liban, 1968; originally published 1863), p. 90.

4 W. Montgomery Watt, *Islamic Political Thought: The Basic Concepts* (Edinburgh University Press, 1968), p. 10; Frederick Mathewson Denny provides a cogent overview of the debates over the relationship between *umma* and *umm*, and is not convinced that the connection is more than 'homonymy and the ramification of kinship groups to peoples and communities'. 'The Concept of "Ummah" in the Qur'an', *History of Religions* 15, 1 (1975): 34– 70 (p. 37).

5 For example, 'Abd al-Rahman al-Sulayman, 'Arabic Translators International', online forum, 17 October 2009, www.atinternational.org/forums/showthread.php?t=7018, accessed 14 November 2017.

6 Leon Zolondek's work points to a slow modern evolution of the idea of the 'people'. He argues that, in the late nineteenth century, reformers such as Muhammad 'Abduh (1849–1905) and 'Abd al-Rahman al-Kawakibi (1855–1902) viewed *al-sha'b* as a secular idea and so preferred *umma* in order to designate the sovereignty of 'the people': 'Ash-Sha'b in Arabic Political Literature of the 19th Century', *Die Welt des Islams*, New Series 10, 1/2 (1965): 1–16 (p. 1). Also see his 'The Language of the Muslim Reformers of the Late 19th Century', *Islamic Culture* 37, 3 (July 1963): 155–62.

7 The Qur'an refers to the early Meccans as a 'transgressing people' (*qawmun taghuna*, 52:32).

8 'Abdullah al-Ahsan points out that the term *umma* can refer to a variety of forms of communal affiliation: *Ummah or Nation? Identity Crisis in Contemporary Muslim Society* (Leicester: Islamic Foundation, 1992), pp. 10–26.

9 Watt says that the *umma* passages in the Qur'an date no later than 625 CE – that is, after the Prophet's migration (*hijra*) to Medina but roughly five years before the conversion of Mecca. *Islamic Political Thought*, p. 10.

10 *Sunan Ibn Majah* (Arabic–English), ed. Hafiz Abu Tahir Zubair 'Ali Za'i, vol. 5, book 36 (*al-Fitan*), *hadith* 3948 (Riyadh: Maktaba Dar us-Salam, 2007), p. 174. This *hadith* has been assessed as *sahih* or authentic.

11 *Sunan Abu Dawud* (Arabic–English), ed. Hafiz Abu Tahir Zubair 'Ali Za'i, vol. 5, book 43 (*al-Adab*), *hadith* 5121 (Riyadh: Maktaba Dar us-Salam, 2008), p. 421. Al-Albani said this is a weak *hadith* but al-Suyuti said it is authentic.

12 *Sahih Muslim* (Arabic–English), ed. Hafiz Abu Tahir Zubair Ali Za'i, vol. 6, book 44 (*al-Birr*), *hadith* 6588 (Riyadh: Maktaba Dar-us-Salam, 2007), p. 451. A similar *hadith* reported by al-Bukhari speaks of the believers as one body (*al-jasad*). *Sahih Al-Bukhari* (Arabic–English),

Conclusion 43

trans. Muhammad Muhsin Khan, vol. 8, book 78 (*al-Adab*), *hadith*
6011 (Riyadh: Maktaba Dar-us-Salam, 1997), p. 36. Both *hadith* are
considered reliable.

13 *Sahih Al-Bukhari*, vol. 1, book 8 (*al-Salat*), *hadith* 481, p. 301. A similar
hadith is found in *Sahih Muslim*, vol. 6, book 44 (*al-Birr*), *hadith* 6585,
p. 450. These are considered reliable.

14 *Jami'at al-Tirmidhi* (Arabic–English), supervised by Abdul Malik Mujahid, vol. 4, book 31 (*al-Fitan*), *hadith* 2167 (Riyadh: Maktaba Dar-us-
Salam, 2007), p. 227.

15 This saying appears in several similar forms. For example, *Sunan Ibn
Majah*, *hadith* 3950, pp. 174–5.

16 See Ahmad S. Dallal, Yoginder Sikand, and Abdul Rashid Moten,
'Ummah', *The Oxford Encyclopedia of the Islamic World*, Islamic Studies Online, www.oxfordislamicstudies.com/article/opr/t236/e0818?_hi=
0&_pos=3#, accessed 17 August 2017.

17 Cited in Muhy al-Din al-Nawawi, *al-Minhaj fi Sharh Sahih Muslim Ibn
al-Hajjaj* [Commentary on *Sahih Muslim*], in *Kitab al-Waqf*, ed.
Muhammad Fu'ad al-Baqi (Beirut: Dar Ibn Hazm, n.d.), p. 91.

18 Toshihiko Izutsu, *God and Man in the Qur'an* (Petaling Jaya: Islamic
Book Trust, 2002; originally published 1964), p. 79.

19 Eric Voegelin, 'The Political Religions', in *Modernity without Restraint*,
vol. 5 of *The Collected Works of Eric Voegelin*, ed. Manfred Henningsen
(Columbia: University of Missouri Press, 2000), p. 185.

20 Isma'il ibn Kathir, *Tafsir al-Qur'an al-'Azim* [Exegesis of the Glorious
Qur'an], vol. 4, 2nd edn. (Riyadh: Dar Tiba li-l-Nashr wa-al-Tawzi',
1420 A.H./1999), pp. 570, 610–11.

21 Muhammad Asad, *The Principles of State and Government in Islam*
(Kuala Lumpur: Islamic Book Trust, 1999; originally published 1961),
pp. 32, 99.

22 'Ali Juma'a, 'Mafhum al-umma' [Understanding the *Umma*], *al-Ahram*,
14 July 2014, reproduced on his website, www.draligomaa.com/index
.php/المكتبة/مقالات/الأهرام/item/358-مفهـــــــوم-الأمة, accessed 8 March 2017.

23 Shaykha Tamara Gray, 'Who Belongs in the Ummah of the Prophet
Muhammad?', YouTube video, 8 March 2016, www.youtube.com/
watch?v=zNeVsJeb_Gk, accessed 5 November 2016.

24 This is variously called a 'constitution' (*dustur*), 'compact' (*sahifa*), or
'charter' (*mithaq*). Many scholars prefer 'treaty'. For example, Michael
Lecker, 'Constitution of Medina', in *The Encyclopedia of Ancient History*, ed. Roger S. Bagnall, Kai Brodersen, Craige B. Champion, Andrew
Erskine, and Sabine R. Huebner (Oxford: Blackwell Publishing, 2013),
pp. 1748–9. Watt and Serjeant believe that it was not one document, but
a series proposed over time. W. Montgomery Watt, *Muhammad at*

Medina (Oxford University Press, 1956), pp. 225–8; R. B. Serjeant, 'The Constitution of Medina', *Islamic Quarterly* 8 (1964): 3–16. For a detailed comparison of the two competing texts of Ibn Ishaq (*Kitab Sirat Rasul Allah*) and Abu Ubayd (*Kitab al-Amwal*), see Michael Lecker, *The Constitution of Medina: Muḥammad's First Legal Document* (Princeton, NJ: Darwin, 2004).

25 Muhammad Hamidullah said it was the world's first constitutional document. *The First Written Constitution in the World: An Important Document of the Time of the Holy Prophet*, 3rd edn. (Lahore: Ashraf Press, 1975); Said Amir Arjomand calls it a 'proto-Islamic public law'. 'The Constitution of Medina: A Sociolegal Interpretation of Muhammad's Acts of Foundation of the *Umma*', *International Journal of Middle East Studies* 41, 4 (2009): 555–75 (p. 555) .

26 For example, Watt, *Muhammad at Medina*, pp. 126, 231–2, 238–49, 261–71; Arjomand, 'The Constitution of Medina', pp. 561, 565.

27 'Inahum umma wahida min dun al-nas' (they are one community distinct from [or to the exclusion of, or apart from] the others). See Uri Rubin, 'The "Constitution of Medina": Some Notes', *Studia Islamica* 62 (1985): 5–23 (pp. 13, 21).

28 'Yahud Bani 'Awf ummat ma'al-mu'minin li-al-yahud dinahum wa lil-muslimin dinahum wa mawalihum', the 30th stipulation of the Constitution. It goes on to list Jews from other clans and tribes to whom this also applies.

29 For example, Watt says that '[t]he Jews of various groups belong[ed] to the community' and were committed to mutual help with Muslims. *Islamic Political Thought*, p. 5.

30 For example, Frederick Mathewson Denny argues that because 'the Constitution was very much a political-military document of agreement designed to make Yathrib [Medina] and the peoples connected with it safe', the Jews likely constituted a 'special sub-group, a "sub-*ummah*"'. 'Ummah in the Constitution of Medina', *Journal of Near Eastern Studies* 36, 1 (1977): 39–47 (p. 44).

31 Banan Malkawi and Tamara Sonn, 'Ibn Taymiyya on Islamic Governance', in *Islam, the State, and Political Authority: Medieval Issues and Modern Concerns, Middle East Today*, ed. Asma Afsaruddin (New York: Palgrave Macmillan, 2011), pp. 111–27.

32 'Abd al-Rahman b. Muhammad b. Qasim and Muhammad b. 'Abd al-Rahman b. Muhammad, *Majmu'Fatawa Shaykh al-Islam Ahmad b. Taymiyya* [Collection of the Fatwas of Ibn Taymiyya], vol. 28 (Cairo: Dar al-Rahma, n.d.), pp. 390–1; Taqi al-Din Ahmad Ibn Taymiyya, *al-Siyasa al-shar'iyya* [Legitimate Governance] (Cairo: Dar al-Sha'b, 1971), p. 185; Henri Laoust, *Le Traité de droit publique d'Ibn Taymiyya:*

Traduction annotée de la Siyasa shar'iyya [Ibn Taymiyya's Public Law Treaty: Annotated Translation of *Siyasa Shar'iyya*] (Beirut: Institut Français de Damas, 1948), p. 172.

33 Invoking Ibn 'Abbas, *Sahih Muslim*, vol. 5, book 33 (*al-Imara*), chapter 13, *hadith* 4790, p. 183.

34 E. I. J. Rosenthal, *Political Thought in Medieval Islam: An Introductory Outline* (Cambridge University Press, 1962), p. 52.

35 Henri Laoust argues that, with the divisions that set in following the period of the Prophet and Rightly Guided Caliphs, Ibn Taymiyya understood that the Caliphate was no longer an obligation. To decree that it was so, would put believers in a dilemma: either they would have to find a leader for a community that had lost its cohesion, or accord legitimacy to an empty institution and a merely formalistic political and social order. *Essai sur les doctrines sociales et politiques de Taḳī-d-Dīn Aḥmad b. Taimïya* [Essay on the Social and Political Doctrines of Taqi al-Din Ahmad ibn Taymiyya] (Cairo: Imprimerie de l'Institut Français d'Archéologie Orientale, 1939), pp. 281–3.

36 Mona Hassan, 'Modern Interpretations and Misinterpretations of a Medieval Scholar: Apprehending the Political Thought of Ibn Taymiyya', in *Ibn Taymiyya and His Times*, ed. Yossef Rapoport and Shahab Ahmed (Oxford University Press, 2010), pp. 338–66.

37 Ovamir Anjum, *Politics, Law, and Community in Islamic Thought: The Taymiyyan Moment* (Cambridge University Press, 2012), p. 269.

38 A. K. S. Lambton, *State and Government in Medieval Islam: An Introduction to the Study of Islamic Political Theory – The Jurists* (Oxford University Press, 1981), p. 172; Muhammad Mahmoud Rabi', *The Political Theory of Ibn Khaldun* (Leiden: E. J. Brill, 1967), p. 94.

39 'Abd al-Rahman ibn Khaldun, *The Muqaddimah: An Introduction to History*, trans. Frantz Rosenthal (Princeton University Press, 1958), pp. 399, 401–2.

40 The commonly cited justification is a *hadith* which says that the 'people follow the Quraysh'. *Sahih Muslim*, vol. 5, Book 33 (*al-Imara*), chapter 1, *hadith* 4701, p. 144. Earlier jurists who provided a variant interpretation to the conventional one include Abu Bakr Muhammad al-Baqillani (d. 1013) and 'Abd al-Qahir al-Jurjani (d. 1078). Ibn Khaldun specifically cites the similar opinion of al-Baqillani (d. 1031).

41 Cornell Fleischer says that the *Muqaddima* was known in Ottoman intellectual circles from the end of the sixteenth century: 'Royal Authority, Dynastic Cyclism and Ibn Khaldunism in Sixteenth Century Ottoman Letters', *Journal of Asian and African Studies* 18, 3–4 (1983): 198–220 (pp. 199–201).

42 Benedict Anderson, *Imagined Communities: Reflections on the Origin and Spread of Nationalism*, rev. edn. (London: Verso, 2006; originally published 1983), especially chapter 3.

43 *Ibret* was a Young Ottoman newspaper that appeared in 1871; *Besiret* was a late nineteenth-century newspaper in Istanbul.

44 M. Naeem Qureshi, *Pan-Islam in British Indian Politics: A Study of the Khilafat Movement, 1918–1924* (Leiden: Brill, 1999), p. 31. Examples of the Urdu press include *Shamsu'l-Akhbar* in Madras and *Awadh Punch* in Lucknow.

45 Volker Adam, 'Why Do They Cry? Criticisms of Muharram Celebrations in Tsarist and Socialist Azerbaijan', in *The Twelver Shia in Modern Times: Religious Culture and Political History*, ed. Rainer Brunner and Werner Ende (Leiden: Brill, 2001), p. 122.

46 Nikki Keddie, *An Islamic Response to Imperialism: Political and Religious Writings of Sayyid Jamal Ad-Din 'al-Afghani'* (Berkeley: University of California Press, 1968), p. 183.

47 Muhammad Imarah, *al-Amal al-kamila: Jamal al-Din al-Afghani* [The Complete Works: Jamal al-Din al-Afghani], part 2 (Beirut: al-Mu'assasa al-'Arabiyya li-l-Dirasat wa-al-Nashr, 1981), p. 35.

48 Hasan Kayali, *Arabs and Young Turks: Ottomanism, Arabism and Islamism in the Ottoman Empire, 1908–18* (Berkeley: University of California Press, 1997), p. 114; Arnold, *The Caliphate*, pp. 177–8.

49 Francis Robinson, 'Islam and the Impact of Print in South Asia', in *The Transmission of Knowledge in South Asia; Essays on Education, Religion, History and Politics*, ed. Nigel Crook (Oxford University Press, 1996), p. 74.

50 The Turkish Grand National Assembly abolished the Ottoman Sultanate on 1 November 1922, but retained the Caliphate until March 1924.

51 For example, Ilyas Sami, Rasih Kaplan, and Halil Hulki, in their *Hakimiyet-i Milliye Hilafet-i Islami* [National Sovereignty and the Islamic Caliphate], rejected the arguments of pro-Caliphate figures, such as Isma'il Şūkrū in *Hilafet-i Islamiye ve Büyük Millet Meclisi* [The Islamic Caliphate and Grand National Assembly]. See Banu Turnaoğlu, *The Formation of Turkish Republicanism* (Princeton University Press, 2017), pp. 230–1.

52 Mehmet Seyyid Bey, *Hilafet ve hakimiyet-i milliye* [The Caliphate and Nationalism] (1339/1923), pp. 3–4; Mehmet Seyyid Bey, *Usul-i Fikh, madhal* [Introduction to Usul-i Fikh] (1333/1917), p. 117; both cited in Michelangelo Guida, 'Seyyid Bey and the Abolition of the Caliphate', *Middle Eastern Studies* 44, 2 (2008): 275–89 (pp. 279, 281).

53 Quoted in Martin Kramer, *Islam Assembled: The Advent of the Muslim Congresses* (New York: Columbia University Press, 1986), p. 117.

54 Collected as Muhammad Rashid Rida, *al-Khilafa aw'l-imama al-'uzma* [The Caliphate or Great Imamate] (Cairo: Matba'at al-Manar, 1923); and Muhammad Rashid Rida, *al-Wahda al-Islamiyya wa-al-ukhuwa al-Islamiyya* [Islamic Unity and Islamic Brotherhood] (Cairo: Matba'at al-Manar, 1925).

55 Malcolm Kerr said his thought was 'often incoherent' in this regard. *Islamic Reform: The Political and Legal Theories of Muhammad 'Abduh and Rashid Rida* (Berkeley: University of California Press), p. 176. But Mahmoud Haddad argues that Rida's reactions to changing political realities account for the permutations in his views. 'Arab Religious Nationalism in the Colonial Era: Rereading Rashid Rida's Ideas on the Caliphate', *Journal of the American Oriental Society* 117, 2 (1997): 253–77 (p. 277).

56 *Al-Manar*, vol. 11, section 4, pp. 268–74, reproduced online, *al-Maktaba al-'Arabiyya al-Kubra* [The Great Arab Library], http://arabicmegalibrary.com/pages-8492-14-3571.html, accessed 11 January 2017.

57 Rida, *al-Khilafa*, pp. 50, 114.

58 Muhammad Rashid Rida, *al-Wahhabiyyun wa-al-Hijaz* [The Wahhabis and the Hijaz] (Cairo: Matba'at al-Manar, 1344 A.H./1925), p. 50.

59 'Ali 'Abd al-Raziq, *al-Islam wa Usul al-Hukm: Bahth fi-l Khilafa wa-l Hukuma fi-l Islam* [Islam and the Roots of Governance: Study on the Caliphate and Government in Islam], book 2, chapter 3, 3rd printing (1344 A.H./1925), ed. 'Ammar 'Ali Hasan (Cairo: Dar al-Kitab al-Misri/ Beirut: Dar al-Kitab al-Lubnani, 1433 A.H./2012), p. 97.

60 Ibid., book 1, chapter 3, p. 51.

61 Ibid., book 1, chapter 1, p, 22.

62 Ibid., book 2, chapter 3, p. 94.

63 Ibid., book 3, chapter 1, p. 112.

64 'Abd al-Razzaq Al-Sanhuri, published as A. Sanhoury, *Le Califat: Son évolution vers une société des nations orientales* [The Caliphate: Its Evolution Towards a Society of Eastern Nations] (Paris: Librairie Orientaliste Paul Geuthner, 1926), pp. 504–9.

65 Ibid., pp. 574–7.

66 Hasan al-Banna, 'Ila al-umma al-nahida 2' [To the Rising *Umma* 2], *Ikhwan Wiki*, www.ikhwanwiki.com/index.php?title=إلى_الأمة_الناهضة_2, accessed 18 August 2017.

67 Christine Sixta Rinehart, *Volatile Social Movements and the Origins of Terrorism: The Radicalization of Change* (Lanham, MD: Lexington Books, 2013), p. 18.

68 Hasan al-Banna, *Mudhakkirat al-da'wa wa-al-da'iya* [Memoirs of the Call and the Preacher, original version, 1950], edited by Abu'l-Hasan 'Ali al-Nadvi, www.kutub-pdf.net/book/2243, accessed 22 July 2017, p. 25.

69 Hasan al-Banna, 'Ila al-umma al-nahida' [To the Rising *Umma*], *Ikhwan Wiki*, https://translate.google.com.au/translate?hl=en&sl=ar&tl=en& u=http%3A%2F%2Fwww.ikhwanwiki.com%2F&anno=2, accessed 18 August 2017.

70 Hasan al-Banna, 'Mawqif al-Imam al-Banna min al-qawmiyya wa-al-wataniyya' [Position of Imam al-Banna on Regional Nationalism and Patriotism], *Ikhwan Wiki*, www.ikhwanwiki.com/index.php?title= موقف_الإمام_البنا_من_القومية_و_الوطنية, accessed 18 August 2017.

71 Hasan al-Banna, 'Bayna al-qawmiyya wa-al-Islamiyya' [Between Regional Nationalism and Islam], *Ikhwan Wiki*, https://translate.google.com.au/ translate?hl=en&sl=ar&tl=en&u=http%3A%2F%2Fwww.ikhwanwiki .com%2F&anno=2, accessed 20 August 2017.

72 Hasan al-Banna, 'Risalat al-mu'tamar al-khamis' [Message of the Fifth Congress], in *Majmu'at al-Risa'il li-l-Imam al-Shahid Hasan al-Banna* [Collected Statements of the Martyred Imam Hasan al-Banna] (Cairo: Dar al-Tawzi', 1992), pp. 142–4.

73 Sayyid Qutb, *Ma'alim fi-al-tariq* [Signposts on the Road] (Beirut and Cairo: Dar al-Shuruq, 1979/1399 A.H.), p. 6.

74 Sayyid Qutb, *Hadha al-din* [This Religion] (Beirut and Cairo: Dar al-Shuruq, 1995), p. 88

75 Qutb, *Ma'alim*, p. 137.

76 Qutb, *Hadha al-din*, p. 88.

77 Qutb here followed the Qur'an (5:48), which referred to God prescribing a 'law and a *minhaj*' (sometimes translated as 'methodology', Qur'anic 'science', or the Islamic 'way').

78 Sayyid Abu A'la Mawdudi, *Witnesses unto Mankind: The Purpose and Duty of the Muslim Ummah*, trans. and ed. Khurram Murad (Leicester: The Islamic Foundation, 1986/1406 A.H.), p. 19.

79 Sayyid Abu A'la Mawdudi, *Towards Understanding the Qur'an*, vol. 1, abridged version of *Tafhim al-Qur'an*, trans. and ed. Zafar Ishaq Ansari (Leicester: The Islamic Foundation, 1988/1408 A.H.), p. 121.

80 Sayyid Abu A'la Mawdudi, published as Siyyid Abul A'la Maududi, *Unity of the Muslim World*, ed. Khurshid Ahmad (Lahore: Islamic Publications, 1967), pp. 45, 48.

81 Sayyid Abu A'la Mawdudi, published as Syed Abul 'Ala Maulana Maudoodi, *Khutabat* [Sermons], 2nd edn. (Chicago: Kazi Publications, 1977), p. 56.

82 In the words of Peter Mandaville, 'Actively embracing technologies that would have made Jamal al-Din al-Afghani, his pan-Islamist forebear, green with envy', al-Qaradawi has established 'something like a global infrastructure for the dissemination of his particular religious

worldview': *Islam and Politics*, 2nd edn. (London and New York: Routledge, 2014), p. 381.

83 See Yusuf al-Qaradawi, *Fiqh al-wasatiyya al-Islamiyya: ma'alim wa manarat* [Islamic Jurisprudence of the 'Middle Way': Milestones and Lighthouses] (Cairo: Dar al-Shuruq, 2010).

84 Yusuf al-Qaradawi, *Dars al-nakba al-thaniyya: li-madha hazamna wakayfa nantasir* [Lesson of the Second *Nakba* (Disaster): Why We Lost and How We Win] (Cairo: Maktabat Wahba, 1993), pp. 52–7.

85 Yusuf al-Qaradawi, *Ummatna bayna qarnayn* [Our *Umma* between Two Centuries] (Cairo: Dar al-Shuruq, 2000), pp. 231–5.

86 Solojuve1897, 'Shaykh Yusuf al-Qaradawi is asked about the aqeedah of al-Azhar', YouTube video, 30 November 2011, www.youtube.com/watch?v=BG8PEU0Iqn8, accessed 16 April 2017.

87 Azzam S. Tamimi, *Rachid Ghannouchi: A Democrat within Islamism* (Oxford University Press, 2001), p. 155.

88 See his speech on 'Secularism and the Relation between Religion and the State from the Perspective of the en-Nahdah Party' (Center for the Study of Islam and Democracy, Tunisia, 2 March 2012), http://anwaribrahim blog.com/2012/03/19/transcript-of-rachid-ghannouchis-speech-at-csid-tunisia-on-2-march-2012-on-secularism-and-relation-between-religion-and-the-state-from-the-perspective-of-the-en-nahdah-party/, accessed 28 September 2017.

89 Rashid al-Ghannushi, *Muqarabat fi-al 'ilmaniyya wa-al-mujtama'al-madani* [Approaches on Secularism and Civil Society] (London: al-Markaz al-Maghribi li-al-Buhuth wa-al-Tarjama, 1999), p. 47.

90 Rashid al-Ghannushi, *al-Hurriyyat al-'amma fi-al dawla al-islamiyya* [Public Liberties in the Islamic State] (Beirut: Markaz Dirasat al-Wahda al-'Arabiyya, 1993), p. 123.

91 Ibid., pp. 162, 310.

92 Iain Stewart, 'The Critical Legal Science of Hans Kelsen', *Journal of Law and Society* 17, 3 (1990): 273–308 (p. 296). For Kelsen, the *Grundnorm* did not exist.

93 *Amman Message* (Amman: Royal Aal al-Bayt Institute for Islamic Thought, 2009), p. 16. The original message calling for unity was delivered by Jordan's King 'Abdullah in November 2004 and the subsequent declaration on the acceptable Muslim schools of thought, the impermissibility of *takfir* or excommunication, and who is authorised to give a *fatwa*, was signed in 2005.

94 Henri Lauzière, *The Making of Salafism: Islamic Reform in the Twentieth Century* (New York: Columbia University Press, 2016), p. 38.

3 | *Shi'a Islam and the* Umma

In its totality, the concept of *umma* is meant to have a common connotation for all Muslims, irrespective of their social, cultural, ethnic, and geographical divisions. In its dominant formulation, it denotes a cluster of believers bounded by their faith and religious and moral responsibilities, in a single borderless community. The concept is transcendental, calling for pan-Islamic ideals, values, and practices, as elaborated in Chapter 2. However, when it comes to the application of the concept of *umma* to the political organisation of that community, the Sunni–Shi'i sectarian division has historically thrown up differences. The invocation and deployment of *umma* by both sects – each of which is internally plural – is underwritten by their sectarian differences. Sunni Islam has provided for a *khalifa* (Caliph) and the institution of *khilafa* (Caliphate) to lead and govern the *umma*. In contrast, Shi'a Islam has cultivated the position of Imam and the institution of *imama* or Imamate, to lead and govern the universal community of believers. In Shi'a Islam, the Imam is projected as having divine authority through blood relations to the Prophet Muhammad. Like the followers of Sunni Islam, their Shi'a counterparts are divided into distinguishable sub-categories. Yet whereas Sunni Muslims are distinguished by the school of jurisprudence (*madhhab*) to which they subscribe, Shi'a Muslims are divided according to which Imams are accepted as legitimate successors to the Prophet and part of his house-hold (*ahl al-bayt*). There are three predominant groups: the followers of the twelve Imams, known as Twelvers, the followers of the seven Imams, known as Isma'ilis, and the followers of the five Imams, known as Zaydis. However, since the Twelvers form the great majority of the Shi'i population, estimated at some 20 per cent of the approximately 1.8 billion Muslims in today's world, it is this category's stance on *umma* and its governance that primarily forms the subject matter of discussion here.

The main purpose of this chapter is threefold. One is to unpack the Shi'i theological-scholarly deliberation on the role of the Imam and Imamate as key to understanding the Shi'i concept of *umma*. Another is to examine the evolution and application of the doctrine of Imamate in the contemporary Shi'i-dominated Iran from 1979, under Ayatullah Ruhollah Khomeini, to the present, under Ayatullah 'Ali Khamenei. The third is to evaluate the cross-sectarian appeal of the Islamic Republic's Imamate within the *umma*.

The Imam and the Imamate Doctrine

Shi'a Islam's conception of the Imam and his leadership of the *umma* is based on a view that the successor to the Prophet Muhammad should be related to him through the bloodline, rather than elected in a popular-based consensual process. Whereas the legitimacy of the *khalifa* in Sunni Islam stems from the consent of the *umma* (as the Islamic community of citizens, whom he is responsible to lead), Shi'a Islam holds that only those leaders who are members of the Prophet's *ahl al-bayt* are legitimate successors to his societal leadership. After the Prophet's death in 632, a gathering of the inner circle of his followers in Medina reached a consensus (*ijma'* – a concept that is in itself a legacy of the Prophet) that his rightful successors would be his four closest companions in order of seniority: Abu Bakr al-Siddiq, 'Umar ibn Khatab, Uthman ibn Affan, and 'Ali ibn Abi Talib. However, a minority subsequently dissented from the Medina consensus over the succession. According to this heterodox group, who became known as the Shi'a, 'Ali's position as the cousin and son-in-law of the Prophet, by marriage to his daughter Fatima, made him the rightful successor. Thus, whilst a majority of the early *umma* remained loyal to the Medina school as the Sunnis or orthodox in Islam, the Shi'a adopted 'Ali as their first Imam or leader. As such, the majority of the Shi'a rejected the first three Caliphs, who did not have direct blood linkage to the Prophet, as illegitimate. As a corollary to this, the concept of *wilaya* (Persian: *velayat*, 'the faculty that enables a person to assume authority and exact obedience') is especially important in Shi'i theology.[1]

Shi'a Islam nonetheless accepts and includes Sunnis in their conception of the *umma*, but posits that only those who follow Imami traditions are real, 'true', or authentic believers.[2] Its concept of the

Imamate, which is analogous to the Sunni *khilafa*, enshrines the role
and position of the Prophet's descendants (beginning with 'Ali) as
Imams – religious and political leaders of the *umma*. Sunni Islam
acknowledges the importance of imams, but in its discourse, the term
refers not to the leader of the *umma* but to spiritual authorities and
religious scholars that lead prayers and provide guidance to a
congregation.[3]

Shi'i scholars have elaborated both traditional and rational proofs to
justify the hereditary nature of leadership (and therefore the legitimacy
of 'Ali's succession) and the existence and purpose of the Imamate.
They cite a number of *hadith* and Qur'anic verses that suggest that the
Prophet had intended to designate 'Ali as his successor. The most
notable of these is the *hadith* of the Ghadir Khumm incident, where
the Prophet took 'Ali's hand and raised it, stating: 'for whomever I am
their lord (*mawla*, or variously *wali*), 'Ali is their lord; O God, befriend
(*wali*) the one who befriends him (*walahu*) and be the enemy (*'adi*) of
the one who is his enemy (*'adahu*)'.[4] The authenticity of this *hadith* is
acknowledged and established in both Sunni and Shi'i traditions.
However, Sunni scholars argue that the Prophet's description of 'Ali
as *mawla* merely ascribes to him fatherly qualities like his own, stem-
ming from their interpretation of a Qur'anic verse (33:6) which states
'the Prophet is closer to the believers than their selves'. They therefore
deny that this *hadith* was an explicit designation of succession. By
contrast, Shi'i scholars interpret the *hadith* as evidence that the Prophet
designated 'Ali as his successor.[5] They have taken this affirmation to
justify a succession of Imams who through the bloodline are transcen-
dentally linked to 'Ali, and through him to the Prophet.

Simultaneously, Shi'i scholars have advanced several arguments for
the necessity of the Imamate not only to embody religious leadership
but also to spawn a system of Islamic governance under the Imam or
those who are qualified to deputise in his absence. For example,
Shaykh Abu al-Qasim 'Ali ibn Husayn al-Sharif al-Murtada
(965–1044), a prominent Shi'i scholar also known as 'Alam al-Huda,
writes that the Imamate was self-evident because 'reason (*'aql*) requires
that there should be a leader at all times, that this leader should be
infallible [and that he is such that] one is secure against his committing
any bad deed'.[6]

The Shi'i conception of the Imam as having divine authority has had
several important influences in shaping the doctrine of the Imamate.

First, it underpins the principle of the Imam being *hujjat Allah* (God's proof). Unlike Sunni Islam, where the *umma* is taken to be proof of the existence of God, for the Shi'a, the Imam is the direct proof of God. The Shi'i philosopher and theologian Sadr al-Din Muhammad Shirazi, also known as Mulla Sadra (1572–1640), wrote:

For as long as the earth sustains in existence and there are people in the world, there should necessarily be for them a Proof (*hujja*) of Allah who is in charge of their affairs and guides them towards the right path and the good Return (*husn al-ma'ād*) in afterlife. And that person is the outer proof who must necessarily possess knowledge of God and His signs/verses [of the Qur'an] that testify to the truth of what he says and his invitation for the people, as well as to the establishment of his rule over them and the proof of his justice among them. [This knowledge] is the esoteric proof (*al-hujja al-bāṭina*), and verily Allah tells the truth and shows the path.[7]

The concept of proof (*hujja*), then, is central to Shi'a Islam because it underpins the legitimacy of the Imamate.

Hujja also implies that the Imam has specific knowledge (*'ilm*). Knowledge became another central requirement for the Imam from the eighth century, although various sects differ in their interpretation of the extent and nature of this knowledge. In the view of Twelver Shi'a Islam, the Imam possesses special knowledge, due to his relationship with God and his position as an intermediary between God and man. It claims that 'Ali ibn Abi Talib stated that 'the door of knowledge has been opened to me by the Prophet and, as a result, thousands of other doors opened'.[8] The Qur'an is complex and, as Mulla Sadra argues, its path to salvation is not accessible to everyone. The Imam, therefore, possesses a necessary and central role in interpreting Scripture and leading the *umma* to salvation through esoteric exegesis, and this role, in Sadra's view, is *hujja*.[9]

In addition to divine and prophetic designation, religious knowledge is one of the sources of the Imam's legitimacy.[10] Abdulaziz Sachedina writes that possession of *'ilm* and knowledge of the traditions was established and theologically elaborated as underpinning an Imam's authority during the Shi'i Buyid dynastic rule in western Iran and Iraq (945–1055).[11] Yet even before this time, the linking of the Imam's authority to his knowledge of Islam had raised issues for Shi'a Muslims. This occurred, for example, when the eighth Imam, 'Ali ibn Musa al-Rida (also called Abu al-Hasan, 'Ali al-Reza or, commonly among Persians, Imam Reza, 766–818) died and was succeeded by his seven-year-old son, Muhammad ibn 'Ali ibn Musa (also called Abu Ja'far, Ibn al-Ridha, al-Jawad, or al-Taqi and commonly known as Imam al-Jawad, 811–35). Said Arjomand writes that 'many prominent figures in the Imami community asked how ... a child of seven, could act as the authoritative teacher of the scripture and the law'.[12] Similarly, another crisis of legitimacy was caused because the followers of another Imam not included among the twelve Imams, 'Abd Allah ibn Ja'far (d. 766) did not view him as being adequately knowledgeable in religious issues.[13]

A combination of the Imam's divine qualities and knowledge means that the Imamate possesses both spiritual and temporal authority and legitimacy. Indeed, the main point of difference between the *khalifa* and the Imam is that the *khalifa* is the socio-political leader of the *umma* and does not need to have a strong theological standing,[14] while for the Shi'a, an Imam is not just a prayer leader, but also wields religious and temporal authority that demands possession of unrivalled and esoteric religious knowledge. In this view, an Imam is the leader of the *umma* and occupies this position both via his descent from the Prophet's bloodline, as well as his knowledge and wisdom as a jurist. Hamid Mavani writes:

Since the Shi'ite theory of authority conceives of Imamate as a continuation of *nubuwwah* [Prophethood], the scope of the authority and the claim to absolute legitimate obedience enjoyed by the divine guides is identical with that of Muhammad and encompasses both the *zahir* (apparent, manifest, exterior) and *batin* (hidden, interior) aspects of Islam.[15]

In reality, the Imamate has only rarely existed as a concrete political and territorial entity. Early notable examples where this occurred were the Fatimid Empire (909–1171), Safavid Iran (1501–1722), and most recently and prominently the Islamic Republic of Iran (1979–), the last of which is discussed and analysed later. Hillel Fradkin writes that Shi'ism is 'a deeply political theological doctrine that lacked a direct political expression'.[16] This relative marginalisation of politics complements the Shi'i concept of *taqiyya* (prudent dissimulation), which permits Shi'a Muslims to lie and deny their religion in the face of persecution while they await the return of the Mahdi (the Guided One or the saviour of mankind).[17] Because Imams were historically politically powerless, several theories emerged to deal with political authority, temporal rule, and 'just' rule.[18] The basis of these theories stems from the conception that the Imamate constitutes a direct continuation of the Prophetic era.

The Shi'i notion of Imams being God's representatives implies that they are 'divinely guided ... infallible leader[s]'.[19] Indeed, the concept of infallibility (*'isma*) is central to Imami (Twelver) Shi'a Islam. According to one *hadith*, the Prophet allegedly stated that 'I, 'Ali, Hasan, Husayn, and the nine of the descendants of Husayn are pure and sinless'.[20] Imams are individuals of impeccable personal and spiritual character, designated by God and divinely guided by him. Moreover, as mentioned above, they are the external proof (*hujja*) of God's existence.[21] Thus, unlike Sunni Islam, there is no provision for the removal of an Imam.

Because the Imam is both God's proof and his chosen recipient for the divine knowledge that is necessary to lead the *umma* to salvation, there can only be one such leader at any time. This argument is reinforced by the fact that the Imam is the vessel of divine knowledge and authority that is transmitted from each Imam to his successor. Arjomand writes that 'science is inherited ... 'Ali was indeed the learned one (*'alim*) of the community; and no learned one among us dies except when there is a successor after him who knows the like of his'.[22] As a result, succession is determined by designation (*nass*). The principle of *nass* is the mechanism for succession and was important in ensuring stability and continuity of the Imamate. The legitimacy of each Imam derived from his designation by his predecessor – this designation, in turn, gave each Imam spiritual authority. This is in contrast to the Sunni *khilafa*, where leadership is derived from the community's consensus, that is, from a temporal rather than a spiritual source. In practice, however, after the reigns of the first four 'Rightly Guided Caliphs' (*al-Khulafa al-Rashidun*), the succession in practice became hereditary in Sunni Islam as well.[23]

The Greater Occultation

While there is arguably a general consensus about the nature of the Imamate, there is much greater disagreement among Shi'a over the leadership of the *umma* after the disappearance of the final Imam. Unlike their Sunni counterparts, the Shi'i *'ulama* never developed a unified theory of statehood until the rise of the Islamic Republic under

Ayatullah Khomeini, as discussed in detail later. This is in part due to the internal disagreements over the succession to the Imamate. There is widespread agreement about the legitimacy of the first six Imams across all Shi'i sects, with the exception of the Zaydis. The latter believe that Zayd ibn 'Ali (695–740), the son of the fourth Imam, 'Ali ibn Husayn (known as Zayn al-Abdin, 659–713) was the next successor to the Imamate instead of his half-brother. Zaydis accept the Caliphates of Abu Bakr and 'Umar as politically expedient, and therefore do not hold the *Rashidun* at fault for usurping the rightful place of 'Ali.[24] In general, Zaydi Islam departs from other sects in asserting that the only criterion for leadership of the Imamate is that an individual be a descendant of the Prophet's grandsons, Hasan or Husayn (that is to say, a *Sayyid*). Furthermore, they reject the principle of infallibility and, unlike their many Imami counterparts who view dissimulation and political quiescence as permissible, take an activist position in viewing rebellion and rejection of corrupt and unjust rule as legitimate and necessary.[25]

A second schism emerged after the death of the sixth Imam Ja'far al-Sadiq (700–65); one group supported his son, Isma'il ibn Ja'far al-Mubarak (719–62), who had died three years before his father. This raised important questions about the concept of *nass* and had potentially problematic implications for the doctrine of *'isma* (moral infallibility or incorruptible innocence). The followers of Isma'il, who became known as the Isma'ilis, argued that succession therefore passed to the seventh Shi'i Imam, Muhammad ibn Isma'il (740–813), who was Isma'il ibn Ja'far's son and Sadiq's grandson. The descendants of this faction established the Fatimid dynasty in Africa, with Egypt as its centre. Others, however, rejected this line of succession, claiming that the Imamate passed instead on to Musa al-Khadim, Isma'il's younger brother. They became known as the Twelver Shi'a, whose last or twelfth Imam, Muhammad ibn Hasan al-Mahdi (July 868–January 874), known as Imam Zaman, disappeared after his father was killed. They affirm that this final Imam, the Mahdi, will one day return and usher in the end of the world.[26]

In both Isma'ili and Twelver Islam, Shi'i philosophers and theologians developed the concept of 'Occultation' (*ghayba*) to account for the continuation of leadership of the *umma* following the disappearance of the final Imam.[27] As Moojan Momen writes, 'the Imam had left no specific instructions as to how the community was to be organised in his absence. In particular, the Imam's role as the head of the community was left vacant and a number of functions invested in him ... thus theoretically lapsed'.[28] The theory of Occultation states that the twelfth Imam did not die, but disappeared, his life preserved and hidden by God (for various reasons, notably for his own protection in the face of a growing number of enemies).

An Imami theologian, Ibn Qiba al-Razi (d. 929), played a definitive role in laying out the theological and rationalist framework for Occultation.[29] During a period of Lesser Occultation, the immediate period after the disappearance of the Mahdi, he communicated with his followers through four *babs* or deputies. Afterwards, the Imamate entered the period of the Greater Occultation, during which the Imam no longer communicated with the outside world, but was still present and involved in its affairs.[30] This doctrine helped resolve many of the crises facing the Imamate, notably the apparent violation of the principle of *nass*, as the death of the twelfth Imam would have meant that there was no Imam present on earth. This in turn would have implied that all the religious and political injunctions of the Imami theologians would have become void, while also contradicting several Shi'i tenets such as *hujja* (proof).

The theory of Occultation did not, however, provide a definitive, comprehensive, or authoritative prescription for how the political and spiritual leadership of the *umma* should be carried out in the interim. With the disappearance of the Mahdi, the functions and responsibilities of the Imam 'lapsed' (*saqit*). Since the eleventh century, various Shi'i scholars have sought to legitimise the transfer of the execution of, at the very least, the Imam's religious duties, to the *'ulama* through the institution of *niyabat al-Imam* (deputyship of the Imam).[31] Between the eleventh and sixteenth centuries, Shi'i theology progressively expanded the scope of the *'ulama*'s authority in carrying out the various religious functions formerly under the provenance of the Imam. This trend reached its culmination with a grand Shi'i scholar, Zayn al-Din ibn Nur al-Din 'Ali ibn Ahmad al-'Amili al-Juba'i, known as Shahid al-Thani (1506–58), who argued that the *'ulama* should be responsible for all religious duties, including collecting taxation and even waging defensive *jihad*.[32] This process was epitomised in the doctrine of *al-na'ib al-'amm* (general deputy to the Imam during the Occultation).

It was during this time that the concept of *wilayat al-faqih* (the rule of supreme jurist; Persian, *velayat-e faqih*) first developed. It took two initial forms: *al-wilaya al-i'tibariyya* (relative or limited authority), which endowed jurists with religious, 'non-litigious' authority over issues such as the collection of a religious tax called *khums* (one fifth) and the management of inheritance; and *al-wilaya al-'amma* (general authority), which is also referred to variously as *al-wilaya al-mutlaqa* (absolute authority) and *al-wilaya al-takwiniyya* (formative authority).[33]

Devolving *wilaya* to jurists therefore has an established precedent in Twelver Islam – the main question and debates have centred on the *scope* of these powers.[34] Shahrough Akhavi traces the earliest proposals of endowing jurists with political powers to the Mullah Ahmad ibn Muhammad Mahdi ibn Abi Dhar al-Naraqi (1771–1829). The latter made the first concerted argument in favour of *wilayat al-faqih* by arguing that the *mujtahids*, who exercised a 'general viceregency' (*niyaba 'amma*), should possess the same political, as well as juristic, authority as the Imams.[35] In his *'Awa'id al-ayyam* ('Outcomes of the Days', what can be described as a basic Shi'i *fiqh* text), he wrote that only *mujtahids* were qualified and authorised to wield the political and religious authority held by the Imams because they are 'the trustees of the Prophet and will not be tied up with the kings'.[36] Similarly, Shaykh Muhammad Husayn Kashif al-Ghita, a nineteenth-century scholar, also proposed some form of political authority for the *'ulama*, albeit of an admittedly more limited character.[37]

Until the *'ulama*'s institutionalisation and empowerment from the sixteenth century under the Safavids, questions of political authority were generally not comprehensively discussed, simply because there was no need. The devolution of religious duties only became practically enforceable with the collapse of the Safavid dynasty (1501–1722), which led the *'ulama* to work in tandem with the ruling Shah in the execution of religious and temporal governance. The breakdown of Safavid power enabled the now institutionalised *'ulama* to become more involved and assertive in religious and political activity.[38] Various *mujtahids* took on increasing roles, such as the collection of religious taxes and even the declaration of *jihad* against Russia during the Russo-Persian War (1804–13). Indeed, retreating state control, combined with the development of independent religious taxation (*khums* and *zakat*), proved pivotal to ensuring the *'ulama*'s independence from the state.[39]

This emerging institutionalisation of the *'ulama*'s political role was further aided by developments under the Qajar dynasty (1785–1925), which cemented an already developing hierarchical clerical structure based on scholarship and knowledge through the concept of *taqlid* (emulation). In Twelver Islam, this connotes that those who have not acquired the religious knowledge needed to practise *ijtihad* must follow the rulings of a jurist – a *mujtahid*. It was also during this time that the position of ayatullah emerged,[40] alongside the bourgeoning of a Shi'i hierarchy led by the most learned scholars: grand ayatullahs, who were referred to as *marja' al-taqlid* (source of emulation).[41] The institution-alisation of the *'ulama* also led to the bifurcation of religious and temporal spheres of authority. While the *'ulama* maintained religious legitimacy under the Qajars, temporal power came from the authority of the state, which was distinctly separate, although it often worked in tandem with the increasingly powerful *'ulama*.[42]

However, disputes over the nature and exercise of political authority continued. This widened an already existing split between quietist and activist currents within Shi'a Islam in general and in Iran in particular. Historically and theologically speaking, Twelver Shi'a clergy have erred on the side of quietism, not pledging allegiance to states while awaiting the return of the Mahdi (a period known as *intizar*).[43] This is a passive approach, however, which legitimises the practice of *taqiyya*. As Calder writes:

Politically, the doctrine of the *Ghayba* [Occultation] and that of *suqut* (lapsing) indicate a denial of legitimacy but an abstention from active opposition: the *shari'a*, in its political aspects, is not being put into effect but there is no one available to implement it. Practically, the Imamis were enabled to establish a perennial *de facto* rapprochement with actual governments.[44]

Momen argues that Shi'i theology and philosophy have demonstrated that the *'ulama* did not constitute one coherent class, and that they evinced varied, plural attitudes towards the question of political authority that typically fell along one of three approaches to the state: (1) cooperation and co-optation; (2) aloofness or separation; or (3) activism and reformation.[45] Adel Hashemi-Najafabadi describes the question of political leadership as dividing the Shi'i *'ulama* between 'traditionalists' (quietists) and 'fundamentalists' (activists).[46]

In the first category, many believed that clerics had only religious and not political authority, and that the role of the *'ulama* was to advise secular authorities on issues of religious and ethical importance. Rosset writes that 'this approach is based on the fundamental

Shiite outlook of anticipating the return of the hidden Imam, who, upon his return, will lead the Umma [the Islamic community] in all aspects'.[47] Thus,

the raison d'être of Imamate is to provide authoritative guidance, not governance (*maqiim-e hidiiyat* and not *maqiim-e pukümat*) with the aim of leading humankind to prosperity, felicity and perfection in this life and the afterlife. Accordingly, it is not necessary for the divine guide to assume a political post in order to validate his station of Imamate.[48]

Thus, for example, Mullah Ahmad Naraqi (1771–1829) advocated for the devolution of political authority onto the *'ulama*, whilst his pupil, Shaykh Murtaza Ansari (1800–64), espoused a typically quietist position that sought to refute his mentor's activist ideas. Ansari argued that it was '[a]bsurd ... to reason that because the Imams should be obeyed in all temporal and spiritual matters, the *faqih* [should] also [be] entitled to such obedience'.[49] He called for restricting the functions of the *faqih* to '1) issuing authoritative opinions; 2) arbitrating disputes; [and] 3) exercising guardianship for the disposal of properties and persons'.[50]

More recently, the Iraqi Grand Ayatullah 'Ali al-Sistani (1930–) argued that governance and popular sovereignty were not incompatible, espousing a democratic conception of Shi'a Islam that acknowledged nation-state boundaries.[51] Similarly, Grand Ayatullah Muhammad Kazem Shariatmadari (1905–86), perhaps the most prolific quietist Shi'i cleric prior to the Iranian revolution of 1978/79, advocated only a limited role for the *'ulama* in the state.[52] He opposed direct political involvement and the concentration of political power in one individual *'alim*. His stance ran contrary to Khomeini's position and as a result he was put under house arrest until his death.

Despite the debate among the Shi'i *'ulama* over the question of political engagement, it is important to note that until the turn of the twentieth century, most of them remained apolitical, seeing their role as religious, concerned with matters such as interpreting *shari'a*, collecting *khums*, and looking after those dependent on them. Those who engaged in religious-based political discourse were limited in number and were mostly confined to the city of Qom, south of Tehran, which had gradually emerged as the bastion of Shi'i learning and seat of the clerics' political influence. However, the political role of the *'ulama* began to change with their growing institutional and social influence and independence against the backdrop of three primary developments. One was the Qajar dynasty's growing concerns about the Shi'i establishment as a potential source of opposition to its repressive rule. Another was the traditional Anglo-Russian rivalry over, and interferences in, Iran, which intensified with the discovery of oil and the rapid domination of this industry by the British. The third was the sociopolitical and economic changes that swept the Muslim world, notably in the face of colonialism. These developments incentivised more *'ulama* to engage in increasingly political interpretations of their role. Fundamentalist activist scholars reinterpreted scriptural sources to support arguments in favour of greater religious supervision over and authority in the state. For example, they reinterpreted a *hadith* that read, 'Concerning the new cases that occur, refer to the transmitters of our Traditions, for they are my *hujja* (proof) unto you and I am God's proof unto them',[53] as a justification for both the religious and political authority of the *'ulama*, although this *hadith* is typically used to justify the devolution of religious authority to the *'ulama* during the Occultation.

The political involvement of the *'ulama* had limited beginnings. In 1891, Grand Ayatullah Muhammad Hasan Husseini Shirazi (1815–96) issued a *fatwa* against the selling of tobacco to the British, but at the same time explicitly stated that he would withdraw from political involvement once the issue had been resolved. Similarly, activist clerics supported Iran's 1906 Constitutional Revolution, for domestic and foreign policy reforms to limit the powers of the Shah and undercut the Anglo-Russian rivalry. However, they sought only a supervisory role whereby senior clerics could oversee legislation to ensure its accordance with *shari'a*.[54] At the same time, a major theoretical development occurred involving the reinterpretation of the traditionally passive Shi'i concept of *intizar* to an active one of:

spiritual, material, and ideological readiness for revolutionary action, belief in the universal change and certainty that justice will become victorious over oppression, that the pauperized and enslaved classes will inherit the earth.[55]

Thus, the

[e]xpectation is no longer simply a hope that one day justice will rule supreme and that men will be delivered through divine intervention. Rather, expectation comes to mean man's deliverance through his own actions.[56]

Even among the activist scholars who advocated for greater political involvement, there emerged a wide variety of different perspectives on the nature and degree of this involvement. During the Constitutional Era (1905–11), the majority of activist clerics went only so far as to advocate for supervision by jurists over government, rather than their direct involvement in its execution. However, a smaller camp took a more extreme position, arguing that the *'ulama* should inherit the political and religious functions of the Imamate. For instance, a prominent cleric and philosopher, Ayatullah Morteza Mutahhari (1919–79), argued for Islam to come out of 'the corner of mosques and temples' to 'become a philosophy of life dominating society'. He proposed that the *'ulama* should 'play the role of true leaders rather than that of indirect followers' and advocate for the 'active involvement' of the Shi'i *'ulama* to establish an ideal Islamic society.[57] In his view, the Shi'a must actively work to establish this society as a precursor and in anticipation of the return of the Mahdi. Similarly, Allameh Tabatabai (1904–81), another prominent Shi'i philosopher, argued that 'no society in any circumstances can be free from the need for guardianship'. He asserted that in lieu of the Imam, leadership should be given to a 'person who is supreme in religious righteousness, sane judgment, and awareness of the situation'.[58] Grand Ayatullah Hussein 'Ali Montezari (1922–2009), too, envisaged a specific role for the *vali-e faqih* (Supreme Leader), yet one that was not directly involved in legislative and executive power, but more as an overseer: 'an unelected jurist does not have any responsibility except to guide and expound his ideas to the people. A jurist cannot impose his ideas – even with the help of the minority – upon the majority of people.'[59] For him, the legitimacy of the jurist stemmed from his election by the people, and the position should have limitations placed upon it to avoid despotism.[60]

In contrast to Montezari, there was 'Ali Shari'ati (1933–77), an innovative Shi'i thinker and activist, who strongly advocated for clerical involvement in affairs of state. He combined religious activism with nationalism in criticising Iran's monarch, Muhammad Reza Shah Pahlavi, and the *'ulama*, whom he admonished for having allied themselves with the Shah in the tradition of 'Safavid Islam', which he regarded as 'debased, quietist, and obscurantist'.[61] He contrasted this with the dynamic, just, and active nature of his revolutionary brand of Islam.[62] Shari'ati influenced a whole generation of mostly young Shi'a scholars and political activists. In the process, he played an important role in public mobilisation and legitimation in support of the forthcoming revolution that finally opened the way for the politically activist clerics whose ambition was to transform Iran into an Islamic Republic.

Iran under the Imamate as the 'Vanguard' of the *Umma*

As the debate over political involvement continued to be waged between Shi'i scholars in the twentieth century, the circumstances in Iran unexpectedly changed in favour of the radical activists, propelling them to political ascendancy and power. This development came about in the wake of the Iranian revolution of 1978/79, which resulted in the overthrow of the pro-Western monarchy of Muhammad Reza Shah Pahlavi. The Shah, who had ascended the throne of Persia in 1941, had ruled the country largely at the behest of the United States from 1953. Although the revolution commenced in pursuit of transforming Iran into a constitutional monarchy, it ended by enabling the radical Shi'i activists to assume the leadership of the state. Leading them was the Shah's chief religious and political opponent and clerical revolutionary, Ayatullah Khomeini (1902–89), who had lived in exile in Iraq since the early 1960s, with a brief period in France. His triumphant return to Iran took place two weeks after the revolution forced the Shah himself to go into exile on 17 January 1979. With overwhelming clerical and popular support, Khomeini declared Iran an Islamic Republic, following the results of a referendum in May 1979. He did so with the clear goal of transforming Iran into an Islamic polity, according to his vision of Islam, for the first time in Iranian history. To establish this Islamic order at home as the foundation for leading the global *umma*, he reformulated and recast the concept of Imamate in Shi'a Islam.

Khomeini was a trained theologian and philosopher, versed in both Islamic and Western philosophy, from a very strict Shi'i religious background. His attitude towards leadership, the state, and the *umma* had nevertheless evolved over time. Initially, he had tacitly accepted the necessity of the state and the monarchy, arguing that 'bad order was better than no order at all'.[63] His activism only emerged publicly following the death of his mentor, Grand Ayatullah Seyyed Hossein Borujerdi (1875–1961), the dominant jurist of his time. Borujerdi had argued against the *'ulama*'s direct involvement in politics, and had only

endorsed their role as overseers of the government in order to ensure its
compliance with *shari'a*. Khomeini had intentionally refrained from
political activism out of respect for his teacher.[64] After Borujerdi's
death, however, Khomeini opted for public criticism of the Shah's rule.
From Qom, he denounced the Shah for violating the constitution,
spreading moral corruption, and serving American and Israeli interests. Khomeini also rejected the Shah's White Revolution or 'the revolution of the Shah and people', which had been designed to implement
a series of pro-Western secular social and economic reforms, commen-
cing in 1962. Meanwhile, he accused the monarch of straying from the
path of Shi'a Islam and pursuing a policy of 'capitulation' to the United
States by allowing Americans who committed crimes in Iran to be tried
under US laws. Meanwhile, he accelerated his call for direct religious
involvement in political affairs.[65] About the same time, Khomeini's
peers, led by Grand Ayatullah Shariatmadari, elevated him to the rank
of ayatullah and *marja'-e taqlid* – the highest ranking positions in the
Shi'i hierarchy. This promotion was largely to protect him against state
punishment.

   Despite these promotions, in 1962, the Shah's notorious secret police
(SAVAK) arrested and incarcerated Khomeini, causing his supporters
to lead the January 1963 uprisings. Although he was released within a
year, his continued anti-Shah activities and rising influence within the
Shi'i establishment led the authorities to banish him in May 1964. He
spent the next fourteen years in exile, mostly in Iraq, where he was
harboured by the Shah's regional rival, the dictatorial Saddam Hussein, and where he preached amongst the Iraqi Shi'a and sharpened the
political edge of his theology. He nonetheless maintained his links with
the *ruhaniyyat* (the clerical stratum) network in Iran, who opposed
what Khomeini now also regarded as the Shah's illegitimate rule. In his
sermons, which were smuggled into Iran and disseminated through this
clerical network, he hearkened to the core Shi'i theme of justice,
tapping into the emotions, sensitivities, and vulnerabilities of the wide
cross-section of Iranians who had accumulated grievances against the
Shah's regime.

   Khomeini contended that Islam presents a comprehensive socio-
political system, and that an Islamic Government led by the scholarly
experts of Islamic law (the *fuqaha*) is necessary to carry out God's
plans. He stated that '[s]ince Islamic government ... is a government
of law, those acquainted with the law, or more precisely, with

religion – i.e. the *fuqaha* – must supervise its functioning. It is they who supervise all executive and administrative affairs of the country, together with all planning.'[66] Going further than any of his predecessors, Khomeini argued that the *'ulama*'s religious and political authority should be concentrated in the theocratic authority of a single learned and qualified jurist (*faqih*).[67] He demonstrated this radical activist position clearly when he wrote:

To offer judgement on a question of law or to expound the laws in general is, of course, one of the dimensions of *fiqh*. But Islam regards law as a tool, not as an end in itself. Law is a tool and an instrument for the establishment of justice in a society, as a means for man's intellectual and moral reform and his purification.[68]

He referred to several Shi'i traditions, notably a *hadith* concerning the sixth Imam,[69] as well as the concept of *toqih sharif* (the Exalted Stamp), where the twelfth Imam, in response to a question about seeking guidance for problems in 'newly occurring circumstances', said that 'you should turn [for guidance] to those who relate to our traditions, for they are my proof to you, as I am God's proof'.[70] As Farhang Rajaee writes, Khomeini argued that these circumstances 'refer to social and political issues, since it was already established practice, even in the lifetime of Imams, to refer questions and issues of a personal nature to the jurists'.[71] This interpretation built on pre-existing arguments justifying the *'ulama*'s religious, and later on, juristic, authority.[72]

   Khomeini relied on four sources to formulate his theory of *velayat-e faqih* (guardianship of the jurist) and Islamic government, which are central to his conception of *umma*. The first and most authoritative, as for all Muslim theologians, was the Qur'an. The second was the *sunna*, which in Twelver Shi'ism includes not only the traditions, sayings, and deeds of the Prophet, but also those of his *ahl al-bayt*. Two particularly influential sources in Twelver Shi'a jurisprudence are the teachings of the sixth Imam, Ja'far ibn Muhammad al-Sadiq (702–65), and Shaykh Abu Ja'far Muhammad ibn Ya'qub al-Kulayni's (864–941) *hadith* collection, *Kitab al-kafi* (The Sufficient Book). Third, Khomeini relied on the concept of the *ijma'* (consensus) of the time of the Prophet and Shi'i Imams, including 'Ali ibn Abi Talib, the Prophet's son-in-law. The fourth source was *'aql* (intellect or reasoning) – a term with a variety of technical meanings in Islamic theology and philosophy. All Sunni and

Shi'i schools of jurisprudence recognise *'aql* as a source of law, yet it has been used more extensively by Shi'i jurists.

Khomeini built his theory of *velayat-e faqih* on the basis of these sources in the context of encapsulating all the scholarship and debates in Shi'a Islam concerning the requirements for governing the *umma* during the period of the Greater Occultation. He concurred with many like-minded assertive predecessors that the Imams' functions – both juristic and political – should be devolved to the jurists, who are the most learned, respected, and just members of Muslim society.[73] Khomeini, indeed, was not the first ayatullah to pioneer the idea of an Islamic Government. Several before him had advocated such a position since the turn of the twentieth century. One of his most prominent and influential predecessors was Ayatullah Kashani (1882–1962), who served as Chairman of the Iranian *majles* (consultative assembly) during Muhammad Mossadeqh's premiership. Known for his advocacy of Islamic Government, he initially made common cause with the political secularist Mossadeqh over the nationalisation of the Anglo-Iranaian Oil Company. However, when Mossadeqh refused to give Kashani's supporters a meaningful share of executive power, he turned against the prime minister, which helped precipitate Mossadeqh's downfall.[74]

However, Khomeini's detailed and innovative exposition of the doctrine of Islamic Government was unique. His writings, statements, and sermons attest to an unwavering conviction in the superiority of Islam as a system for governing all aspects of human life, and in the unique authenticity of his own theological interpretation.[75] Khomeini was the first Shi'i leader to provide a unified theory of *velayat-e faqih* as a system of Islamic governance. His idea of a single jurist possessing direct leadership in the state constituted a major revolution within Shi'i theology, which had hitherto only flirted with the idea.[76] For this reason, his theory of Islamic Government, particularly in its later stages after several revisions that progressively centralised power in the hands of the *faqih*, is sometimes referred to as *velayat-e motlagheye faqih* (the absolute guardianship of the jurist, as opposed to the limited guardianship of the jurist, which is restricted to non-public, religious non-litigious issues).[77] In effect, the concept of *faqih* can generally be described as 'supreme political and religious leader' or a prototype of the Platonic concept of the 'philosopher king'.

Importantly, in Khomeini's view this jurist, or Supreme Leader, is invested with similar roles to that of the Imam, but not necessarily the same status. He wrote: 'When we say that after the Occultation, the just *faqih* has the same authority that the Most Noble Messenger and the Imams had, do not imagine the status of the *faqih* is identical to that of the Imams and the Prophet.'[78] Be that as it may, 'the true rulers are the *fuqaha* themselves, and rulership ought officially to be theirs, to apply to them, not to those who are obliged to follow the guidance of the *fuqaha* on account of their own ignorance of the law'.[79] He argues, in effect, that the *faqih* possesses the same functions as the Imams, if not their divine qualities, and that this authority is 'a grave responsibility' that is akin to 'the appointment of a guardian for a minor'.[80] Nonetheless, the inevitable divisions that have arisen between the *faqih*, or Supreme Leader, and the *fuqaha*, or the jurists underneath him, have underpinned debates about the extent of the former's authority, which is enshrined in the following section of Article 5 of the constitution of the Islamic Republic of Iran:

During the Occultation of the Wali al-Asr [the Mahdi] (may God hasten his reappearance), the *wilayah* and leadership of the Umma devolve upon the just ('*adil*) and pious (*muttaqi*) faqih, who is fully aware of the circumstances of his age; courageous, resourceful, and possessed of administrative ability, [he] will assume the responsibilities of this office in accordance with Article 107.

It should be noted that Khomeini's conception of Islamic Republicanism was primarily based on divine, and not popular, sources of legitimacy.

In his theory of the guardianship of the jurist, Khomeini changed the basis of sovereignty and legitimacy of the Iranian state, because now, as Ali Gheissari and Vali Nasr note, 'religious knowledge define[s] the worth of political leadership'.[81] Khomeini justified this on the grounds that 'since Islamic government is a government of law, [therefore] knowledge of the law is necessary for the ruler'.[82] As a result, the central requirement and qualification to be the Supreme Leader is 'knowledge of the [religious] law and justice'. Khomeini wrote that:

If a worthy individual possessing these two qualities arises and establishes government, he will possess the same authority as the Most Noble Messenger ... in the administration of society, and it will be the duty of all people to obey him ... government devolves instead upon one who possesses the qualities of knowledge and justice.[83]

In this, he drew on the longstanding emphasis that Shi'a theologians had placed on knowledge (*'ilm*) and jurisprudence (*fiqh*) as prerequisites for leadership of the *umma*. Indeed, the constitution of the Islamic Republic of Iran, which was adopted in 1979 and amended a decade later, states that the jurist must possess these very qualifications.[84]

If the doctrine of *velayat-e faqih* placed the jurist at the head of the state, it also placed the state at the forefront of an Islamic society. Khomeini developed his theory in the context of the growing politicisation of the *'ulama* and massive social upheavals – both of which were a reaction to the Shah's autocratic modernisation policies. The prominence of the state's powers over society, elucidated in his theory of *velayat-e faqih,* displays his *ijtihadi* tendencies or creative interpretation and application of Islam based on independent human reasoning. In fact, after the revolution and the 1 May 1979 referendum endorsing the Islamic system, Khomeini moved to endow the *faqih* with absolute, extra-constitutional powers. Initially, he had defined the *faqih* as a first-among-equals with fellow jurists, who had the authority to appoint the head of the judiciary, endorse presidents, issue pardons, and designate the head of the Joint Chiefs of Staff.[85] Several subsequent constitutional revisions extended this authority, however,[86] empowering the *faqih* to influence and veto policy, to select members of an Expediency Council, and to wield greater control over the judiciary.[87] Another example of Khomeini's *flexible* approach were the amendments to the constitution. For example, the original constitution stipulated that only a *marja' al-taqlid* was qualified to be Supreme Leader. When it transpired that no single *marja' al-taqlid* remained who supported his political system, the constitution was amended to remove this provision.[88] Indeed, Khomeini's endorsed successor, 'Ali Khamenei, who remains in the position of Supreme Leader to date, was not a *marja'* or even an ayatullah.

Khomeini's *ijtihadi* approach is epitomised in the most extreme innovation of the *velayat e-faqih* – his argument that the jurist can supersede *shari'a*:

The government can unilaterally abrogate legal ... agreements that it has made with the people ... The government can – when it sees fit to contravene the good of the Islamic country – prevent the pilgrimage, which is one of the important divine duties ... If the government can exercise its authority only within the bounds of the peripheral divine laws, then the bestowal of the divine ordinances through absolute deputyship upon the Prophet … would be hollow and meaningless.[89]

Thus, the *faqih* is empowered to make extra-religious decisions and rulings in the interest of protecting or advancing the interests of the *umma*. Khomeini underscored this shift by redefining the system as 'the *absolute* guardianship of the jurist'.[90] In this, he privileged political exigencies over theological standards,[91] stating that 'the government, which is part of the absolute deputyship of the Prophet, is one of the primary injunctions of Islam and has priority over all other secondary injunctions, even prayers, fasting and hajj'.[92] In this way, he gave precedence to the institution of the Imamate over all other aspects of Shi'i practice, insisting that the '[l]ogic behind the absolute empowerment notion is that the establishment of an Islamic state supervenes in its importance every other facet of Islam, because without such a state, the very existence of Islam itself is in question'.[93]

In stressing the primacy of the Imamate, embodied in the Islamic Republic, over religious tradition, Khomeini's conception of *velayat-e-faqih* sought to appeal to two audiences: the broader *umma* (through its pan-Islamic discourse) and more specifically to Shi'i Muslims, particularly in Iran. Frederic Volpi writes that 'one can also see in Khomeini's concept of veliyat-i-faqih an attempt to articulate a Caliphate that is acceptable to Shi'a opinion and thus able to transcend divisions between Shi'a and Sunni political thought'.[94]

On the one hand, Khomeini's theory of *velayat-e faqih* asserted the *faqih*'s leadership of the whole *umma*, not just Iran, on the grounds that nationalism had created artificial divisions between Muslims. Indeed, he wrote:

Together, the imperialists and the tyrannical self-seeking rulers have divided the Islamic homeland. They have separated the various segments of the Islamic *umma* from each other and artificially created separate nations.[95]

He went on to state that it is necessary to establish an Islamic government in order to 'assure the unity of the Islamic *umma*'.[96] Indeed, Khomeini envisaged the Iranian Revolution as an Islamic Revolution that would lead to a united *umma*.[97] According to the constitution, the Supreme Leader is legally the leader of the *umma* as a whole, taking on a role, as we have seen, similar to that of an Imam (if not with more powers).[98] Article 11 of the constitution states:

In accordance with the sacred verse of the Qur'an ('This your community is a single community, and I am your Lord, so worship Me' [21:92]), all Muslims form a single nation, and the government of the Islamic Republic of Iran has the duty of formulating its general policies with a view to cultivating the friendship and unity of all Muslim peoples, and it must constantly strive to bring about the political, economic, and cultural unity of the Islamic world.

This is a clear and typical example of the pan-Islamic discourse that Khomeini and his followers employed.

On the other hand, whilst emphasising the omnipotence of the *faqih*, Khomeini was cognisant of the fact that for the *velyat-e faqih* system and the Islamic Republic of Iran to function and endure effectively in the modern world, both would require popular support and therefore worldly legitimacy. As such, he conceded that there was a critical role for the public and nation-state to play in enabling the Islamic Republic to be the vanguard that could lead the *umma* towards eventual unification.

The Islamic constitution thus enshrined a role for the people to elect jurists that they deemed acceptable, requiring that the supreme jurist be approved not only by his peers but by the population at large. Thus, while the legitimacy of a jurist exists independently of popular opinion, the population has the right to reject the jurist. In this manner, elections are a measure of the acceptability of the government amongst the population, rather than its legitimacy.[99] However, reformists such as Ayatullah Montazeri and Abdul Karim Soroush have argued that the consent of the governed is a legitimate source of authority.[100] This underlines a recurring (and still present) tension within the Iranian religious establishment over questions of sovereignty and legitimacy.

Khomeini's Cross-Sectarian Appeal and Its Drawbacks

Once in power and ensconced firmly in the position of *faqih*, with extraordinary divine and constitutional powers as well as public support, Khomeini initially shaped his messages in support of universal features of Islam and the need for the unity of the *umma*. He proclaimed that the Shi'a and Sunnis were Muslim brothers and equals, who shared a common bond through their belief in the Qur'an and *tawhid* (oneness of God) – the central principle from which flow all other principles in Islam. He warned Muslims against discord, which he claimed was the work of the enemies of Islam who wanted to divide and weaken the Muslim world, for their self-centred geopolitical ends. The main targets of his criticism were the United States and Israel, as well as ruling elites in Muslim countries. The latter he called the *mostakbareen* (the haves, or the oppressors), who had sold their countries and honour to world powers by suppressing their own people, the *mostazafeen* (the have nots, or the oppressed). The *mostakbareen*, in Khomeini's thinking, referred primarily to the surrounding pro-Western autocratic Arab monarchies, as well as the repressive regime of Saddam Hussein in Iraq and, indeed, the Soviet-backed communist groups that ruled in Afghanistan from 1978 to their overthrow in 1992.

Within his dichotomous view of the world as divided between the *mostakbareen* and the *mostazafeen*, Khomeini condemned the United States as a hegemonic and imperialist power, invoking America's history of interference in Iran and dominance in the region since the Second World War. In 1953, the Central Intelligence Agency (CIA), with assistance from the British MI6, had intervened in Iran in order to overthrow the elected government of Prime Minister Mossadeqh and prevent the nationalisation of Iran's oil industry by restoring the Shah, who was a loyal ally and linchpin for US influence in the region over the next twenty-five years. This experience, along with other US interventions in the Middle East, equipped Khomeini with ample evidence to support his adversarial attitude towards Washington. He was equally damning of Israel for its 'illegitimate' usurpation of Palestinian lands, including most importantly Jerusalem (the third holiest site of Islam, after Mecca and Medina). While branding the United States 'the Great Satan', he had no sympathy for the ideological disposition of the Soviet Union as a Godless communist power either. He opposed the pro-Soviet communist cluster that seized power in Afghanistan in April 1978 and the Soviet invasion of the country that took place twenty months later.

Khomeini's appeal for cross-sectarian pan-Islamic solidarity of Muslim peoples was not premised on religion alone. It also carried strong geopolitical undertones. He sought to enforce his stance for the unity of the mosaic Muslim *umma* with a declaration of Iran's foreign policy as neither 'East' nor 'West' but pro-Islamic, calling on Muslims in the region to emulate Iran's example by transforming their countries into revolutionary Islamic states with anti-American and anti-Israeli postures. To this end, he advocated a two-pronged and interconnected approach, which could be described as *jihadi* in the sense of assertive/ combative policies and *ijtihadi* in the more positive sense of reformist- pragmatist-internationalist action, to reshaping not only the Iranian landscape, but also that of the Muslim domain. While leading Iran down the path of his Shi'i vision, he sought to foment popular upris- ings in the Sunni-dominated region, similar to those that catapulted him and his radical clerical supporters to power. Meanwhile, to com- pensate for Iran's newfound isolation that resulted from the confron- tation with the United States and its allies, Khomeini demonstrated a balancing measure of political expediency, allowing his Islamic Gov- ernment to forge closer ties with secularist states whose political systems and ideological dispositions were at odds with his pan-Islamic stance. Those forces included Syria, Soviet Russia, the People's Repub- lic of China, and India. In effect, he aspired to create a sovereign and self-reliant Islamic state of Iran, free from political and cultural influ- ences of outside powers, most importantly the United States. To achieve this, however, he was willing to receive whatever degree of support the Islamic Republic could foster from the *umma* and Amer- ica's adversaries in the region and beyond.

Khomeini signalled his pan-Islamic aspirations in a number of ways. His call for pan-Muslim solidarity was symbolised through the insti- tution of an annual Islamic unity day – on 17 August. This event was designed to highlight the Israeli occupation of the Palestinian lands, East Jerusalem in particular, as this was an issue that resonated and continues to resonate with a significant cross-section of the Muslim population. Khomeini's desire to position himself as the spiritual leader of the global *umma* was also reflected in the *fatwas* that he issued on behalf of the international Muslim community. The best-known example – to be discussed further in Chapter 4 – is his 1989 *fatwa* calling for the execution, in the cause of *jihad*, of the Indian-born British writer Salman Rushdie. Khomeini's proclamation against the author made clear his pretensions to leadership over the entire Muslim community:

I am informing all brave Muslims of the world that the author of *The Satanic Verses*, a text written, edited, and published against Islam, the Prophet of Islam, and the Qur'an, along with all the editors and publishers aware of its contents, are condemned to death. I call on all valiant Muslims wherever they may be in the world to kill them without delay, so that no one will dare insult the sacred beliefs of Muslims henceforth. And whoever is killed in this cause will be a martyr, Allah Willing. Meanwhile if someone has access to the author of the book but is incapable of carrying out the execution, he should inform the people so that [Rushdie] is punished for his actions.[101]

Khomeini's approach succeeded in inspiring and enticing some Shi'i minorities to follow his path, and encouraged some of their Sunni counterparts to become receptive to his messages and methods. Most prominent among them were the Lebanese Shi'a, who with direct Iranian assistance, set up their own organisation of Hizbullah (Party of God). Since its foundation at the turn of the 1980s Hizbullah has become a very powerful pro-Iranian political and paramilitary force in Lebanon. Hizbullah, along with the Syrian regime of Bashar al-Asad and Iraqi Shi'i militias, not to mention the Houthis in Yemen, have now become important parts of the Islamic Republic of Iran's regional security architecture. However, not all these forces have simply acted as Iranian proxies. Moreover, intra-sectarian differences have existed. Muhammad Husayn Fadlallah (1935–2010), the spiritual head of Hizbullah, criticised Iranian attempts at religious and cultural hegemony among the Lebanese Shi'a and called Iranian domination of the *marja'iyya* (top clerical leadership) 'racist'.[102] In Yemen, the Houthis belong to the Zaydi sect, which, in some respects, is closer to Sunni Islam than Twelver Shi'ism, and religious relations between Iran and the Yemeni Zaydis have historically been limited.[103] While Iran is, and was, thus not the 'Vatican of Shi'ism',[104] Khomeini clearly advanced ambitious goals that were both religious and political.

Whatever his pan-Islamic stance, Khomeini was ultimately a Shi'i essentialist in matters of religion and a realist in matters of state. He believed that his Shi'i version of Islam was most authentic and applicable to the modern era, and he had an unwavering commitment to the sanctity and preservation of Iran as a nation-state. While proclaiming the existence of a global borderless *umma*, he nevertheless recognised the nation-state as a reality and an enduring building block in the prevailing international order. His *velayat-e faqih* system of leadership and governance, along with his promotion and rebuilding of Iran as a sovereign political, economic, and territorial entity, testified to this fact. As he progressed in his tenure as Supreme Leader, he combined his brand of Shi'i political activism with traditional fierce Iranian nationalism to transform and defend Iran as an Islamic Republic. During the eight-year-long war with Iraq, he drew on the need to protect not only Islam but also the noble nation of Iran against Iraqi aggression.

Khomeini did not appear to be cognisant that his Shi'i essentialism and geopolitical objectives presented major obstacles to persuading the Sunni majority of the world's Muslim populations to tilt to his side and rise against their 'oppressive regimes' in support of Islamic revolution. If anything, his pan-Islamist approach paradoxically caused more divisions among Muslims and turned many powerful ruling elites in the region against Iran. The Arab regimes, with the exception of those of Syria and Libya, rapidly found Khomeini's Shi'i-based Islamism threatening enough to put aside their own deep-seated differences and line up in a common cause against the Islamic Republic. They did so with full US backing and to Israel's policy advantage. Taking the lead in this opposition was Saddam Hussein, who decided to attack Iran in the midst of the post-revolutionary turmoil of mid-1980, in 'defence of the Arab nation'. The invasion triggered the longest, bloodiest, and costliest war in the history of the modern Middle East, which ended in stalemate and in a UN-brokered truce in 1988. Despite all their former misgivings about Saddam Hussein's regional ambitions, the oil-rich Gulf Arab states, along with Egypt and Jordan, found it expedient to support him financially and logistically in his war against the Islamic Republic as their newfound common enemy. Their objective was to cause the demise of the Khomeini regime and its replacement with a less hostile government. Even the West's most potent critic of Saddam Hussein's rule, the United States, joined the chorus in support of the Iraqi leader's war efforts, despite having previously condemned him for his dictatorial rule, challenges to America's regional allies (including the former Shah), and anti-US, and periodically pro-Soviet, stance in the context of the Cold War.

Herein lay the fundamental contradiction between Khomeini's appeal for pan-Islamic unification and his Shi'i essentialism and Iranian nationalism. On the one hand, he desired the unity of the *umma* and denounced the divisions of the Muslim community as the effect of imperialist designs. On the other hand, however, he insisted on the primacy of Shi'a Islam and his interpretation of it as the only legitimate model for instituting a revolutionary Islamic Republic, which was to lead the way for similar developments throughout the region in opposition to the United States and its regional allies. In addition, he emphasised the integrity and identity of the Iranian nation-state. In other words, he wanted to have it both ways.

The Islamic state that Khomeini left behind after his death in 1989 has remained subject to a tremendous amount of hostility from regional states, the United States, and Sunni Muslim leaders. Khomeini's ambition to spread Islamic revolution throughout the region has fallen flat; no state has emulated the Iranian model of governance or Khomeini's alternating combative and pragmatist approaches to domestic and foreign policy behaviour. Khomeini's successor, Ayatullah 'Ali Khamenei (1989–), has basically followed Khomeini's path. However, under him the Islamic regime has become less ideological and more pragmatic in its functioning. This development was made possible by the distinctive assertive-reformist framework that Khomeini deployed in generating the power structures and system of governance in the Islamic Republic. Khomeini delivered Iran a two-tiered system of Islamic governance, with one tier embodying the 'sovereignty of God' through a largely appointed and partially elected *faqih*, and the other representing the 'sovereignty of people' through a universally elected president and national assembly (*majles*). The main purpose of this bifurcated system was to provide for both divine and popular legitimacy. However, within the Islamic framework laid down by Khomeini, the latter was to operate in subordination to, and in organic relation with, the former.

As such, the structure of the Islamic Republic contained a degree of internal elasticity that by the time of Khomeini's death had given rise to three main factions within the system: the traditionalists or hardliners; the reformists or internationalists; and the pragmatists, who stood between the first two. This internal elasticity also provided for some external flexibility to enable the regime to make adjustments and engage in some reinvention whenever necessary for regime preservation. These features of the regime have been crucial in enabling Khamenei to ensure the continuation of his predecessor's legacy within a politically pluralist Shi'a theocratic framework, and to maintain the

Islamic Republic as a relatively stable and secure state in a very turbulent region.

As for Khamenei's stance regarding the *umma*, he has continued Khomeini's rhetoric in support of Muslim unity, but he has been even less successful than his predecessor in reaping tangible results. The Iranian regime earned a measure of broad popular approval in the Hizbullah–Israel war of July 2006, even among Sunni Arabs who appreciated the external support for Palestinians during the conflict. But, if anything, under Khamenei the Islamic Republic has become increasingly embroiled in regional hostilities and its record of influence beyond its borders is mixed. This is partly because of the Republic's transnational sectarian and forward defensive involvement in Iraq, Syria, Lebanon, and Yemen, and partly due to the US-led regional opposition to alleged Iranian expansionism and Tehran's pursuit of a nuclear programme. However, to improve economic conditions at home and soften the image of the Islamic Republic abroad and widen its appeal within the Sunni-dominated and largely pro-Western segments of the Muslim domain, Khamenei found it expedient to back the newly elected moderate President Hassan Rouhani (2013–) to reach a settlement of Iran's nuclear dispute with the United States.

As a result, during the presidency of Barack Obama (2009–17) the level of US–Iranian tension de-escalated, as the two sides entered direct talks for the first time since the advent of the Islamic Republic. These talks resulted in the signing of the historic July 2015 Joint Comprehensive Plan of Action (JCPOA) or 'nuclear agreement' between Iran and the five permanent members of the United Nations Security Council, plus Germany (P5+1), which was to curb Iranian military nuclear ambitions in return for the lifting of international sanctions. However, the 'America first' populist leadership of Obama's Republican successor, Donald Trump (2017–), saw the United States withdraw from the deal in May 2018 and reimpose American sanctions, at the same time threatening to punish any third party that conducted business with Iran. Trump's actions, backed strongly by the Israeli and Saudi governments, were opposed by other signatories, who remained committed to the agreement on the grounds that Iran had kept its end of the bargain since the implementation of the agreement in January 2016, and that the maintenance of the agreement was critical for regional and international security. Khamenei had backed the agreement as a demonstration of what he called 'heroic flexibility', but in response to the events of 2018, he promised to re-engage Iran's nuclear programme at a higher level should other signatories fail to hold to their commitment or allow America's withdrawal to affect their economic and commercial dealings with Iran. As the European, Russian, and Chinese signatories scrambled to save the agreement, it was not clear whether they would succeed in satisfying Tehran on this score and reducing the tensions between Iran and the United States and its regional allies.

Conclusion

As Chapter 2 and this chapter have shown, Sunni and Shi'i thought commonly assume that the *umma* is the community of 'believers' and that it needs proper leadership. They diverge with regard to who are proper believers and what kind of leadership is required. While both accord 'Ali ibn Abi Talib immense respect as the fourth Caliph, the Shi'a find in his blood relationship to the Prophet a hereditary principle that validates the line of succession after him. While the Caliph has wide political and religious authority in Sunni Islam, the Shi'i Imams are considered divinely designated and even infallible and thus have much greater authority in leading the community of the faith. When the Imams are no longer present, their successors who purport to speak in their name inherit immense influence.

The implication of *de facto* rather than *de jure* rule hovered, however, over the Shi'a for centuries. Most of the religious class, the *'ulama*, remained apolitical, preferring (especially in relation to the Twelver Shi'a school) to wait for the physical return of the last Imam who had gone into Occultation. With exceptions, apoliticism was the norm, but the twentieth century brought together a number of ideas about governance that had been implicit. Ayatullah Khomeini articulated a powerful vision that the clergy should not only advise but rule. Rather than abstract theory, this was the engine of a revolutionary movement and the template for the construction of an 'Islamic republic' that would serve as a beacon for Muslims elsewhere.

Khomeini, like other modern Islamic thinkers, aspired to what he saw as the restoration of pan-Islamic unity. Muslims must unite around God's sovereignty and oppose blasphemy, and the anti-Islamic position taken by Western powers. In his view, Iran, as the vanguard of the *umma*, bears a special responsibility to propagate Islam to the world and thus needs to be protected. The 'rays' of Islam spread from Iran: 'We should safeguard this source; we should protect the centre of these rays.'[105]

This ecumenical appeal was, however, undermined to a considerable extent by such sectarian allusions as the need for the Imam Mahdi to return to complete the revolution started by the Prophet – a reference that would have struck many Sunnis as undermining the idea of Muhammad's final prophecy. In the early days of the revolution, there was also a political sub-text: Iran, locked in battle with the secular Arab nationalist and dictatorial Iraq of Saddam Hussein, projected itself as its alternative – that is, both Muslim and progressive.

Indeed, the aspiration to promote the Islamic Republic of Iran, with its Shi'i system of governance (*velayat-e faqih*), as the catalyst for uniting the *umma*, has remained very much at the rhetorical level. By 2019, no Muslim country had adopted the Iranian religious and political *modus operandi*, and the *umma* had never been so divided, polarised, and demoralised. The Saudi–Iranian sectarian and geopolitical rivalries and proxy conflicts had reached a very high pitch, undermining any chance of regional cooperation, let alone unity within the *umma*. The Organisation of Islamic Cooperation, which had originated in 1969 to act as a credible venue for promoting solidarity among Muslim countries and which will be discussed further in the next chapter, has proved ineffective. The Islamic Republic of Iran has been marginalised in the Saudi-led Sunni-dominated organisation. With little or no meaningful ideological or geopolitical capability to unite the *umma*, the best that the Islamic Republic of Iran has been able to do is to look after itself in the face of mounting domestic and foreign policy challenges to its survival.

Notes

1 Abdulaziz Abdulhussein Sachedina, *The Just Ruler* (*al-Sultan al-'adil*) in *Shi'ite Islam: The Comprehensive Authority of the Jurist in Imamite Jurisprudence* (Oxford University Press, 1988), p. 119.
2 Moojan Momen, *An Introduction to Shi'i Islam: The History and Doctrines of Twelver Shi'ism* (New Haven: Yale University Press, 1985), p. 192.
3 Manzooruddin Ahmed, *Islamic Political System in the Modern Age: Theory and Practice* (Karachi: Saad Publications, 1983), p. 57.

4 Maria Massi Dakake, *The Charismatic Community: Shi'ite Identity in Early Islam* (Albany: State University of New York Press, 2007), p. 34.

5 Ibid., p. 35.

6 From al-Murtada's *Risalat al-Ghayba* (Treatise on the Occultation [of the Twelfth Imam]), as translated by Abdulaziz Sachedina, 'A Treatise on the Occultation of the Twelfth Imamite Imam', *Studia Islamica* 48 (1978): 109–24 (p. 118).

7 Quoted in Sayeh Meisami, 'Mullā Ṣadrā's Philosophical Arguments for the Necessity of the Imamate', *Religion Compass* 10, 10 (2016): 247–56 (p. 250).

8 Takamitsu Shimamoto, 'Leadership in Twelver Imami Shi'ism: Mortaza Motahhari's Ideas on the Imamate and the Role of Religious Scholars', *JISMOR* 2 (2006): 37–57 (p. 44).

9 Meisami, 'Mullā Ṣadrā's Philosophical Arguments', p. 250.

10 Said Amir Arjomand, 'The Crisis of the Imamate and the Institution of Occultation in Twelver Shiism: A Sociohistorical Perspective', *International Journal of Middle East Studies* 28, 4 (1996): 491–515 (p. 497).

11 Sachedina, *The Just Ruler*, pp. 62–3.

12 Arjomand, 'The Crisis of the Imamate', p. 497.

13 Ibid.

14 Sunni jurists agree that the Caliph exercises only temporal authority. Ahmad Vaezi, *Shi'a Political Thought* (London: Islamic Centre of England, 2004), p. 62.

15 Hamid Mavani, 'Doctrine of Imamate in Twelver Shi'ism: Traditional, Theological, Philosophical and Mystical Perspectives' (PhD dissertation, McGill University, 2005), p. 6.

16 Hillel Fradkin, 'The Paradoxes of Shiism' (report, Hudson Institute, Washington, DC, 29 May 2009), www.hudson.org/research/9885-the-paradoxes-of-shiism, accessed 20 July 2017.

17 Shahrough Akhavi, 'Contending Discourses in Shi'i Law on the Doctrine of Wilāyat al-Faqīh', *Iranian Studies* 29, 3/4 (1996): 229–68 (p. 230).

18 Said Amir Arjomand, 'Introduction: Shi'ism, Authority and Political Culture', in *Authority and Political Culture in Shi'ism*, ed. Said Amir Arjomand (Albany: State University of New York Press, 1988), pp. 3–4.

19 Vivienne S. M. Angeles, 'The Development of the Shi'a Concept of the Imamate', *Asian Studies* 21 (1983): 145–60 (p. 149).

20 Momen, *An Introduction to Shi'i Islam*, p. 155.

21 Angeles, 'The Development of the Shi'a Concept of the Imamate', p. 149.

22 Arjomand, 'The Crisis of the Imamate', p. 497.

23 Momen, *An Introduction to Shi'i Islam*, p. 147.

24 Ibid., p. 49.

25 Ibid., p. 50.

26 Angeles, 'The Development of the Shi'a Concept of the Imamate', p. 150.
27 Arjomand, 'The Crisis of the Imamate', p. 501.
28 Momen, *An Introduction to Shi'i Islam*, p. 170.
29 Arjomand, 'The Crisis of the Imamate', pp. 504–5.
30 Momen, *An Introduction to Shi'i Islam*, p. 165.
31 Sachedina, *The Just Ruler*, p. 119.
32 Momen, *An Introduction to Shi'i Islam*, p. 190.
33 Akhavi, 'Contending Discourses in Shi'i Law', p. 233.
34 Sachedina suggests that Qur'anic notions of justice underpin questions of political authority because it was the Imam's responsibility to uphold and implement the Qur'anic injunction of 'commanding the good and forbidding the evil'. This informs the conception of juristic authority as not just forming an opinion based on jurisprudence, but also taking action (arbitration) and executing these laws. *The Just Ruler*, pp. 120–35.
35 A *mujtahid* in Shi'a Islam is a qualified scholar who is empowered to interpret legal Islamic issues, based on independent human reasoning or *ijtihad*, that are not explicitly elaborated in the Qur'an. In Shi'a Islam, *mujtahids* are often an ayatullah or 'Sign of God' – the highest rank bestowed upon a Shi'i *'alim* or learned scholar, who is accepted as an original authority in Islam by his peers.
36 Mullah Ahmad al-Naraqi, quoted in Zackery M. Heern, *The Emergence of Modern Shi'ism: Islamic Reform in Iraq and Iran* (London: Oneworld Publications, 2015), p. 101.
37 Akhavi, 'Contending Discourses in Shi'i Law', p. 234.
38 Momen, *An Introduction to Shi'i Islam*, p. 191.
39 Perwez Shafi, 'Towards a General Theory of Islamic Revolution: The Problem of Legitimacy and the Transformation of the Contemporary Muslim Nation-State System' (PhD dissertation, Walden University, 1993), p. 483.
40 Ibid., p. 17.
41 Christoph Marcinowski, *Twelver Shi'ite Islam: Conceptual and Practical Aspects* (Singapore: Institute of Defence and Strategic Studies, 2006), p. 34.
42 Momen, *An Introduction to Shi'i Islam*, p. 193.
43 In fact, Khomeini argues that the decline of Muslim society is a result of the *'ulama*'s marginalisation from political power. He states: 'Indeed, it is precisely because the just *fuqaha* have not had executive power in the lands inhabited by Muslims and their governance has not been established that Islam has declined and its ordinances have fallen into abeyance.' Ruhollah Khomeini, *Islamic Government: Governance of the Jurist*, trans. and ed. Hamid Algar (Tehran: Institute for Compilation

and Publication of Imam Khomeini's Work, 2002; originally published as *Velayet-e Faqih*, 1970), p. 47.

44 Norman Calder quoted in Akhavi, 'Contending Discourses in Shi'i Law', p. 230.

45 Momen, *An Introduction to Shi'i Islam*, p. 193.

46 Adel Hashemi-Najafabadi, 'Imamate and Leadership: The Case of the Shi'a Fundamentalists in Modern Iran', *Canadian Social Science* 6, 6 (2010): 192–205 (p. 195).

47 Uri Rosset, 'Hizballah and Wilayat al-Faqih' (working paper, Eleventh Annual Herzliya Conference, The Interdisciplinary Center, Herzliya, Israel, 6–9 February 2011), p. 1.

48 Mavani, 'Doctrine of Imamate in Twelver Shi'ism', p. 16.

49 Said Amir Arjomand, 'Revolution in Shi'ism', in *Islam and the Political Economy of Meaning*, ed. William R. Roff (Sydney: Croom Helm, 1987), p. 116.

50 Akhavi, 'Contending Discourses in Shi'i Law', p. 237.

51 Yitzhak Nakash, *Reaching for Power: The Shi'a in the Modern Arab World* (Princeton University Press, 2006), p. 9.

52 Foody, 'Thinking Islam', p. 59.

53 Arjomand, 'Introduction', p. 5.

54 Ervand Abrahamian, *Khomeinism: Essays on the Islamic Republic* (London: I. B. Tauris, 1993), p. 19.

55 Ayatollah Shariati, quoted in Shafi, 'Towards a General Theory of Islamic Revolution', p. 506.

56 Ali Reza Sheikholeslami, 'From Religious Accommodation to Religious Revolution: The Transformation of Shi'ism in Iran', in *The State, Religion, and Ethnic Politics: Afghanistan, Iran, and Pakistan*, ed. Ali Banuazizi and Myron Weiner (Syracuse University Press, 1986), p. 249.

57 Ibid.

58 Hashemi-Najafabadi, 'Imamate and Leadership', p. 196.

59 Naser Ghobadzadeh, *Religious Secularity: A Theological Challenge to the Islamic State* (Oxford University Press, 2015), p. 50.

60 Adel Hashemi-Najafabadi, 'The Shi'i Concept of Imamate and Leadership in Contemporary Iran: The Case of Religious Modernists', *Studies in Religion* 40, 4 (2011): 479–96 (p. 487).

61 L. Carl Brown, *Religion and State: The Muslim Approach to Politics* (New York: Columbia University Press, 2000), pp. 168–9.

62 Ibid.

63 Abrahamian, *Khomeinism*, p. 20.

64 Hashemi-Najafabadi, 'Imamate and Leadership', p. 195.

65 Ibid., pp. 197–8.

66 Brown, *Religion and State*, p. 172.

67 Arjomand, 'Revolution in Shiʻism', p. 117.
68 Khomeini, *Islamic Government*, p. 46.
69 Akhavi, 'Contending Discourses in Shiʻi Law', p. 238.
70 Farhang Rajaee, *Islamism and Modernism: The Changing Discourse in Iran* (Austin: University of Texas Press, 2007), p. 177.
71 Ibid.
72 Said Saffari, 'The Legitimation of the Clergy's Right to Rule in the Iranian Constitution of 1979', *British Journal of Middle Eastern Studies* 20, 1 (1993): 64–82 (p. 65).
73 Shafi, 'Towards a General Theory of Islamic Revolution', p. 503.
74 See Abbas Milani, *Eminent Persians: The Men and Women Who Made Modern Iran, 1941–1979* (New York: Syracuse University Press/Persian World Press, 2008), p. 348.
75 See the section on 'Islamic Government' in Ruhollah Khomeini, *Islam and Revolution I: Writings and Declarations of Imam Khomeini (1941–1980)*, trans. and ed. Hamid Algar (Berkeley: Mizan Press, 1981), pp. 27–68.
76 Ibid.
77 Ali Siyar Rezai, 'Velayat-e Faqih: Innovation or Within Tradition' (Master's dissertation, Arizona State University, 2016), p. 34.
78 Khomeini, *Islamic Government*, p. 62.
79 Ibid., p. 32.
80 Ibid., p. 63.
81 Ali Gheissari and Vali Nasr, *Democracy in Iran: History and the Quest for Liberty* (Oxford University Press, 2006), p. 107.
82 Khomeini, *Islamic Government*, p. 31.
83 Ibid., p. 62.
84 Specifically: 'a. scholarship, as required for performing the functions of mufti in different fields of fiqh; b. justice and piety, as required for the leadership of the Islamic Ummah; c. right political and social perspicacity, prudence, courage, administrative facilities and adequate capability for leadership'. Article 109, Constitution of the Islamic Republic of Iran, as reproduced at Iran Chamber Society, *Iranian Laws and Government*, www.iranchamber.com/government/laws/constitution_ch08.php, accessed 4 June 2018.
85 Hosssein Seifzadeh, 'Ayatollah Khomeini's Concept of Rightful Governance: The *Velayat-e-Faqih*', in *Islam, Muslims, and the Modern State*, ed. Hussin Mutalib and Taj ul-Islam Hashmi (London: Macmillan, 1994), p. 205.
86 Mohsen Milani writes that the constitution was changed in forty-nine areas, including 'strengthening the presidency and demolishing the post of prime minister, destroy[ing] the collective leadership of the judiciary

by centralizing all power in the hands of a man appointed by the Leader, establish[ing] a mechanism for the future revision of the Constitution, solidif[ying] the fusion of the state with Shi'ism, and tak[ing] a few steps further away from popular sovereignty'. 'Shiism and the State in the Constitution of the Islamic Republic of Iran', in *Iran: Political Culture in the Islamic Republic*, ed. Samih K. Fasoun and Mehrdad Mashayekhi (London: Routledge, 1992), pp. 150–1.

87 Ibid., p. 206.
88 Foody, 'Thinking Islam', p. 60.
89 Quoted in Foody, 'Thinking Islam', p. 48.
90 He marked this doctrine by emphasising the word *motlaqeh* ('absolute'). Mojtaba Mahdavi, 'The Rise of Khomeinism: Problematizing the Politics of Resistance in Pre-Revolutionary Iran', in *A Critical Introduction to Khomeini*, ed. Arshin Adib-Moghaddam (Cambridge University Press, 2014), p. 43.
91 Seifzadeh, 'Ayatollah Khomeini's Concept of Rightful Governance', p. 198.
92 Hamid Mavani, 'Khomeini's Concept of Governance of the Jurisconsult (*Wilayat al-Faqih*) Revisited: The Aftermath of Iran's 2009 Presidential Election', *The Middle East Journal* 67, 2 (2013): 207–28 (p. 209).
93 Akhavi, 'Contending Discourses in Shi'i Law', p. 276.
94 Salman Sayyid, 'The Islamist Impasse?' in *Political Islam: A Critical Reader*, ed. Frédéric Volpi (Abingdon: Routledge, 2011), p. 130.
95 Khomeini, *Islamic Government*, p. 24.
96 Ibid.
97 Rosset, 'Hizballah and Wilayat al-Faqih', p. 2.
98 Eva Patricia Rakel, *Power, Islam, and Political Elite: A Study on the Iranian Political Elite from Khomeini to Ahmadinejad* (Leiden: Brill, 2009), p. 26.
99 In this perspective, elections are for the purposes of acceptability and functionality, or *maqbuliyyat*, not determining righteousness and legitimacy, or *mashru'iyyat*. Hashemi-Najafabadi, 'Imamate and Leadership', p. 202.
100 Naser Ghobadzadeh and Lily Zubaidah Rahim, 'Islamic Reformation Discourses: Popular Sovereignty and Religious Secularisation in Iran', in *Religion and Political Change in the Modern World*, ed. Jeffrey Haynes (London: Routledge, 2014), p. 141.
101 'Ayatollah Sentences Author to Death', *BBC News*, 14 February 1989, http://news.bbc.co.uk/onthisday/hi/dates/stories/february/14/newsid_2541000/2541149.stm, accessed 16 November 2018.
102 Roschanack Shaery-Eisenlohr, 'Iran, the Vatican of Shi'ism?', *Middle East Report* 233 (Winter 2004): 40–3 (p. 43).

103 Thomas Juneau, 'Iran's Policy Towards the Houthis in Yemen: A Limited Return on a Modest Investment', *International Affairs* 92, 3 (May 2016): 647–63 (p. 655). Juneau generally argues: 'Iran does not choose its partners on the basis of a common adherence to Shi'i Islam' (p. 649).
104 Shaery-Eisenlohr, 'Iran, the Vatican of Shi'ism?'
105 'Speech at the Guards' Day Celebration' as reported by Tehran Home Service, 24 April 1985, *Foreign Broadcast Information Service*, SAS-85-080, 25 April 1985, p. 12.

4 | *Saudi 'Guardianship' of the* Umma

Saudi Arabia promotes itself as the premier Muslim country. As guardian of the Holy Places of Mecca and Medina, it has assiduously crafted an image as leader of the *umma*. Its international activities and the apparatus of the state have been devoted to this cause. At times this self-representation has had a legitimising effect; more often, it has had the ironic opposite effect. States, non-state actors, and individuals across the Muslim world have routinely criticised the Kingdom for its sectarian assertiveness and elite hypocrisy, and yet innate conceptions of centre and periphery among millions of Muslims have seemingly endowed it with a kind of natural pre-eminence – the centre of the Muslim world, just as the Ka'ba is regarded as the hub of Islam.

This chapter first considers the importance of 'Islam', in a historically contingent, puritanical mode and a more generic one, to the legitimisation of the ruling family and Saudi state. Their control of the pilgrimage to Mecca, which is indisputably central to Muslim beliefs and practice, has provided, in their eyes, a straightforward claim to guardianship of the *umma*. Yet the chapter shows that this claim has been vulnerable to managerial inefficiencies of the ritual and Holy Cities and inequities in the treatment of pilgrims. It moves on to consider the tensions within the formalisation of a Saudi-Wahhabi ideological position: on the one hand, it purports to be applicable to all Muslims and yet, on the other, it has shown hostility to other Muslims, especially the Shi'a, and ambivalence towards other monotheists, customarily acclaimed as fellow 'People of the Book' (*ahl al-Kitab*). The discussion turns, finally, to the effects of transnational institutionalisation. Organs such as the Organisation of Islamic Cooperation (OIC) and Muslim World League channel Saudi state influence beyond its borders, but Wahhabi-orientated teachings do not always find favourable local reception and may, in fact, undermine state interests. This chapter thus sets out to explore the possibilities and contradictions inherent in outsized Islamic ambition.

Entwined Legitimacies

At the core of the Saudi state is a narrowly-based regime. Lacking democratic, even historically rooted national, *bona fides*, the regime's security is not automatically assured and significantly rests on claims to domination over political rivals and people. To give these claims normative preference, they are, in turn, framed as appeals to legitimacy. There are two interlocking spheres – domestic and foreign – and two principal kinds of legitimacy – religious and functional. Each impacts on the other, and each is instrumentalised.

The current state is generally perceived as the third iteration, with the first two in the eighteenth and nineteenth centuries. The official narrative is centred on what is presented as a seminal alliance around 1744 between a reformer and ruler, thus fusing religion and politics in one mighty force as had the Prophet in Medina. This Wahhabi–Sa'udi partnership is thought to explain both the creative impulse behind the development of the modern state and its enduring source of strength. Saudi texts are full of this foundational history and there is no doubt that it unleashed local energies. The story is more complex, however. Muhammad ibn 'Abd al-Wahhab (1703–92) at first saw no need for political support, but his mission to purify a wayward region soon alienated the local *'ulama* (religious officials) who, in turn, pressured the *amir* to intervene against him. Ibn 'Abd al-Wahhab's campaign found protection in what might be termed Sa'udi territory near Riyadh in central Najd under the control of Muhammad ibn Sa'ud (d. 1765) and later his son. Yet the building up of a political institution was not immediate or based on an equal partnership. It emerged over time, largely between 1747 and 1758, in response to a series of hostile attacks, in which the Sa'ud chieftain provided the protective arm to a more influential force, Ibn 'Abd al-Wahhab, who viewed this defensive shield not as an end in itself but as means to propagate a purified Islam. While the Wahhabi message would come to have an impact across much of the Muslim world in later centuries, it was, as Nabil Mouline points out, an essentially local movement at its origins.[1]

With the steady accretions of territory, however – control over Riyadh in 1773 and Mecca in 1803 – wider opposition grew, and the Egyptian-Ottoman forces of Muhammad 'Ali invaded the new Wahhabi-Saudi emirate in the Najd and sacked it in 1818. The emirate was reconstituted between 1824 and 1891, with the *amirs* – having inter-married with the Ibn 'Abd al-Wahhab family – legitimised as Imams. While the Wahhabis consistently supported the Sa'uds, they did not always speak with one voice, as differing views on cooperation with the Ottomans, who had occupied what is now the Eastern Province in 1871, indicate. Nor were they adverse to an accommodation with the local Najdi rivals of the Sa'uds, the Rashids. As David Commins notes of the Najd, by the 1880s 'the strict monotheistic doctrine had been naturalized as the native religious culture'.[2]

Stories of the 'third state' – the current one – have become mythologised. 'Abd al-'Aziz ibn Sa'ud (1875–1953; more commonly known in the West as Ibn Sa'ud) is routinely characterised in heroic terms, stealing in at the dead of night at the beginning of the twentieth century to recapture Riyadh from rivals and slowly building state structures. Personal cunning and tribal loyalties played a significant role, but so too did religious validation. But if, arguably, one could say that the Wahhabi–Sa'udi partnership was, in the eighteenth century, unequally tilted in favour of the religious reformers, the political dimension became dominant over the thirty years of 'Abd al-'Aziz's rule. While the alliance continued to produce mutual benefits, 'Abd al-'Aziz's territorial and political ambitions were paramount, seeking to expand his control at the expense of local rivals and to deflect unwanted Ottoman and British influence.

The core of the developing Saudi state was a working coalition of disparate elements. Tribal chiefs maintained personalistic and *ad hoc* arrangements with each other but were, broadly, accepting of the larger Saudi chieftain. Tribesman provided the emerging order with military backbone, and the *'ulama* validated it against local and regional enemies. Extension of Wahhabi practices into the formerly Sharifian province of the Hijaz from 1924 was designed to satisfy the religious elements, but the Wahhabis did not have an unfettered hand. 'Abd al-'Aziz's policy towards the Holy Places in the western part of the peninsula and the Shi'a in the east did not always follow strict Wahhabi guidance. Rather, he moderated his approach in the hope of appeasing broader Muslim sentiment and avoiding direct challenges to his expansionist aspirations.[3]

The Mecca conference of 1926, ostensibly designed to consider the management of the *hajj* pilgrimage, was expected to legitimise 'Abd al-'Aziz's control of the Hijaz. The involvement of Muslims from other parts of the Muslim world was crucial to this legitimisation;

they would approve his *de facto* guardianship of the Holy Cities. In the event, however, dispute ensued over the freedom that non-Wahhabis would have in their religious observances. The Saudi ruler made clear the limits of pan-Islamic openness: the beliefs of pilgrims would not be examined, but wayward practices would not be tolerated. In the end, as Martin Kramer details, the meeting and its follow-up activities confirmed that, in the period of 'Abd al-'Aziz's rule ending with his death in 1953, 'there remained in effect an inviolable prohibition against any more formal demonstration of Muslim solidarity at Mecca'.[4]

The domestic scene was also unpredictable, in part because of the solidifying regime's interaction with foreigners. Part of the Sa'ud success was due to the creation of a powerful movement, the Ikhwan (Brotherhood). Its tribal members formed small communities that, while not supra- or even trans-tribal, had a defined religious grounding. Each was designated a *hijra*, the symbolically-charged name for morally enjoined migration, and instruction in the Wahhabi creed formed part of communal life. The motivation for this sedentarisation was religious, but also economic: the tolerance towards raiding other Bedouin. Ikhwani sentiment had approved of the prohibition on grave visitations and shrines in the Hijaz. But the Ikhwan's relationship with the Sa'uds deteriorated when 'Wahhabisation' stalled in the Hijaz and, perhaps more importantly, when limitations were placed on their raiding as a result of both increased Saudi control over the peninsula and concern about an adverse foreign reaction.[5]

'Abd al-'Aziz was forced to consider disquiet from two sources – Muslims across the world, not least from India; and, not unrelated, the British. He was impelled to assure the former that, while the *shari'a* would be applied in the Hijaz, no damage would be done to the Grand Mosque in Mecca and the Prophet's Mosque in Medina and that the *'ulama* across the Muslim world would be consulted in their governance.[6] With regard to the latter, the official historical narrative extols a mutually beneficial relationship between the emerging Saudi order and the British: 'Abd al-'Aziz appreciated the importance of friendly imperial power on his borders, and the British understood that, as his realm included the Holy Places, he could exert influence 'among Muslims everywhere'.[7] Yet, at the same time, these dealings with the British seemed, to many in the Ikhwan, an abandonment of core religious beliefs. 'Abd al-'Aziz, in turn, viewed this criticism as not only disloyal but also unnecessarily antagonising of a Great Power. The Ikhwan had brought much success, but expansion into British-controlled Trans-Jordan, Iraq, and Kuwait heralded its demise. The battle was now joined, defeat came by 1929, and *raison d'état* triumphed over religious ideology.

The State and Islam

In the succeeding decades, a modern state developed as centralisation, bureaucratisation, and international alliances solidified the power of the ruling house and its associated elites. Joseph Kostiner explains the interweaving of factors: centralisation weakened rivals of the Sa'uds and, as state institutions coalesced around the regime, key government portfolios were assigned to members of the ruling family, reinforcing personalistic rule:[8] institutionalisation and neo-patrimonialism became two sides of the governmental coin. The survival of the royal family became paramount, therefore, and identifiable with the national interest.

It is not surprising that loyalty is a running theme of Saudi commentaries; it was, in one account of 'Abd al-'Aziz's successes and even triumph over 'fanatics', 'the key to victory'.[9] This loyalty is thought to be assured through related functional and religious claims. The functional takes two forms: the regime deserves allegiance because it unfailingly provides security to the realm and protection for the millions of 'guests of God' who perform the *hajj* annually; and it advances the cause of social welfare and development through its beneficence. Saudi historical accounts routinely invoke the importance of avoiding disorder (*fitna*) and praise the security that the government has brought over the decades. The cessation of lawlessness, protection of borders, and receipt of diplomatic support from outside powers resulted from this commitment. A tenth-grade textbook outlines the by-product of such a stable order: 'mutual consultation between the rulers and ruled ensures rights and obligations and promotes loyalty and allegiance'.[10] Although the regime does not explicitly invoke rentierism, it repeatedly reinforces the view that it not only provides for its people but does so effectively. It seeks to counter both the conventional view that it is incapable of change and thus extols the benefits of modernising reforms, and the charge that international alliances undermine its Islamic *bona fides*. A legendary convocation of *'ulama* in 1928 certified that 'Abd al-'Aziz's use of radios, telephones, automobiles, and air-planes was consistent with Islam, and it also endorsed treaties with non-Muslins as 'desirable if they brought peace and freedom to Muslims'.[11] Today Crown Prince Muhammad ibn Salman (b. 1985) has staked his and family's future on an expanding programme of social change and economic development officially encapsulated in 'Vision 2030' and enthusiastically supported by the United States.

Religious legitimacy is based, in large part, on an instrumentalisation that combines the ideological with the functional. The Saudi management of the *hajj* is one such example. Long projecting them-selves as guardians of the pilgrimage, the Saudis have invoked a 'spiritual, moral, and historical responsibility' to do so.[12] From 1984, the Saudi King has assumed the Ottoman title of Servant of the Two Holy Places (*khadim al-haramayn al-sharifayn*). The King's *hajj* speech is tantamount to a 'state of the *umma*' address, allowing the ruling family to link themselves directly to a primary obligation of the faith and to range across issues affecting Muslim societies broadly.

But, in addition to this automatic claim to Muslim leadership, approbation is predicated on efficient management of the *hajj*, as measured by numbers of pilgrims safely accommodated and the suc-cessive expansions of the two holy mosques. Numbers now exceed two million a year, and their security is considered a religious obligation, enshrined in Article 24 of the Basic Law of Governance, which, if effected, is likely to produce a political dividend. 'Tranquillity' (*al-hudu'*), 'civilised conduct' (*mazhar hadari*), and respect for the governing system (*al-nizam*) are enjoined on all pilgrims.[13] Saudi media routinely report on the large number of police and security personnel who are charged with providing a safe environment. If they somehow missed the message, the pilgrims are prompted at the final sermon at Mount 'Arafat to leave with a favourable view of the Saudi regime: 'You came here to a sacred place. It is safe and secure, and everything is provided.'[14]

Additions to the sacred enclaves in Mecca alone have occurred over decades. At the time of the founding of the Saudi Kingdom in 1932, the Grand Mosque was able to hold no more than 48,000 worshippers at one time. In 1955, the government launched its first expansion project, enveloping the Ottoman architectural configuration and quadrupling the size of the complex. It raised and covered the yard with white marble and added a second level for additional pilgrims. The surrounding area was 'redeveloped' and tunnels and culverts were constructed to guard against flash flooding.

The most ambitious reform project began in 1989. Over the succeeding ten years, more than 70 billion Saudi riyals (US$18.7 billion) were expended on expansion of both the Grand Mosque in Mecca and the Prophet's Mosque in Medina: 'no expense has been considered too high and no effort too great'.[15] The Prophet's Mosque had increased tenfold and was able to accommodate 700,000. A further expansion has been ordered by King Salman involving the expansion of all facilities and using state-of-the-art technology. When completed, the mosque complex will accommodate 1.85 million pilgrims over six floors.

But Saudi control over the *hajj* has been a matter of fierce contention across the Muslim world. Alarm was expressed as far back as the mid-1920s when Saudi forces were closing in on the Hijazi Hashimites, and criticisms intensified from the early 1980s after the Iranian revolution. The International Hajj Seminar of 1982 in London proclaimed that 'no single nation-State or a group of States based on sentiments and philosophies of local or regional nationalism can perform the task of the liberation of Al-Quds [Jerusalem] and the defence of the Haramain'.[16] From 1987 when more than four hundred people died in clashes between Iranian pilgrims and Saudi security officials, charges of heresy and illegitimacy have flown back and forth across the Gulf. The Saudis convened a meeting of the Muslim World League in October 1987 to denounce Iran, and Iran countered with an International Congress on Safeguarding the Sanctity and Security of the Haramayn Sharifayn in November, which demanded that the Holy Places be placed under international Muslim control. Iranians and others have continued to call for internationalisation, such as in 1990 when one thousand were killed or in 2015 when a large number of deaths – likely over two thousand – occurred, owing to stampedes.[17]

Since the deterioration of relations in the Arab Gulf from mid-2017 and the Saudi-led blockade of Qatar, critical voices have come from that shayhkdom as well. Recognising that nothing less than the Kingdom's legitimacy was at stake, the Saudi Foreign Minister denounced these particular calls for internationalisation from an ostensibly fellow member of the Gulf Cooperation Council as tantamount to a 'declaration of war'.[18] The Mufti, 'Abd al-'Aziz ibn 'Abdullah ibn

Muhammad Al al-Shaykh (b. 1943), also hit back saying the Saudis have worked hard and honourably to protect the sacred shrines, a fact universally recognised and attested to. But the 'unity of [this] Muslim word' (*wahdat al-kalimat al-Muslimin*) has been maliciously targeted with the goal of sowing confusion and dissent.[19] In August 2018, Yusuf al-Qaradawi issued a *fatwa* that appeared to question the need for the *hajj* itself – a startling view that must be seen as having been intended to question Saudi control of the pilgrimage and, thus, was a by-product of Gulf regional tensions. It was promptly denounced as 'strange'.[20] There is no doubt that a raw nerve had been hit.

As this section shows, the legitimacy formula of a narrowly based regime can produced ironic consequences. From the beginning, a particularist mode of Islam, Wahhabism, helped to advance the cause of a local family, but, as a state coalesced around them, power and wealth afforded opportunities to enhance their rule, and dangers in doing so. The claim that the Sa'uds had a larger mission to protect the Holy Places and pilgrimage and to lead the broader community of Islam has provided them with the concrete benefits of deference and respect from many Muslims elsewhere. But the manner in which this self-imposed mission has been carried out has also incited controversy and even outright opposition from others. The *umma* coin of the realm, as it were, has two sides.

Ideologisation of the *Umma*

As this appropriation of the *hajj* suggests, Saudis routinely assign to themselves leadership of the *umma* and invoke it in a virtually automatic way. While the concept is proposed as an almost obvious vision of both Islamic unity and universalism, the Saudi perspective on the larger Muslim world has clearly been shaped by broad doctrinal views, however. Two debates have become central to this worldview. The first deals with the proper attitude to take towards believers when sectarian and territorial considerations are considered. It involves principally the Shi'a on the one hand, and Muslims in a minority situation on the other. The second debate, to which we turn later in this chapter, concerns the proper attitude to take towards adherents of other faiths or, broadly, 'unbelievers'. The first concerns the unity of the *umma*; the second, its universality.

Fellow Muslims on the 'Outside'

Early on in the history of the third Saudi state, questions had been raised about the faith of other groups, such as the Shi'a, the Ahmadiyya, and Sufi brotherhoods. The religious establishment has had to tread carefully between upholding censorious Wahhabi views of innovators, and affirming the inclusiveness of the state in its guardianship of the *hajj*. In response to a formal query about who constituted the 'saved sect' (*al-firqa al-najiyya*) prefigured in Prophetic tradition and retold by Ibn 'Abd al-Wahhab, the Permanent Committee for Scholarly Research and Ifta' (al-Lajna al-Da'ima li-al-Buhuth al-'Ilmiyya wa-al-Ifta') argued, on the one hand, that Ibn 'Abd al-Wahhab's teachings were correct: the saved would be those who follow the Qur'an, Sunna, '*ijma*' of the umma', and *shari'a* while avoiding false interpretations. But, on the other hand, the Saudi government, in allowing all to perform the *hajj* – except the Ahmadiyya who openly recognise prophecy after the final Prophet Muhammad – has not deviated from the true path. The state-driven interpretation has clearly evolved from the rigid Wahhabi interpretation: the government judges Muslims on 'what is apparent and not what is in their hearts' (*bi-zawahirim wa lam tunqib 'an qulubhim*).[21] In a contest of legitimacy formulas, the promotion of a worldwide duty seems to trump that of a provincial ideology, not least because the former implicitly rejects the judgemental *takfiri* approach of radical Islamist groups like ISIS. The current Mufti, 'Abd al-'Aziz Al al-Shaykh concedes that *takfir* (excommunication) does exist in the Qur'an and Sunna, but was not part of Ibn 'Abd al-Wahhab's 'project'. It, rather, was '*da'wa* for the good' (*da'wa ila al-khayr*).[22]

Despite such relative flexibility in interpretation, the Wahhabi attitude and Saudi state policy towards the Shi'a has been consistent in its hostility. A minority based in the oil-rich Eastern Province,[23] the Shi'a have been subject to discriminatory, even repressive, measures from the beginning of the modern state. Saudi concern over Iranian 'export of the revolution', Hizbullah's predominance in Lebanon, and majority Shi'i agitation in neighbouring Iraq and Bahrain have all redounded to the disadvantage of the Saudi Shi'a whose allegiance is questioned. Underlying this suspicion of disloyalty is the persistent Wahhabi anathematising of the Shi'a as 'rejectionists' (*rafidun*) or 'extremists' (*ghulw*). Ibn 'Abd al-Wahhab was clear in his view that they were heterodox and therefore, regardless of later attempts to smooth over his views, were subject to *takfir*.[24] Pre-eminent Shaykhs, since the founding of the third Saudi state, have repeated that the Shi'a reject orthodox inter-pretations and have made of 'Ali and the Imams quasi-divine figures and so committed the cardinal sin of worshipping multiple gods (*shirk*). The very influential religious scholar Shaykh 'Abdullah ibn Jibrin (1993–2009) also emphasised their rejection of scriptural sources and practice of 'hypocrisy' (*al-nifaq*), relegating them to the category of *kuffar*.[25] The law professor 'Abd al-'Aziz ibn Fawzan al-Fawzan has denounced Shi'i rituals like 'Ashura as *bid'a*, a negative term for unacceptable innovation.[26]

Shaykh Nasir ibn Sulayman al-'Umar (b. 1952) seems to have objected to the Shi'a as an obstreperous minority in the Kingdom, as much as a deviant sect of Islam. In his view, while they erroneously exaggerate their communal strength in the Kingdom, they are in fact over-represented in the universities and have 'penetrated' government ministries. Their rituals such as grave visitations and emotive mourning for the martyred grandson of the Prophet are offensive to the vast majority of Saudis, even visitors, who are subjected to such a 'manifestation of evil' (*al-jahr bi'l-munkar*).[27] In a similar manner, Shaykh Safar al-Hawali (b. 1950) denounced the unreasonable demands of a minority on the majority. He noted not only that the Shi'a 'disbelieve (*yukafiruh*) everywhere', but also that they are in alliance with communists and secularists, 'enemies of the *umma*', they threaten to enlist external assistance – presumably from Iran – and they have already the unwarranted sympathy of the Americans. The Saudi 'land' (*bilad*) would be undermining both its *raison d'être*, if it made concessions to this minority, and the 'unity of the *umma*'.[28]

The stakes, Saudi worldwide leadership, are thus high, and the concern is both religious and political: the Shi'a do not adhere to the central doctrine of 'oneness' (*tawhid*), but also with their relative geo-graphical proximity in varying strengths – Lebanon, Syria, Iran, Iraq, Afghanistan, Pakistan, Turkey, Bahrain, and Yemen – they potentially constitute a dangerous encirclement. *'Ulama* political views of Shi'ism have often been viewed through an Iraqi or Syrian prism in particular. Thirty-eight Saudi religious figures, including al-'Umar and al-Hawali, signed a statement in December 2006 denouncing the 'octopus-like' conspiracy among 'Crusader, Safavid [Iranian], and Rafidi', anti-Sunni elements in Iraq and the region generally.[29] The implied criticism of the

American occupation, coupled with a traditionally Wahhabi scorn for both interventionist unbelievers and the Shi'a, now benefiting from the intervention, diverged from the government's cautious navigation between its American ally and a Shi'i-dominated Iraqi neighbour. Al-Hawali gave clear expression to the dual religious and political concerns about sectarianism when denouncing 'the great rejectionist arc' (*al-qaws al-kabir qawsan rafidan*) of the Shi'a.[30] This view overlaps with the regime's anxiety over the purportedly Iran-led 'Shi'i crescent' (*al-hilal al-shi'i*), an anxiety that existed for some time but became acute in Saudi and broader Sunni circles after the battle of Qusayr in 2013 in the Syrian civil war;[31] the victory then of Syrian government forces and the Shi'i Lebanese group, Hizbullah, was widely seen as tipping the balance against Sunnis in the region. Yet, caution has prevailed and, consistent with views on Iraq, the view of both the religious establishment and other *'ulama* has been that Syria should not be thought of as a *jihad* requiring the enlistment of Saudi youth.[32]

A political issue such as the position to take on Hizbullah produced over time a kind of dissonance on the issue of unity, however. On the one hand, Hizbullah's sectarian affiliation and support from Iran were objectionable in themselves, but its firm opposition to Israel suggested to some Sunni Islamist circles the need for support. The Egyptian-Qatari intellectual Yusuf al-Qaradawi, whom we cited in Chapter 2, was one such notable defender, as was Salman al-'Awda (b. 1956), Qasim branch dean at the establishment Imam Muhammad ibn Sa'ud University and a leader of the reformist Awakening (Sahwa) movement in the Kingdom.[33] Yet, Hizbullah's decisive backing of the Asad regime in Syria, particularly after 2013, led to revision of this view. Al-Qaradawi then argued that he had reached a 'more mature' (*anduj*) and 'more discerning' (*absar*) judgement in accord with the prudent Saudi position. The Saudi Mufti, Al al-Shaykh, welcomed al-Qaradawi's change of heart and appealed to Muslim scholars generally to cooperate for the sake of an *umma* of 'unity and strength' (*wahdatha wa quwatha*).[34] As we saw above, his attitude towards al-Qaradawi was to change again when the dispute with Qatar unfolded in 2017.

The question of Muslim migration to the West has also raised Saudi-Wahhabi concerns consistent with aspirations to lead the *umma*. Such movement ostensibly runs counter to a fundamental belief that Muslims should reside in *dar al-Islam* (the realm or abode of Islam), but the reality of the modern world is extensively of travel in the opposite direction. This recognition perhaps accounts for a bifurcated Saudi-Wahhabi view. The harder edge of the Wahhabi establishment has demonstrated hostility to the idea of both permanent migration and a separate juridical status for migrants. In their view, since the West is conventionally understood in conservative circles to be *dar al-harb* (the ream or abode of war), permanent migration is unacceptable: 'If it is not possible to gain a livelihood except by what Allah has forbidden, namely through the mixing of men and women, then this livelihood must be abandoned.' Muslims should not take non-Muslim wives.[35] Presence in a non-Muslim society, however temporary, must be valorised by proselytising for Islam (*da'wa*).

If circumstances are unfavourable to the faithful and hindrances are put in their way, Muslims need to migrate (*hijra*) to Muslim lands. But if a kind of security is possible, then Muslims have a duty to proselyt-ise – through active campaigns or moral example – to decrease the number of unbelievers in the world.[36] While this is ongoing, Muslims are not relieved of their obligation to Islamic law, nor do their circum-stances allow for special legal considerations. Contrary to what some have been arguing since the 1970s, therefore, a dedicated legal frame-work, *fiqh al-aqalliyyat* (minority jurisprudence), is not permissible.[37] This Wahhabi objection is clearly based on an assumption that the *umma* is at least jurisprudentially undivided and, by implication, that its own interpretation is paramount. The fact that one of the minority *fiqh*'s primary proponents is al-Qaradawi, noted for both his Ikhwani and Qatari sympathies and thus a target of overt Saudi criticisms since the blockade of Qatar in 2017,[38] no doubt confirms the antipathy.[39]

But the Saudi-Wahhabi orbit has also included more approving voices. For instance, Taha Jabir al-Alwani (1935–2016) is also con-sidered a co-founder of the minority jurisprudence movement. Though not Saudi-born, he lectured at Imam Muhammad ibn Sa'ud University from 1975 to 1985, and when he moved to the United States, headed the International Institute of Islamic Thought, supported by the Saudi-financed SAAR Foundation;[40] he was also a member of the Inter-national Fiqh Council in Jidda associated with the OIC. He drew on a well-established argument that since Muslims were free to practise their faith in non-Muslim lands, living there was permissible. But he also found justification in *da'wa*, making a positive virtue out of the reluctant concession made by the higher *'ulama*. Invoking the Shafi'i jurist al-Qaffal al-Shashi (904–76), for example, he argued, similar to the views of the Shaykh of al-Azhar noted in Chapter 1, that lands such as North America and Europe are *dar al-da'wa* – in effect, the realm of potential Muslims.[41] While the logic varies in Saudi-led religious circles, their common, perhaps self-reassuring, assumption is that the community of Muslims *should* be unified and universal.

Non-Muslims and the Umma

But the universality of the *umma*, as we have seen in prior chapters, is a vaguer idea than presumed. It relates to the second debate over doctrinal views of the *umma* – whether and to what extent it can accommodate and perhaps eventually incorporate non-Muslims. Following Ibn 'Abd al-Wahhab, the bulk of the religious class adheres to a form of dissociation from the 'unbelievers'. He conceived of those to be excluded as the 'polytheists', the classical exclusionary category in keeping with Qur'anic injunctions. Qur'an 60:4 approves of Abraham's dissociation from polytheists and declares 'enmity and hatred' (*al-'adwa wa-al-baghda'*) for those who do not accept the One God. For most of the higher *'ulama*, 'loyalty and disavowal' (*al-wala' wa-al-bara'*) is a fundamental element of the Islamic creed. According to an influential religious scholar popular in Salafi circles, Shaykh Salih ibn Fawzan ibn 'Abdullah al-Fawzan (b. 1933), a member of the Council of Senior 'Ulama (Majlis Hay'at Kibar al-'Ulama), Muslims should not take non-Muslims as friends or receive support from them. He invokes Qur'an 60:1: 'O you who believe, do not take my enemies and your enemies as allies, showing them affection'. Particularly objectionable is imitation (*tashabbuh*) of the unbelievers' way of life – their dress, comportment, even language. In a similar vein, Shaykh Muhammad ibn Jamil Zaynu (1925–2010), a faculty member of Imam University in Riyadh, warned against attempts to resemble the unbelievers through dress and custom.[42] While a ninth-grade textbook in the early 2000s lumped *kafir* and *fasiq* (unrighteous or Godless) together, a tenth-grade textbook explicitly discussed *al-wala' wa-al-bara'*: Muslims are led astray by the unbelievers' activities and culture and so neglect to worship God and do good deeds. The doctrine is, in fact, central: 'The place of *al-wala' wa al-bara'* has great standing in Islam, and is the strongest bond of belief.'[43] Right-thinking Muslims bear a clear responsibility to correct fellow Muslims who 'love the unbelievers' (*yuhibun al-kuffar*) and to teach them the importance of this principle.[44] The broad category of unbelievers (*kuffar*) seems to include other monotheists and followers of deviant Muslim sects.

While a common refrain, such as expressed by Muhammad ibn Salah al-Uthaymin (1925–2001), is the obligation of Muslims to avoid, even hate, the unbeliever, the confrontational dimension has been somewhat softened in some formulations. Dissociation is called for when unbelievers display hostility to or are aggressive towards believers; it is a kind of self-defence. This was reflected in secondary school textbooks reviewed in 2017–18 where Christians and especially Jews are depicted as plotting against and dividing Muslims and so dissociation has to be the 'firmest handle of the faith' (*awthaq 'ara al-iman*).[45] Moreover, as Salih ibn 'Abdullah al-Fawzan for instance says, there is a clear need to dissociate from unbelievers, but Muslims should show mercy towards them (*al-tarahum 'alayhim*).[46] 'Abd al-Aziz ibn Fawzan al-Fawzan reaffirms the importance of the 'hate the sin, not the sinner' approach. He calls for 'positive hatred', with compassion towards the infidels and the hope to reform them to the guiding principles.[47] Abd al-'Aziz ibn Baz (1910–99) and others have emphasised the underlying logic: if Islam was the one true religion, then adherents of other faiths were not on an equal footing. Moreover, the West through its education, Orientalism, religious missions, and co-optation of Muslim elites was constant in its efforts to undermine the unity of the *umma*.[48] The 'hate' to be directed at them should be in the heart, and not take physical form, provided that the non-Muslims do not fight the believers or expel them from their homes.[49]

Even terminology has been subject to intense debate. Discussions at the National Dialogue (al-Hiwar al-Watani), which has been ongoing since 2003, have aired concerns that categorising terms (*tasnif*) like believer and infidel is constraining and may encourage radicalisation. It might also undermine the public image the Kingdom wishes to project, as, arguably, is the intent of motorway signage in the Hijaz that indicates where 'non-Muslims' (*ghayr Muslimin*), as opposed to unbelievers (*kuffar*), must exit before approaching Mecca. But some members of the *'ulama* have expressed disquiet. Shaykh Salih ibn 'Abdullah al-Fawzan argued that God had created differences and distinguishing labels like 'polytheist' (*al-mushrik*) and 'monotheist' (*al-muwahhid*), 'hypocrite' (*al-munafiq*) and 'obedient' (*al-muti'*). A 'settlement' (*al-taswiyya*) between the two 'factions' – believers and unbelievers – was forbidden. Relations with non-Muslims could be regularised, even respectful, but Muslims were obligated not to submit to them or even seek to please them, but to call them to the true faith.[50]

Ibn Baz directly, though controversially, dealt with the political implications. After the Iraqi invasion of Kuwait in 1990 and the sending of foreign troops to Saudi Arabia, his position was largely based on establishing a critical distinction: are non-believers helpful to, or attacking, the believing realm? He had endorsed 'Abdullah 'Azzam's tract, *al-Difa'i 'an ard al-muslimin* (Defence of the Land of the Muslims), which justified *jihad* against the Soviet Union for its invasion of the Muslim territory of Afghanistan. But in the Gulf War of 1990–1, coalition forces came to the aid of Muslims in need.

His argument validated the arrival of 'diverse nationalities among the Muslims and others for the resistance of aggression and the defence of the country'.[51] The Council of Senior 'Ulama also pronounced in a formal *fatwa* that a Muslim ruler was obligated to 'seek the help of whoever has the power that enables them to perform the task'. Another *fatwa* in January 1991 declared that, in the ensuing *jihad* against Saddam, non-Muslim soldiers would help to defeat Saddam Hussein, 'the enemy of God'.[52] Hatim ibn 'Arif al-'Awni, in a work distributed by the Muslim World League, further justified aid from outside by arguing that loyalty to fellow Muslims is not impinged by such external assistance unless there is certainty that the outsiders have clear unbelief in their hearts.[53]

Ibn Baz had spoken circuitously of 'others' (*ghayrhum*) in referring to the Western troops, but even the avoidance of more evocative terminology such as 'unbelievers' did not still criticism. Safar al-Hawali, then dean of Islamic studies at Umm al-Qura University in Mecca and a well-known popular preacher, condemned what seemed like a trusting embrace of an American-led coalition that harboured hopes of occupying the holy peninsula.[54] This turn to outsiders to defend the Kingdom unleashed a storm of criticism from a number of quarters, including many religious figures, throughout the ensuing decade. Al-'Awda, for instance, suggested that the rulers, and by implication, the establishment *'ulama* had failed in their basic duty to consult with and protect the wider community.[55]

The American invasion of Iraq in 2003 precipitated another lively debate. On the one hand, a group of religious authorities proclaimed in November 2004 that, in line with the *shari'a* and international law, armed resistance against occupying 'aggressors' was legitimate. The *fatwa* did not call for Saudis to join the *jihad*, as one of the signatories, al-'Awda, pointed out. But he simultaneously reaffirmed that the occupied had a right to resist whether in Palestine or Iraq. On the other hand, Shaykh 'Abd al-Muhsin al-'Ubaykan (b. 1952), representing the government position, argued that what was occurring in Iraq was not a *jihad* but a kind of 'chaotic resistance' (*muqawama fawdawiyya*) against a functionally legitimate (though provisional) government.[56] But ambivalence persisted. Even the Mufti, asserting that the question of resistance was best left to the Iraqi *'ulama* to decide, directly referred to the American presence as an 'occupation',[57] and at least one Western news source believed that then Chief Judge of the Supreme Judicial Council (Majlis al-'Ala li-al-Qada'), Shaykh Salih al-Luhaydan, was approving of Saudis joining the Iraqi *jihad* despite the official prohibition policy.[58] Saudis did in fact go to Iraq and this is often invoked as an indication of *societal* pan-Islamic sentiment, regardless of state policy. But, while figures are elusive, Thomas Hegghammer argues that, taking a maximal calculation, no more than 1,500 Saudis engaged in the conflict.[59]

As we have seen in this section, Saudi views of the *umma* are at least partially influenced by formal doctrinal discourses that are tantamount to ideological framing. One position, concerning the unity of the *umma*, articulates hostility towards those considered aberrant, such as the Shi'a and Ahmadiyya. In addition, Muslims living outside the Islamic realm – generally considered today to be where Muslims constitute a majority (rather than, traditionally, where the *shari'a* is law of the land) – are viewed with varying degrees of wariness. The second discourse reviewed here deals with the universality of the *umma* or, simply, whether non-Muslims inspire inherent antagonism as *kuffar* or 'unbelievers'. Not for the first time, hard-line Wahhabis have advanced an antipathetic view that is at odds with the benign image the state wishes to promote and to which, as we will see in Chapter 5, radical Islamists are happy to subscribe.

Institutionalisation of Leadership Claims

National Institutions

In addition to the *hajj*, the Saudis use sponsorship of various organisations to promote their larger claims to Islamic leadership. These are both national and international in form.

The views of the official religious establishment, the Council of Senior 'Ulama, are advanced through various publications and other media of the Permanent Committee for Scholarly Research and Ifta' (al-Lajna al-Da'ima li-al-Buhuth al-'Ilmiyya wa-al-Ifta'). It distributes *fatwas* on a wide range of topics and its opinions are sought from various parts of the Muslim world. Its portal, www.alifta.net, provides easy access to these *fatwas* as well as those of the former Mufti, Ibn Baz and the current one, 'Abd al-'Aziz ibn 'Abdullah ibn Muhammad Al al-Shaykh (b. 1943), which are available in Arabic, Urdu, Turkish, Farsi, Bahasa Indonesian, English, French, Spanish, and Chinese. Ibn Baz had noted with approval that the Committee has been very active worldwide in *da'wa* activity, particularly in Africa and Asia, where it distributes Qur'ans, provides financial assistance to minority communities, and spreads the word of God.[60]

Two Saudi universities are particularly active in promoting Saudi Arabia's Islamic credentials. Imam Muhammad ibn Sa'ud Islamic University in Riyadh was founded in 1974 as an amalgam of several existing colleges and institutions. There are now eleven constituent colleges and two institutes in Riyadh, and six extension colleges elsewhere in the country – in Medina, al-Qasim, al-Hasa, and the 'Asir region. Students are predominantly Saudi, many recruited from over sixty pre-university schools throughout the country. In keeping with its mission to exert an impact on the world and 'increase the global understanding (*al-fahim al-'alami*) of Islam', the university has affiliated institutions in the United States, Japan, Indonesia, Mauritania, Djibouti, and Ras al-Khayma.[61] The Institute of Islamic and Arabic Sciences in America (IIASA), which was established in Fairfax, Virginia, in 1988, aims to train teachers, imams, and *du'a* (callers to Islam) to work in the Muslim communities of America. An example of the importance that the government has attached to the extension of this network overseas was the gift of US$1.3 million that King Fahd gave for the rebuilding of the affiliated Islamic Institute in Tokyo.[62]

The university and its affiliate organisations have been accused of fostering an intolerance towards Christians and Jews and even of promoting terrorism. There is no doubt that controversial views are expressed, such as those of 'Abd al-'Aziz ibn Fawzan al-Fawzan who argued that the American system was collapsing under the weight of its own arrogance and criminality.[63] Whether in Virginia, Tokyo, or Riyadh, students have certainly been exposed to conservative

interpretations while, unexceptionally, required to master the traditional canon. This latter includes the major compilations of *hadith*
and the exegetical commentaries (*tafsirs*) of Ibn Kathir, al-Qurtubi,
and al-Shawkani. But there is a discernibly Wahhabi component as
well: predictably, *Kitab al-tawhid* (The Book of Oneness) of Muhammad ibn 'Abd al-Wahhab and numerous writings of Ibn Taymiyya, but
also various works by modern scholars such as Shaykh al-Uthaymin (for
example, *al-Qawa'id al-muthla*, 'Exemplary Principles'). Students are
expected to know something of the four main Sunni schools of law, yet
because the university produces nearly all of the judges in the Kingdom,
the firmest grounding is in Hanbali *fiqh*. Given political sensitivities, the
Shi'i Ja'fari school of jurisprudence is invoked only rarely.

The university's publications programme, in the main, covers the
usual pious topics, such as the Prophet's biography, or guidance on
how to cope with the challenges of 'Christianisation' (*al-tansir*).[64]
Occasionally, there is the hint of approved political engagement, such
as speaking out against jihadist movements, 'extreme' *hijra*, and
takfir[65] – a message that, if not always identifiably Wahhabi, is nonetheless consistent with an endorsed Salafi quietism. Perhaps in part
because of the traditional appeal of the university's educational
approach to 'lower class' elements,[66] the concern that such a clearly
orthodox education might unintentionally encourage anti-regime
sentiment has long been present.

While Imam University primarily targets Saudi students at its home
campuses, the University of Medina (al-Jami'a al-Islamiyya bil-Madina
al-Munawwara) is the flagship internationalised education enterprise
of the Kingdom. Founded in 1961, encouraged by both influential
Saudi figures, as well as non-Saudis such as Abu al-Ala Mawdudi
and Abu al-Hasan Ali Nadwi, it proclaims that it is an 'international
Islamic institution' in 'purpose' (*al-ghaya*) and a Saudi Arabian one in
'dependency' (*al-taba'iyya*).[67] It has eight faculties, including, since
2012, one dedicated to the sciences, and it runs a primary and intermediate school system. The university has not admitted women, but a
member of the Council of Senior 'Ulama, 'Abdullah ibn Mani'
(b. 1931), has publicly called for the establishment of a women's
branch.[68] Inverting the proportion of foreign to Saudi students at
Imam University, Medina has had roughly 80 per cent of its student
body from outside the Kingdom – an achievement proudly displayed in
a map on its website.[69]

Prominent Muslim writers and activists have studied there. While their views vary of course, most are broadly Salafist and many are politically engaged. These include Bilal Philips (b. 1946), a Canadian preacher living in Qatar; Yasir Qadhi (b. 1975), the American head of the Al-Maghrib Institute in Houston, Texas; Ismail ibn Musa Menk (b. 1975), Grand Mufti of Zimbabwe; Haji Abdul Hadi ibn Awang (b. 1947), head of the oppositional Islamist Parti Islam Se-Malayisa (Malaysian Islamic Party); and Hidayat Nur Wahid (b. 1960), former Speaker of the Indonesian People's Consultative Assembly and leader of the Islamist-nationalist Partai Keadilan Sejahtera (Justice and Prosperity Party).

From the start, the university has had an expansive vision and exercised broader, external influences. Its founding overlaps with crackdowns by the Egyptian state on the Muslim Brotherhood, which – ironically, given the Saudi antipathy towards the Brotherhood that was to develop a few decades later – led to the discernible influence of 'religious migrants' in the teaching of the university. The government drew on their 'spiritual capital' as accepted religious authorities,[70] as well as the aura of the second holiest city of Islam, and expended large sums of money, particularly after the dramatic increases in oil income from the mid-to-late 1970s, to create an institution that might rival the centuries-old educational centre in Cairo, al-Azhar. Today the government devotes 1.5 billion riyals (over US$400 million) per year to the university, which provides free tuition, housing, meals, and one trip home a year.[71]

The Ikhwani influence has lessened, but the ethos is less Wahhabi and more cosmopolitan than at Imam University – and what might be expected of a Saudi institution. The jurisprudential teaching is a subtle but nonetheless discernible variation from standard Wahhabi practice, in part due to the outside influences of teaching staff and students. There has been evolution over time in the adoption of some modern forms of pedagogy, but also in nuanced variations of content. Internationalisation of the university is a critical explanatory factor in this evolution, but jurisprudential and even doctrinal eclecticism emerged in society as a whole from at least the 1970s. Trans-*madhhab* (legal school) approaches and generic appeals to 'public interest' (*maslaha*), rather than simply Hanbali texts, for example, appeared in the legal system, at least through the *nizams* or official ordinances, just as the hybrid though undeniably conservative ideas of intellectuals such as

Muhammad Qutb (1919–2014) inspired individuals across the spectrum.[72] Indeed, the university's evolved teaching occurred in large part because of the oversight of the official state bureaucracy.

While the university has indisputably an international mission, it is not simply engaged in the export of a Wahhabi ideology but in that of a broadly Salafi ethos, and the expansion, if not of an exclusive or narrow 'Wahhabi missionary project',[73] then at least of Saudi religious networks. The regime's intent has clearly been to harness a worldwide conservative Islam in the service of its own legitimacy, rather than to stimulate, as has occurred, a political, even radical, activism that might undermine the status quo, including its own.[74] A cautionary note had been sounded as early as late 1979. Several of the insurrectionists at the Grand Mosque in Mecca in December had been students at Medina University and came to question official interpretations as displacing literal readings of the Qur'an and Sunna, even though Ibn Baz was rector of the university. Some members of the religious establishment felt that such 'an atmosphere favourable to heresy' had been created by the large numbers of foreign students in Medina.[75]

International Institutions

The OIC owes its very existence, in considerable part, to the outrage of King Faysal (r. 1964–75), over a fire at the al-Aqsa mosque in Jerusalem in 1969. One Saudi author notes that, in response, the King called for 'anger and an Islamic renaissance' (*ghabida wa nahda islamiyya*) free of nationalism, racism, and political partisanship.[76] Although the fire was set by a deranged Australian, Muslim anger was directed squarely at Israel – then the occupying power. The summit called to deal with the matter agreed on the establishment of a new international organisation. It has grown to fifty-seven members and, proclaiming itself 'the collective voice of the Muslim world', it ostensibly 'has the singular honor to galvanize the Ummah into a unified body'.[77]

Aspirational rhetoric aside, however, its mission is constrained by the offsetting principle of respect for members' sovereignty (Article 1.3 of the Charter) and the reality of Saudi pre-eminence.[78] The OIC is headquartered in Jidda until 'the liberation of Al-Quds [Jerusalem]' (Article 21), despite the view of some who believe it should be based in a less authoritarian setting. Saudi Arabia contributes the largest financial share to its broad network,[79] and Secretaries-General have formally been Saudis since 2014 but acceptable to the Kingdom before that. Iyad ibn Amin Madani (b. 1946), a former Saudi Minister of Hajj (1999–2005) and Minister of Information and Culture (2005–9), was Secretary-General from 2014 to 2016, when he was reportedly removed because he had offended the Egyptian president, a close ally of the Saudi regime; and Yusuf ibn Ahmad al-'Uthaymin, who was Saudi Minister of Social Affairs (2007–15), was appointed in 2016. The larger network significantly includes the Islamic Development Bank (IDB), whose heads have been Saudis since the establishment of the bank in 1975. From 1975 to 2016, Ahmad Muhammad 'Ali al-Madani (b. 1934), a former Saudi Deputy Minister of Education and rector of King 'Abd al-'Aziz University, was the IDB's president. He was replaced by the former Saudi Minister of Hajj (2011–15), Bandar ibn Muhammad al-Hajjar (b. 1953) in 2016 after the *hajj* disaster of 2015. Saudi Arabia contributes the largest share, by far, of the bank's capital; its subscription at the end of 2017 was 23.5 per cent of the total, compared to Iran's 8.25 per cent, the third largest subscriber.[80] Saudi Arabia is also a principal funder of the Islamic Solidarity Fund, which provides humanitarian, social, cultural, and educational assistance across the Muslim world, not least to Palestine.[81]

The OIC's many conferences and vigorous media routinely promote awareness of 'Muslim' issues on which there is broad trans-sectarian interest, such as the concerns of Muslim youth and inter-religious dialogue. The *OIC Journal* is published in Arabic, English, and French and hardcopies are distributed free to member state embassies, universities, other institutions, and individuals who express interest. All publications are available on their website and social media, such as Facebook, are also extensively used.[82] Saudi ministers and royal personalities figure prominently in these OIC media. In one 2014 issue, for example, Prince Faysal ibn Salman (b. 1970), Governor of Medina Province, and Princess 'Adila bint 'Abdullah were singled out for their contributions, respectively, to urban redevelopment and women's empowerment; the then-new Secretary-General, Iyad Madani, was welcomed for his promise to 'work for the benefit of the Ummah'; King 'Abdullah's initiative to establish a Centre for Dialogue among the Islamic Doctrines was praised as part of the campaign to defeat extremists who had 'hijacked Islam'; and 'Abd al-'Aziz 'Uthman al-Tuwayjri (b. 1950), the Saudi director-general of the Islamic Educational, Scientific and Cultural Organization (ISESCO), part of the OIC network, endorsed King 'Abdullah's 'initiative for inter-faith and inter-cultural dialogue' and noted the common need 'to reconstruct the civilizational edifice of the Ummah'.[83]

Claims to leadership of the *umma* proved contentious after the Iranian revolution established a rival, Shi'i, claimant. When even an ostensibly pan-Islamic issue arose, such as blasphemy towards the Prophet in Salman Rushdie's *Satanic Verses*, a Saudi–Iranian rivalry affected the OIC response. Protests had broken out in South Asia and Europe denouncing the book, and Ayatullah Khomeini issued his infamous *fatwa* pronouncing death on the author in February 1989. The Saudis took a somewhat more nuanced view, arguing that, while Rushdie was likely guilty of apostasy, he had first to stand trial to answer the charge. The Saudi Imam of the main Brussels mosque was murdered by a group with links to Iran when he argued that, given that Belgium was a democracy, the novel should not be banned there.[84] The *'ulama* argued that, contrary to what Khomeini had ordered, Rushdie's life was sacred until a court rendered a guilty judgement. The Iranians urged the OIC to act more decisively and the organisation affirmed that Rushdie was an apostate. But the Foreign Ministers took a middle position overall. They appealed to 'all members of the international community to ban the sale or distribution of this book' and to publishers to cease production of it. Their call on members to bar Rushdie from entering their countries meant that a trial, as the Saudis had argued, would be impossible. But they also failed specifically to endorse the *fatwa* and merely called for legislation to protect religious belief.[85] The spokesman for Iran's Council of Guardians complained that the OIC should have gone further,[86] and it is clear that the Saudis, hopeful of regaining pre-eminence among Muslim states, were intent on denying the Iranians a victory in the OIC.

At times the OIC is direct in its support of Saudi positions, as seen in its repeated endorsements of Saudi efforts to defuse Islamist radicalism. In addition to favourable mentions in its periodical literature as mentioned above, the OIC's landmark blueprint for the next decade, its 'Programme of Action', singled out the King 'Abdullah ibn 'Abd al-'Aziz International Centre for Interreligious and Intercultural Dialogue, based in Vienna, as of 'critical importance' in fostering dialogue across and within religious traditions as a way of combating extremism.[87] Moreover, weighing in on a longstanding conflict, the Assistant Secretary-General for Political Affairs, 'Abdullah 'Abd al-Rahman 'Alam, did not refrain from expressing a view on a contro-versial internal Afghan matter that would have been welcome in the Saudi foreign policy bureaucracy where he had long served. He acknowledged that the Afghan government's 2016 rapprochement with Gulbuddin Hekmatyar's Hezb-e Islami, a group the Saudis had heavily financed during the anti-Soviet *jihad*, was not universally welcomed, but concluded that it was nonetheless a positive development.[88] The Saudis also sponsored an international convoca-tion of *'ulama* in July 2018 that supported the Kingdom's equivocating policy on the Afghan conflict: presuming to be a mediator and officially supportive of a ceasefire and negotiated settlement, but critical of the Taliban. The conference condemned suicide bombings and intra-Muslim fighting as 'prohibited by Allah and His Prophet'; they have only led to disorder and undermined the 'principles of unity, solidarity and preservation of the cohesion of Muslim society' (*tumasik al-muj-tama' al-muslim*). Saudi influence was expressly acknowledged in the declared gratitude to the King and Crown Prince for their part in arranging a temporary truce and generally 'for their interest in Muslim issues everywhere'.[89]

The OIC's support for Saudi political positions has at times risked controversy with other Arab states and Iran. Relations with Iran had improved under the presidency of Mohammed Khatami, who hosted a summit in Tehran in December 1997 and paid a state visit to Saudi Arabia in May 1999, but tensions soon resurfaced. Unusually for the OIC, it suspended Syrian membership in August 2013, to the conster-nation of Iran, which supports the Bashar al-Asad regime. Iran claimed that the move was counter-productive and, in any case, in violation of the OIC's Charter,[90] but it reflected the Saudi hard-line opposition to the Syrian government and its ability to influence the inter-state organisation. In addition, reflecting the Saudi concern over Iranian and Qatari criticisms of Bahrain, the OIC has warned 'all external parties' against interference in Bahrain's internal affairs and, contrary to much international opinion, praised its government for upholding 'the rule of law and promoting the exercise by Bahraini citizens of all their legitimate rights'.[91] Emphasising the personal commitment of King Salman and President Trump, the OIC has also warmly endorsed the Saudi initiative, strongly backed by the United States and regional ally Egypt, to 'unite the Islamic world against extremism and terrorism'.[92] In congratulating the new Crown Prince on his appointment, the Secretary-General singled out his success in fostering US–Arab relations.[93]

The case of Yemen is also instructive. Secretary-General al-'Uthay-min congratulated the Saudi King for donating US$2 billion in aid to the Yemeni people in light of difficulties created by the conflict there – a situation, some would argue, in large part due to Saudi actions. But the Secretary-General singled out the anti-Houthi, Saudi-led 'Arab Alliance' for praise and condemned the 'crimes of the Houthi militias'.[94]

While the OIC is not simply an adjunct of the Saudi Ministry of Foreign Affairs and it does not merely follow Saudi policy, it is nevertheless a useful instrument for upholding broader Saudi interests. For example, OIC declarations on Palestine provide a kind of safety valve for the Saudis: they allow the appearance of consistency with broad Arab and Muslim sentiment – proclaiming members 'United for a Just Solution' as they did at a 2016 summit – without the burden of definitive action that might endanger relations with the United States. The OIC used its size within the non-aligned movement to secure a United Nations General Assembly censure of Israel for its Basic Law that declared Jerusalem the capital of Israel in July 1980. The emotive issue of the US embassy transfer to Jerusalem in December 2017 brought widespread condemnation from all quarters with no substantive response – an outcome prefigured in the absence of King Salman at a special summit in Istanbul to deal with the issue.

Of more direct use to the Saudis has been the Muslim World League (Rabitat al-'Alam al-Islami) network. Founded in 1962, it was intended, in part, to give expression to the pan-Islamic policy of then Crown Prince Faysal. But, given the marked regional hostilities of the time, it had a direct political function in opposing the Arab nationalist ambitions of Egypt's Gamal 'Abd al-Nasser. King Faysal followed this in late 1965 with an appeal to several countries, including Iran, for a Muslim alliance, but was thwarted by an adverse political climate. An allied institution, the World Assembly of Muslim Youth (WAMY, al-Nadwa al-'Alamiyya li-al-Shabab al-Islami), was founded in 1972. It has operated across the world and is especially prominent in Europe, with a focus on youth and student activities. Its headquarters, like the League, is in Saudi Arabia, its Secretary-General is a Saudi, and it is overtly supportive of Saudi policies such as an inter-faith initiative of King 'Abdullah. WAMY has at times coordinated programming with organisations such as the Forum of European Muslim Youth and

Student Organizations, and it has provided a large number of scholarships for study at such universities as Imam University in Riyadh and al-Azhar in Cairo. It also issues publications on understanding the faith, some of which have been accused of fostering Wahhabi values such as antipathy to the Shi'a.[95]

The Muslim World League advances a conservative, though not necessarily Wahhabi, version of Islam. It has principally done so through such periodical publications as *al-Rabitah* (The League) and *al-Nahdah* (The Renaissance), the journal of the allied Regional Islamic Da'wah Council of Southeast Asia and the Pacific, which is funded by Saudi Arabia and Malaysia.[96] These have heightened awareness on broader, pan-Islamic issues like Palestinian resistance, the *jihad* in Afghanistan, and especially the condition of endangered Muslim minorities such as the Rohingyas, Chechens, and Moros. For Muslim oppositional movements, it has been important to enlist League support, or at least sympathy, and thus to plug into the financial and diplomatic reserves of the Kingdom. To give one example, Salamat Hashim, head of the Moro Islamic Liberation Front, visited the League in September 1984 to publicise the Philippines regime's 'genocidal campaign and its duplicity and treachery', which prompted in turn a visit to the Moro area six months later of the League's Secretary-General who was later to become deputy head of the Consultative Assembly (Majlis al-Shura), 'Abdullah 'Umar Nasif (b. 1939).[97] The League's publications and social media routinely document the largesse of the Saudis in providing disaster relief, building mosques, and distributing Qur'ans.

The ascendancy of Crown Prince Muhammad ibn Salman has reinforced the League's political mission while reorienting its attitude towards Islam. For years critics have accused conservative Saudi Arabia of unwittingly fostering Islamist radicalism through its export of a Wahhabi-Salafi version of Islam. In somewhat disingenuously arguing that the country needs to return to the 'moderate Islam' (*al-Islam al-wasati*) of its roots, he positions the Kingdom in stark opposition to the deviant radicals. Their pernicious ideology must be eliminated: 'We will not spend the next 30 years of our life combating destructive ideas (*afkar mutatarifa*). We will destroy them today and immediately.'[98] The head of the League, Muhammad ibn 'Abd al-Karim al-'Issa (b. 1965), formerly Saudi Minister of Justice (2009–15) and member of the Council of Senior 'Ulama, has unequivocally placed his organisation at the service of this new – and sweeping – project. The past is past, he has said, and now 'We must wipe out this extremist thinking through the work we do. We need to annihilate religious severity and extremism which is the entry point to terrorism. That is the mission of the Muslim World League.' He promised to review League support for mosques, such as the central mosque of Geneva, that were regarded as recruitment centres for radical ideologies. The League's new role is consistent with Saudi presumptions to lead the *umma*: 'What we are doing and want to do is purify Islam of this extremism and these wrong interpretations and give the right interpretations of Islam. Only the truth can defeat that and we represent the truth.'[99] At the inaugural meeting of the Saudi-created Islamic Military Counter Terrorism Coalition (al-Tahaluf al-Islami al-'Askari li-Muharabat al-Irhab) in November 2017, al-'Issa applauded Saudi efforts to overcome the 'lack of synergy in the Muslim World in terms of institutionalized mechanisms' and to solidify a larger pan-Islamic cause.[100]

Less grandly, but intensely political nonetheless, the League has strongly supported the Saudi position on Iran. It has denounced Iran's 'criminal' activities in supporting radical groups across the region such as its 'sectarian agents', the Houthis and Hizbullah. In terminology reminiscent of the Bush II administration, it denounces Iran's 'axis of evil' (*mihwar al-shar*).[101] It has vehemently denounced Iranian support for the Asad regime in Syria as well condemning the actions of the regime itself, which, like those of the Nazis, have shaken 'every living conscience' (*kul damir hayy*). It has also expressed its confidence in the Saudi ability to withstand Houthi missile attacks on Riyadh and other Saudi cities; these merely showed the level of 'miserable aggression' (*al-'adwan al-ba'is*) from the Yemeni rebels and their international backers.[102]

To summarise, the Saudis have relied on a variety of institutions to support their religious and political ambitions. The training of Muslims from across the world at tertiary educational institutions such as Imam Muhammad ibn Sa'ud University and the University of Medina is presented as consistent with obligations to the *umma*. While the curricula are mixed and several theological perspectives are presented, there is a broadly Wahhabist bent to the teaching – that is, a form of the puritanical and conservative teachings of traditional Wahhabism that reflects changing social mores and political preferences.

Any hope that the universities would churn out ambassadors for a Saudi-Wahhabi leadership of Islam has been clouded by the inadvertent radicalisation of some students. The Saudis have had somewhat greater success in using institutions like the OIC and Muslim World League. Dependent on the Kingdom's funding, they provide a forum for its views and a showcase for its leadership. These organisations are dedicated to enhancing pan-Islamic solidarity and have contributed to the shaping and promotion of 'Islamic' issues such as the cause of the Palestinians and embattled minorities and opposition to terrorism. But the Saudis have also used these fora to put forward partisan views, such as on Iran, Syria, and Yemen. In short, institutionalisation has magnified Saudi claims to leadership of the *umma* while advancing foreign policy interests.

'Export' of Wahhabism

Regardless of the supportive political position that such institutions as the OIC or League provide, the Saudis argue that their larger motivation is religious. The King Fahd Printing Complex distributes many thousands of Qur'ans in several languages each year as part of its commitment to *da'wa*.[103] Financing for mosques, religious schools, and publications is routinely committed via such institutions as the League and other government-sponsored agencies. To give the example of Indonesia, money from the mid-1960s was principally channelled from the League to its branch, Dewan Dakwah Islamiyah Indonesia (Indonesian Council for Islamic Propagation, DDII). After the Iranian revolution, the Saudis established Lembaga Ilmu Pengetahuan Islam dan Bahasa Arab (Institute for the Study of Islam and Arabic, LIPIA) as an affiliate of the Imam Muhammad ibn Sa'ud University in Riyadh. Its head is a Saudi, it promotes texts in line with the Wahhabi perspective, such as those of Ibn Taymiyya and Ibn 'Abd al-Wahhab, and students are taught the views of modern Wahhabi scholars such as Ibn Baz as well as those of Muhammad Nasir al-Din al-Albani (1914–99), whose scholarship was intermittently in favour in the Kingdom. Many are sent to Imam University and Medina University for further study, and some of the early cohort returned to set up a number of religious organisations that have established mosques and *pesantren* (traditional religious schools). Saudi money has provided a large proportion of their funding, such as from al-Mu'assasat al-Haramayn al-Khayriyya (Haramayn Charitable Foundation) under the Ministry of Islamic Affairs, Endowments, Da'wa, and Guidance.[104]

The Saudi international involvement has been extensive. Considerable support went to Bosnia, particularly during the 1992–5 war. The Saudi High Committee for Aid to Bosnia funded cultural centres in Sarajevo and Mostar, mosques in Sarajevo, Tuzla, and Bugojno, an Islamic teacher training school in Bihać, and the Active Islamic Youth.[105] Saudi *Arab News* reported in April 2018 that Bangladesh would build 560 mosques, each costing around US$1.8 million. The billion dollars required for this massive programme would come, at least in part, from Saudi Arabia.[106] Given that the aim is to counter radical ideologies and that the Muslim Brotherhood has been identified as a troublesome source, it is likely that the Saudis will provide the majority of the funding. One French writer said that the Kingdom spent as much on its 'religious diplomacy' as it did on defence, and compared Medina University with the Soviet-era Patrice Lumumba University as an ideological training ground, especially for Africans.[107] There have also been criticisms of the King Fahd Academy network in several countries of the West, such as the United States, Britain, Germany, and Australia. Ostensibly set up for the children of Saudi diplomats abroad but also local Muslims, these schools have been criticised for their Wahhabi curriculum.

It has become commonplace to criticise the Saudis for encouraging a conservative, Salafist version of Islam throughout the Muslim world. This is thought to have, in turn, encouraged a radicalisation that has led directly to acts of violence. As Chapter 5 indicates, the genealogy of ISIS, as with al-Qa'ida, can be traced back to the more rigid teachings of Wahhabism. As noted above and implicitly acknowledged by Crown Prince Muhammad ibn Salman, such radicalisation has not redounded to the advantage of a conservative Saudi state, especially one that recognises its security is closely tied to American and broadly Western power.

While there are countless examples of Saudi support for religious institutions throughout the Muslim world, they do not amount to an attempt at 'Wahhabization of the *umma*'.[108] Two reasons account for this. First, as we have seen, there is no uniform doctrinal reading of Wahhabism. Its interpretation has been affected by variant understandings at times among the *'ulama*, but it is also in large part affected by the views of the regime, which, history suggests, is more concerned

with legitimising its base of power than promoting orthodoxy. Moreover, the modern Wahhabi narrative has been shaped by broader
influences – encapsulated in the term 'Wahhabist' used in this chapter.
These influences, not least, have come from the currently officially
despised Muslim Brotherhood. Indeed, Stéphane Lacroix argues that,
rather than exporting a form of Islamism, the Saudis have *imported*
Islamist ideas – first from disciples of Muhammad 'Abduh and Rashid
Rida who assisted with the establishment of the state in the early
twentieth century, and then in the 1950s and 1960s, when Muslim
Brothers faced persecution in Egypt,[109] as we have seen with the
establishment of Medina University.

Second, localisation has proven to be a powerful counter-force. As
Noorhaidi Hasan points out, the Saudi desire to affirm its leadership of
the Islamic world, particularly after the Iranian revolutionary challenge, needed receptive local agents. These have been both local groups
with existing political roots, such as DDII in Indonesia, that was
associated with the proscribed Masyumi party, and new activist-
intellectuals, urban and educated in modern-style (though conservative) universities. But the Saudi 'export' has been resource-based – the
provision of money and other support – which seemingly created a
'new generation of Wahhabis',[110] but it, in fact, has induced broadly
conservative, even Salafist, trends rather than exclusively a narrow
Wahhabi one. The case of Malaysia suggests the coexistence of trends.
The Al-Madinah Islamic University, established in Selangor state,
advances a Wahhabi-style curriculum and has close relations with
Saudi institutions.[111] Yet, at the same time, the curriculum, staffing,
and student affiliation of the International Islamic University of Malaysia, which was set up in 1983 with Saudi funds and even had a Saudi
rector for a decade, could not be considered Wahhabi. The same could
be said of PERKIM (Muslim Welfare Organisation of Malaysia),
whose aim to bring non-Muslims into the fold has cut across secular
and Islamic lines and whose role in an ongoing project of Islamisation
reflects Malaysian government influence rather than external prescription.[112] The influx of Saudi money and influence may therefore be
welcomed by local groups, but it does not necessarily, and often, in
fact, does not, mean that there is a simultaneous ideological
conversion.

In sum, much has been made of the Saudi efforts to spread their
version of Islam. Commentators have adopted the post-1979 rhetoric

of the 'export of the [Iranian] revolution' to bring this point home. There is no doubt that the Saudis have built, financed, and otherwise encouraged extensive networks of schools, mosques, cultural centres, publications, and scholarships; some of this has been channelled through the transnational institutions discussed in the last section, some of it through the state religious bureaucracy. While this activity may have had discernibly conservative effects on the religious identity of some recipients, the evolution of ideas and locally grounded reactions suggest that a 'Wahhabised' or even 'Saudised' *umma* has not occurred and is unlikely to do so. However much the Saudis may see themselves as at the centre, their efforts at radiating outwards have, at best, provided financial and political links that have helped to instil a larger sense of Muslim cosmopolitanism, but not necessarily approval of their *umma* contentions.

Conclusion

The Saudi-Wahhabi establishment misses no opportunity to espouse the cause of Islamic unity and to extol the Saudi commitment to that cause. Leadership of the *umma* is in fact central to the regime's legitimacy formula, a formula that places Islam and functional modernisation as two sides of the same coin. This is the message that underlay the central bargain that King Faysal struck in the 1960s in response to the tension between those who wished to bring the Kingdom into the modern age and the *'ulama* who were anxious about open-ended change.[113] Integral parts of this ideological package have been linkages with the outside. Validation of the regime required religious bureaucratisation and social welfare institutionalisation at home, and its wider certification as the leader of the Islamic community abroad. However, the Saudi search for an *umma*-driven legitimacy has had built-in limitations.

The first is that the Wahhabi ideological narrative has been inherently constraining. The *'ulama* have not always spoken with one voice and in fact have often presented variant interpretations, and there has also been an admixture of views that are, at times, difficult to disaggregate as Wahhabi, Salafi, or even Ikhwani. But there has been a larger ethos that is censorious and even divisive, rather than uniting. The chief target of this hostility has been the Shi'a but, from both political and religious sources, there have also been Sunni targets such as the

Muslim Brotherhood. Attitudes towards Muslims living in a minority situation have been, at best, confused and, at worst, patronising.

Second, the desire of the Saudi regime for larger validation has at times been undermined by its own ostensibly co-dependent religious establishment. In perhaps the most dramatic example, al-Qaʻida and ISIS have been depicted as threatening the stability of the state, but their ideologies are, broadly, Wahhabist. It is also evident that, contrary to official policy, some religious scholars have been sympathetic towards youth joining *jihad*s in Iraq and Syria – just as they had been when the government, in a stance markedly different to the present, supported the *jihad* in Afghanistan. To the extent that there has been some popular sentiment in favour of joining larger causes, it may be indicative of a kind of societal pan-Islamism at odds with the state-defined version.

Third, geopolitical considerations have countered Saudi assertions of pre-eminence in the *umma*. Any presumptive right to lead it has been challenged by an equally assertive Shiʻi Iran, as Chapter 3 makes clear. Saudi usage of organisations such as the OIC and the Muslim World League is minimally successful, but there are built-in drawbacks: inter-member competition within and light international weight externally in the case of the OIC; hybrid religious messaging and localisation in the case of the League and its affiliates.

Even leadership of Sunnis is not guaranteed. The Turkey of an assertive President Recip Tayyip Erdoğan (b. 1954) appears to many Saudis as a direct challenge to the mantle of Sunni-world leadership, and designations such as 'sultan of the *umma*', that have been ascribed to him,[114] clearly rankle. His encouragement of the Palestinian cause has won him many admirers, and he appeared to have gained the public relations upper-hand when he sponsored the Istanbul summit of the OIC in December 2017, after the American decision to move its embassy in Israel to Jerusalem. Moreover, his support for the Muslim Brotherhood after the military coup deposed it in Egypt in 2013 stands in stark contrast to the vilifications of the movement that have come from the Saudi political and religious establishments. The October 2018 brutal murder of the Saudi journalist and critic Jamal Khashoggi (1958–2018), in Istanbul, further strained relations between the Kingdom and Turkey and appeared to have given President Erdoğan advantages over the Saudi regime, which, in effect, he accused of complicity in, if not outright commissioning of, the crime. This competition for the moral high ground has complicated the rivalry over political advantage.[115] In February 2019, Erdoğan's forthright criticism of the Chinese government's harsh treatment of the Uighurs, calling it a 'shame for humanity'[116] in distinction to the Saudi Crown Prince who paid a state visit to China, has compounded the sense that the Turkish regime now represents the conscience of the Muslim world.

One further geopolitical consideration is the disjunction between a Kingdom that presumes to speak for global Islam and one that is increasingly dependent on and allied with non-Muslim powers, not least the United States and Israel. In the regional turmoil that has unfolded broadly since the American invasion of Iraq in 2003 but accelerated since the Syrian civil war broke out in 2011, Saudi Arabia has formed an integral part of a US–Israel–Egypt axis against a Russian–Iran–Hizbullah coalition, with Turkey the outlier balancer. Iran and Hizbullah, as well as some Sunni Salafists, routinely point to this Saudi diplomatic and military alignment as an invalidating contradiction of its *umma* role. Muhammad ibn Salman's public acknowledgement of an Israeli right to their own land and of the appeal of an economic relationship with Israel, once peace is established, has also been widely criticised. He accepted that 'we have religious concerns about the fate of the holy mosque in Jerusalem and about the rights of the Palestinian people',[117] but many feel he has undermined the central plank of the pan-Islamic agenda since 1948: a united pro-Palestinian front.

The authoritarian disposition of the state, such as the imprisonment of critics like Nasr ibn Hamad al-Fahd (b. 1968), doubtless accounts for the lack of overt domestic antipathy to this foreign policy. However, a debate over whether its international relationships are consistent with the doctrine of 'loyalty and disavowal', discussed above, has swirled in certain circles.[118] Do these links constitute a form of loyalty (*al-wala'*) to the unbelievers and, if so, is this tolerable when dissociation (*al-bara'*) would be expected? The deliberations are often cast in religious-historical terms, deconstructing the story of the Prophet's forgiveness of the Muslim Hatib ibn Abi Balta'a (586–650), who felt compelled to betray the Medinan Muslims to the enemy Meccans. While some see an implicit acquiescence in enemy power when exceptional circumstances demand, others see treachery to the Muslim cause in any support for and assistance to infidel forces. The political implications of such a lively, and unfinished, debate for the Saudi regime could not be clearer.

As Madawi Al-Rasheed points out, the state ideology links the Al Sa'ud simultaneously with religious tradition and modernisation.[119] But, as the latter suffers the turbulence of late rentierism, legitimisation based on the former has renewed importance. And, yet, a double irony ensues. Legitimisation is integral to regime security, but the security is undermined by the seeming incongruities: the regime was founded as a purifying one with a universalist message, but its Islamic credentials have been called into question and the message has seemed parochial, confronting, and even dangerous. In a related irony, the allure of the idea of the *umma* guarantees that the *claim* to guide it will persist, but for the Saudi regime, the compelling interest in being seen to lead has created conditions that subvert the realisation of that pre-eminence. Muslim unity remains a spiritually charged goal, but the assertion of leadership that has come from the Kingdom has been instrumentalised and self-limiting.

Notes

1 Ira Lapidus refers to its later influence in Islamic India, Indonesia, and much of Africa. *A History of Islamic Societies* (Cambridge University Press, 2002), p. 572; but Nabil Mouline notes that Ottoman officials were largely unconcerned with the movement and left it to the *amir* of Mecca to handle. *Les clercs de l'Islam: Autorité religieuse et pouvoir politique en Arabie Saoudite, XVIIIe–XXIe siècles* [The Clerics of Islam: Religious Authority and Political Power in Saudi Arabia, 18th–21st Centuries] (Paris: Presses Universitaires de France, 2011), pp. 84–5.

2 David Commins, *The Wahhabi Mission and Saudi Arabia* (London and New York: I. B. Tauris, 2009), p. 69.

3 The Wahhabis opposed the veneration of the Prophet at his tomb in Medina, and viewed the Shi'a as heretics.

4 Kramer, *Islam Assembled*, pp. 117, 122.

5 A contemporary observer, Muhammad Asad, explained the Ikhwan's rebellion by a combination of factors: reversion to tribal competitions; a power grab by the chief opponent, Faysal al-Dawish; and religious ignorance, 'Abd al-'Aziz's 'earlier failure to impart education to the *Ikhwan* and turn their religious fervour to positive ends began to bear its tragic fruit'. *The Road to Mecca*, 4th and rev. edn. (Gibraltar: Dar al-Andalus, 1980), p. 225.

6 Joseph Kostiner, *The Making of Saudi Arabia, 1916–1936: From Chieftaincy to Monarchical State* (Oxford University Press, 1993), p. 103.

7 See, for example, Shafi Aldamer, *The Visit of HRH Princess Alice, Countess of Athlone and the Earl of Athlone to the Kingdom of Saudi Arabia, 25 February–17 March 1938*, trans. Richard Mortel (Riyadh: King Abdulaziz Public Library, 2007), p. vi.

8 Kostiner, *The Making of Saudi Arabia*, p. 100.

9 Saifuddin H. Shaheen, *Unification of Saudi Arabia: A Historical Perspective*, 2nd edn. (Riyadh: Dar al-Utuq, 1414 A.H./1993), p. 28.

10 From the 1995 Ministry of Higher Education policy booklet, *Siyasat al-ta'alim fi-al-mamlaka al-'arabiyya al-sa'udiyya* [Education Policy of the Kingdom of Saudi Arabia], cited in Eleanor Abdella Doumato, 'Manning the Barricades: Islam According to Saudi Arabia's School Texts', *Middle East Journal* 57, 2 (Spring 2003): 230–47 (p. 244).

11 Asad, *The Road to Mecca*, p. 225.

12 Kingdom of Saudi Arabia, *The March of Progress* (Riyadh: Ministry of Information, n.d., 2000 [?]), p. 57.

13 See for example, the instructional pamphlet, *Mu'assasat hujjat Turkiyya* [Institution of Turkish Hajjis], n.d., n.p.

14 Michael Wolfe, *The Hadj: An American's Pilgrimage to Mecca* (New York: Grove Press, 1993), p. 324.

15 Kingdom of Saudi Arabia, *The March of Progress*, p. 57.

16 International Hajj Seminar, *Hajj: A Ritual or the Heart of the Islamic Movement* (London: The Open Press, 1983), p. 56.

17 For Iranian calls for internationalisation in 1990, see 'Après la catastrophe de La Mecque, Téhéran invite le monde islamique à retirer la garde des lieux saints à l'Arabie saoudite' [After the Catastrophe at Mecca, Tehran Asks the Islamic World to Take Custody of the Holy Places in Saudi Arabia], *Le Monde*, 6 July 1990; *Crescent International*, a pro-Iranian newspaper published in Canada and Britain, repeated the call regularly. See, for instance, 'Hajj Beyond Rituals', 27 Dhu-al-Qa'da–12 Dhu-al-Hijja 1416 A.H./16–30 April 1996; Arab, particularly Saudi, oppositional elements have joined in this demand. Haroon M. Jadhakhan, ed., *The Thieves of Riyadh: Lives and Crimes of the Al Sauds* (London: The Muslim Chronicle, 1990), p. 87. Reflecting on the 2015 incident, Ayatullah 'Ali Khamenei, Iran's Supreme Leader, said, in 2016, 'Because of these (Saudi) rulers' oppressive behavior towards God's guests (pilgrims), the world of Islam must fundamentally reconsider the management of the two holy places and the issue of haj.' Quoted in 'Iran, Saudi Spar over Running of Haj Pilgrimage', *Reuters*, 5 September 2016, www.reuters.com/article/us-saudi-haj-iran-idUSKCN11B0Y0, accessed 2 July 2018.

18 'Al-Jubayr: talab Qatar tadwil al-masha'ir al-muqadasa 'udwani wa i'lan harb dad al-Sa'udiyya' [Al-Jubayr: Qatar's Request to Internationalise the Holy Places Is Aggressive and a Declaration of War against Saudi Arabia], *al-Sharq al-Awsat* [The Middle East], 6 Dhu-al-Qa'da 1438 A.H./30 July 2017, https://aawsat.com/home/article/986271/, accessed 20 July 2018.

19 'Mufti al-Sa'udiyya li-*al-Sharq al-Awsat*: da'wat tadwil al-haramayn 'haqida wa dala' [The Saudi Mufti to *al-Sharq al-Awsat*: Calls for the Internationalisation of the Holy Places Are Spiteful and Aberrant], *al-Sharq al-Awsat*, issue 14126, 9 Dhu-al-Qa'da 1438 A.H./1 August 2017, https://aawsat.com/home/article/987646/-الشرق«-ل-السعودية-مفتي «وضالة-حاقدة»-الحرمين-تدويل-دعوات-الأوسط», accessed 25 August 2018.

20 Jubayr al-Ansari, 'Fatwa "gharuba" li-al-Qaradawi hawl al-hajj tuthir ghadban [Al-Qaradawi's "Strange" Fatwa on the Hajj Raises Anger], *al-Sharq al-Awsat*, 11 Dhu al-Hijja 1439 A.H./22 August 2018, https://aawsat.com/home/article/1370436/غضباً-تثير-الحج-حول-للقرضاوي«-غريبة»-فتوى, accessed 18 October 2018.

21 Kingdom of Saudi Arabia, *Fatawa al-lajna al-da'ima li'l-buhuth al-'ilmiyya wa-al-ifta'* [Fatwas of the Higher Committee for Research and Guidance], vol. 2 (*al-'Aqida*), *fatwa* 830, 3rd edn. (Riyadh: Dar al-Mu'ayyad, 1421 A.H./2000), pp. 220–9, quotation at p. 229.

22 'Abd al-'Aziz Al al-Shaykh, 'Hal da'wa al-Shaykkh Ibn 'Abd al-Wahhab da'wa takfiriyya?' [Was the Da'wa of Shaykh Ibn 'Abd al-Wahhab a Takfiri Da'wa?], *Riyasat al-'Amma li-idarat al-buhuth al-'ilmiyya wa-al-iifta'* [General Presidency of Scholarly Research and *Ifta'*], www.alifta .net/Fatawa/FatawaChapters.aspx?languagename=ar&View=Page&Page ID=53&PageNo=1&BookID=6, accessed 24 April 2018. He specifically denied that Ibn 'Abd al-Wahhab espoused *takfir* in two works, *Kashf al-Shubuhat* and *al-Durar al-Saniyya*.

23 Estimates of their demographic strength vary, but most place it between 10 and 15 per cent of the total Saudi population. See, for example Toby Matthiesen, *Sectarian Gulf: Bahrain, Saudi Arabia and the Arab Spring that Wasn't* (Stanford University Press, 2013), p. 3.

24 He devoted a treatise to refuting Shi'i views. *Risala fi-al-radd 'ala al-rafida* [A Response to the Rejectionists] (Riyadh: Dar Ṭayyiba, n.d.). His son, 'Abdullah, and grandson, Sulayman, expanded on the deviations of the Shi'a. See, for example, the latter's *Taysir al-'Aziz al-Hamid fi sharh Kitab al-Tawhid* [Facilitating the Explanation of *Kitab al-Tawhid* (Book on Oneness)] (Riyadh: Dar al-Sumai'i li-al-Nashr wa-al-Tawzi', 2007).

25 He also referred to them as *mushrikun*. See *fatwa* of Shaykh Ibn Jibrin, 'Radd 'ala man qal 'ana 'awam al-rafida muslimun' [Answer to Those Who Say the Shi'a Are Muslims], *DD-Sunnah.Net*, 26 July 2010,

www.dd-sunnah.net/forum/showthread.php?t=104067, accessed 18 January 2018.

26 'Bi-al-Fidyu: al-da'ia 'Abd al-'Aziz al-Fawzan yukshaf 'an bid'atayn ibtalayat bi-hima al-umma al-islamiyya bi-yawm 'Ashura' [Video: Caller 'Abd al-'Aziz al-Fawzan Reveals Two Innovations Plagued the Islamic *umma* on the Day of 'Ashura], *al-Marsad*, 1 October 2017, https://al-marsd.com/160501.html, accessed 22 November 2017.

27 Nasir ibn Sulayman al-'Umar, *al-Rafida fi bilad al-tawhid* [The Rejectionists in the Land of Tawhid (Oneness)] (n.p., n.d.), https://ar.islam way.net/book/3165, accessed 2 June 2018.

28 'Jawab al-Shaykh Safar al-Hawali 'ama qadamathu al-ta'ifa al-Shi'a min matalib li-wali al-'ahd' [Shaykh Safar al-Hawali's Response to the Demands Made by the Shi'i Sect to the Crown Prince], *DD-Sunnah. Net*, www.dd-sunnah.net/forum/showthread.php?t=16329, accessed 14 July 2018. Raihan Ismail points out that this was in response to a charged sermon from the Saudi Shi'i leader, Shaykh Nimr al-Nimr (1959–2016; he was executed on 2 January by the Saudi government), who threatened Shi'i secession from the Kingdom, and also that al-Hawali's rejoinder has been popular with other Saudi *'ulama. Saudi Clerics and Shi'a Islam* (Oxford University Press, 2016), pp. 120–1.

29 Cited in Sumedha Senanayake, 'Istanbul Conference Enflames Sectarian Tensions', *Religioscope:* www.religion.info, 23 December 2006, https://english.religion.info/2006/12/23/iraq-istanbul-conference-enflames-sectarian-tensions/, accessed 9 January 2018.

30 In a letter to Shaykh Ibn Baz, cited in https://hawamer.com/vb/hawamer 2110742, accessed 15 May 2018.

31 See, for example Jamal Khashoqji [Khashoggi], 'Lam ya'ud hilalan shi'yyan' [It Is No Longer a Shi'ite Crescent], *al-Hayat*, 15 June 2013, www.alhayat.com/article/436712/, accessed 22 July 2018.

32 'Mufti al-Mamlaka al-Sa'udiyya 'Abd al 'Aziz Al al-Shaykh yufti bi-wujub al-jihad fi Suriya madiyyan wa ma'nawiyyan' [Mufti of the Kingdom of Saudi Arabia Pronounces on the Necessity of Jihad Morally and Materially in Syria], broadcast on al-Qanat al-Hikma, YouTube, 9 March 2014, www.youtube.com/watch?v=lvzOZEtvwJU, accessed 26 July 2018; since 2012, Safar al-Hawali had also argued against foreign fighters going to Syria and in favour of financial assistance instead, as did the Mufti. We are grateful to Raihan Ismail for pointing this out. Raihan Ismail, 'The Saudi 'Ulama and the Syrian Civil War', in *The Arab World and Iran: A Turbulent Region in Transition*, ed. Amin Saikal (New York: Palgrave Macmillan, 2016), p. 93.

33 See Toby Jones, 'Saudi Arabia's Not So New Anti-Shi'ism', *Middle East Report* 242 (Spring 2007): 29–32 (p. 31). Al-Sahwa al-Islamiyya

opposed American military forces on Saudi soil during the Iraq–Kuwait war. He called for limitations on the regime's power, and defended the rights of the religious class. It has been denounced as 'Qutbist' – following the radical ideas of Sayyid Qutb – and, generally, as inspired by the Muslim Brotherhood. See Stéphane Lacroix, *Awakening Islam: The Politics of Religious Dissent in Contemporary Saudi Arabia* (Cambridge, MA: Harvard University Press, 2011). For the argument that it was a Brotherhood front but now moribund because of the Crown Prince's policy of smashing extremism, see Mashari al-Dhayadi, 'Hal intahat 'al-Sahwa' fi al-Sa'udiyya?' [Has the Sahwa Ended in Saudi Arabia?], *al-Sharq al-Awsat*, issue 14220, 13 Safar 1439 A.H./3 November 2017, https://aawsat.com/home/article/1072011/مشاري-الذايدي/هل-انتهت-«الصحوة»-في-السعودية؟, accessed 23 August 2018.

34 Zayid al-Sari', 'Mufti al-Sa'udiyya li-al-Qaradawi: mawqifik yadhkaruna bi-kibar al-'ulama' 'abr al-tarikh' [Saudi Mufti on al-Qaradawi: Your Attitude Reminds Us of the Great Scholars of History], *Elaph*, 6 June 2013, http://elaph.com/Web/news/2013/6/816758.html, accessed 2 June 2018.

35 Muhammad b. Saalih al-'Uthaymeen, 'Inviting to Allah in Communities Where There Are Muslim Minorities' and 'Questions and Answers', in *Muslim Minorities: Fatawa Regarding Muslims Living as Minorities*, ed. 'Abdul Azeez b. Baaz and Muhammad b. Saalih al-'Uthaymeen (Hounslow: Message of Islam, 1988), p. 75. For the point about marriage, see 'Abdul Azeez Ibn Baaz, 'The Importance of Muslim Minorities Adhering to Islaam' and 'Questions and Answers', in *Muslim Minorities: Fatawa Regarding Muslims Living as Minorities*, ed. 'Abdul Azeez b. Baaz and Muhammad b. Saalih al-'Uthaymeen (Hounslow: Message of Islam, 1988), pp. 29–30.

36 'Abdul Azeez Ibn Baaz, *Majmu'fatawa wa maqalat mutanawwi'a* [Collection of Fatwas and Miscellaneous Articles], vol. 2 (Riyadh: Maktabat al-Ma'arif li-al-Nashr wa-al-Tawzi', 1992), pp. 377–9.

37 Ibn Baaz, 'The Importance of Muslim Minorities Adhering to Islam'. For a standard explanation of the jurisprudential genre, see Yusuf al-Qaradawi, *Fi fiqh al-aqalliyyat al-Muslima* [On Islamic Minority Jurisprudence] (Cairo: Dar al-Shuruq, 2001).

38 One example of Saudi criticism is the post-facto accusation that al-Qaradawi's support for the Muslim Brotherhood during the Egyptian Arab Spring of 2011 was tantamount to the extremists' penchant for *takfir*. They called his actions 'quasi-takfiri' (*shibh takfiriyya*), Abd al-Sattar Hatayta, '"Layihat al-irhab" tabruz "wahdat al-hadaf" bayn al-mutatarifin [The "Terrorist List" Highlights "Unity of Purpose" among Extremists], *al-Sharq al-Awsat*, issue 14074, 10 June 2017/15 Ramadan

1438 A.H., https://aawsat.com/home/article/947911/«-تبرز-»لائحة-الإرهاب
«وحدة-الهدف-»«بين-المتطرفين, accessed 7 August 2018; in another example, Hamza al-Salim wrote in *al-Jazira* newspaper that, among his hypocrisies, al-Qaradawi was a 'political person who dominates over religion' (*shakhs siyasi yuhukim fi-al-din*). 'Al-Qaradawi!' *al-Jazira*, 16324, 13 Ramadan 1438 A.H./8 June 2017, www.al-jazirah.com/2017/20170608/lp3.htm, accessed 19 August 2018.

39 Alexandre Caeiro notes that a number of Saudi jurists have denounced *fatwa*s of the European Council for Fatwa and Research as un-Islamic and falling under the influence of the Ikhwan. 'The Power of European Fatwas: The Minority Fiqh Project and the Making of an Islamic Counterpublic', *International Journal of Middle East Studies* 42, 3 (2010): 435–49 (p. 449).

40 The SAAR Foundation was established by the influential Saudi banker and businessman Sulayman ibn 'Abd al-'Aziz al-Rajhi (b. 1929), who has close links to the Saudi establishment and won the King Faysal International Prize in 2012. The Foundation was accused of terrorist funding in 2002 in the aftermath of September 11, but an American investigation was wound down in 2003 without reaching a conclusive result. Critics, however, continued to associate the Foundation and its successor, the Safa Group, with 'providing tremendous logistical and financial support to a variety of international terrorist groups'. See, for example Matthew Levitt, 'Charitable Organizations and Terrorist Financing: A War on Terror Status-Check', Washington Institute for Near East Policy, *Policy Analysis*, Washington, DC, 19 March 2004.

41 Taha Jabir al-Alwani, *Maqasid al-shari'a* [The Foundational Goals of *Shari'a*] (Beirut: Dar al-Hadi, 2001), pp. 55–8. Also see his *Fi fiqh al-aqalliyyat al-Muslima* [On the Jurisprudence of Muslim Minorities] (Cairo: Nahdat Misr, 2000). Qaffal's terminology, cited by Fakr al-Din al-Razi, was *ummat al-da'wa*.

42 For example his *Majmu'at risa'il al-tawjihat al-Islamiyya li-aslah al-fard wa-al-mujtama'* [Collection of Letters on Islamic Guidance for Reform of the Individual and Society], 9th edn., vol. 2, section 1 (Riyadh: Dar al-Sami'i li-al-Nashr wa-al-Tawzi',1417 A.H./1997), p. 122.

43 Doumato, 'Manning the Barricades', pp. 236, 239.

44 Kingdom of Saudi Arabia, *Fatawa al-Lajna*, vol. 2 (*al-'Aqida*), *fatwa* 6541, p. 95.

45 In textbook *Tafsir*, vol. 2, pp. 78, 116; quotation in *Tawhid*, vol. 1, p. 163, as cited in 'Study Revealed Numerous Passages in Saudi Textbooks Advocating Intolerance and Violence', report, United States Commission on International Religious Freedom, Washington, DC, May 2018, p. 3.

46 Salih ibn 'Abdullah al-Fawzan, *al-Wala' wa-al-bara'* [Loyalty and Disavowal] (Cairo: Dar al-Imam Ahmad, 1434 A.H./2013), p. 14.

47 'Saudi Professor of Islamic Law Abd al-Aziz Fawzan al-Fawzan Calls for "Positive Hatred" of Christians', clip number 992, *MEMRI TV*, Middle East Media Research Institute, 16 December 2005, www.memri.org/tv/saudi-professor-islamic-law-abd-al-aziz-fawzan-al-fawzan-calls-positive-hatred-christians, accessed 18 November 2017.

48 'Abd al' 'Aziz Ibn Baz, 'Ma haya al-wasa'il alati yastakhdimuhi al-Gharb li-tarwij afkarhu?' [What Are the Means Used by the West to Promote Its Ideas?], question 3, part 3, pp. 442–6, al-Mamlaka al-'Arabiyya al-Sa'udiyya, *al-Riyasa al-'amma li-idarat al-buhuth al-'ilmiyya wa-al-ifta'*, www.alifta.gov.sa/Ar/IftaContents/Pages/IbnBaz Subjects.aspx?languagename=ar&View=Page&HajjEntryID=0&HajjEntry Name=&RamadanEntryID=0&RamadanEntryName=&NodeID=11094& PageID=246&SectionID=4&SubjectPageTitlesID=38375&MarkIndex= 0&0#؟الوسائلالتييستخدمهاالغربلترويجأفكاره, accessed 22 February 2018.

49 This was the view of 'Abdul Azeez Ibn Baaz, 'al-Raja' min fadilatikum tawdih al-wala' wa-al-bara' li-man yakuna?' [Your Excellency, Please Clarify to Whom Does *al-Wala' wa-al-Bara'* Apply?], *al-Imam Ibn Baz* [official website of Shaykh Ibn Baz], https://binbaz.org.sa/old/37631, accessed 24 March 2018. It has even been expressed by Salih ibn 'Abdullah al-Fawzan, whose views are generally regarded as hostile to non-Muslims. For example, Alberto M. Fernandez, '"Kufr" and the Language of Hate', *MEMRI Daily Brief* 98, 25 July 2016, www.memri.org/reports/kufr-and-language-hate, accessed 12 February 2018. Al-Fawzan's relatively tolerant position is conditional and is based on Qur'an 60:8, which says that God does not forbid treating unaggressive Muslims with kindness and justice (*an tabarruhum watuqsitu ilayhim*), *al-Wala' wa-al-Bara'*, p. 19.

50 'Al-Shaykh al-Fawzan yu'qib 'ala iqtirahat al-Hiwar al-Watani …' [Shaykh al-Fawzan follows the proposals of the National Dialogue …], *al-Watan*, 30 June 2005, reproduced at www.awbd.net/article.php?a=34, accessed 17 February 2018. Mark Thompson provides information on such discussions in the National Dialogue of 2010. 'Assessing the Impact of Saudi Arabia's National Dialogue: The Controversial Case of the Cultural Discourse', *Journal of Arabian Studies* 1, 2 (2011): 163–81 (pp. 173–4).

51 'Kalimat al-Shaykh 'Abd al-'Aziz ibn 'Abdullah ibn Baz 'an mawqif al-Shari'a al-Islamiyya min al-ghazu'al-'Iraqi li'l-Kuwayt' [Words of Shaykh 'Abd al-'Aziz ibn 'Abdullah Ibn Baz on the Islamic Legal Position concerning the Iraqi Invasion of Kuwait] (mimeographed, n.p., n.d.), especially p. 6.

52 According to Saudi newspaper *al-Muslimun*, 18 January 1991. As reported in Judith Miller, 'War in the Gulf: Muslims; Saudis Decree Holy War on Hussein', *The New York Times*, 20 January 1991, p. 18.

53 Al-'Awni, *al-Wala' wa-al-bara' bayna al-ghuluw wa-al-jifa' (fi Daw' al-Kitab wa-l-Sunna)*. See Joas Wagemakers, 'The Enduring Legacy of the Second Saudi State: Quietist and Radical Wahhabi Contestations of *al-Wala' wa-l-Bara'*, *International Journal of Middle East Studies* 44 (2012): 93–110 (pp. 98–9). Al-'Awni has been a member of the Saudi Majlis al-Shura and is General Supervisor of the International Committee for the Support of the Final Prophet (ICSFP).

54 Safar al-Hawali, *Kashf al-ghumma 'an 'ulama' al-umma* [Revealing the Sorrow to the Umma's Scholars] (n.p.: Dar al-Hikma, 1991), pp. 16, 69–71, 75–9, 83, 101, 131; and Mamoun Fandy, 'The Hawali Tapes', *The New York Times*, 24 November 1990.

55 This is found in his lecture of 7 Safar 1411 A.H./28 August 1990, the relevant part of which is 'Asbab suqut al-duwal' [Causes of the Fall of Sates], *islamweb.net*, http://audio.islamweb.net/audio/index.php?page=FullContent&audioid=13759#119704, accessed 12 March 2018.

56 Salih al-'Ubaykan, 'Ma yajri fi-al-Iraq laysa jihadan' [What Is Going on in Iraq Is Not *Jihad*], *al-Sharq al-Awsat*, issue 9473, 20 Ramadan 1325 A.H./4 November 2004, http://archive.aawsat.com/leader.asp?article=263861&issueno=9473#.W1k56FUzaUk, accessed 16 October 2017; Khalid al-Dhakil, a professor at King Sa'ud University in Riyadh, questioned the argument's critical premise that the American-imposed Bremer government could be considered legitimate. 'Al-'Ubaykan bayna rafad al-jihad wa-al-ta'yush ma'al-ihtilal' ['Ubaykan between the Rejection of *Jihad* and Coexistence with the Occupation], *al-Ittihad*, 24 November 2004, www.alittihad.ae/wajhatdetails.php?id=8261, accessed 16 October 2017.

57 'Reactions and Counter-Reactions to the Saudi Clerics' Communiqué Calling for Jihad in Iraq', *MEMRI*, Special Dispatch No. 896, 21 April 2005, www.memri.org/reports/reactions-and-counter-reactions-saudi-clerics-communiqu%C3%A9-calling-jihad-iraq#_ednref4, accessed 2 November 2017.

58 Lisa Myers et al., 'More Evidence of Saudi Doubletalk?', *NBC News.com*, 26 April 2005, www.nbcnews.com/id/7645118/ns/nbc_nightly_news_with_brian_williams-nbc_news_investigates/t/more-evidence-saudi-double talk/#.W1ked1UzaUk, accessed 12 October 2017; he reportedly said that 'if someone knows that he is capable of entering Iraq in order to join the fight, and if his intention is to raise up the word of God, then he is free to do so'. When contacted by NBC, he said that he meant that the Iraqis were

capable of fighting for themselves. Al-Luhaydan was removed from his post in February 2009.

59 Thomas Hegghammer, 'Saudis in Iraq: Patterns of Radicalization and Recruitment/Combattants saoudiens en Irak: modes de radicalisation et de recrutement', *Cultures & Conflits*, 12 June 2008, file:///C:/Users/u4442428/Downloads/conflits-10042.pdf, accessed 23 September 2017, pp. 2, 4.

60 Ibn Baz, *Majmu'fatawa*, vol. 2, pp. 370–9. Here he used a slightly variant title for the agency: General Presidency of the Departments of Scientific Research and Issuing Fatwas (Riyasat al-'Amma li-Idarat al-Buhuth al-'Ilmiyya wa-al-Ifta').

61 'Al-Ahdaf' [Objectives], *Jami'at al-Imam Muhammad ibn Sa'ud al-Islamiyya*, university website, www.imamu.edu.sa/about/Pages/targets3.aspx, accessed 16 November 2018. This is listed as one of the university's objectives for 2014–20.

62 Kingdom of Saudi Arabia, *Kingdom of Saudi Arabia* [English-language newsletter issued by Saudi embassy in Washington], 28 December 2000, p. 3.

63 'Saudi Cleric Who Taught in U.S. On Al-Majd TV: "Allah Be Praised, America Is Collapsing ..."', translated transcript of televised interview, *MEMRI* Special Dispatch no. 2097, 30 October 2008, www.memri.org/reports/saudi-cleric-who-taught-us-al-majd-tv-allah-be-praised-america-collapsing-will-wes, accessed 22 June 2018. He taught for a few years at IIASA in Virginia.

64 Qasim al-Samrani, *al-Fihris al-wasfi li-makhutat al-sira al-nabawi wa muta'laqatuha* [Index of Manuscripts of the Prophet's Biography and Addenda] (Riyadh: Jama'at al-Imam Muhammad ibn Sa'ud al-Islamiyya, 1416 A.H./1995); 'Abd al-'Aziz al-Nimla, *al-Tansir fi-l-adabiyyat al-'arabiyya* [Evangelisation in Arabic Literature] (Riyadh: Jama'at al-Imam ibn Sa'ud al-Islamiyya, 1415 A.H./1994), pp. 109–44.

65 For instance: 'Abd al-Rahman al-Mutayri, *al-Ghulu fi-al-din fi hayat al-muslimin al-mu'asara* [Extremism in the Life of Today's Muslims] (Riyadh: Kulliyat al-Shari'a, Jami'at Imam Muhammad Ibn Sa'ud University, 1990), published MA thesis. This work has been translated as: *Religious Extremism in the Lives of Contemporary Muslims*, trans. Jamaal al-Din al-Zarabozo (Denver: Al-Basheer Company for Publications and Translations, 2001).

66 Mordechai Abir, *Saudi Arabia: Government, Society and the Gulf Crisis* (London: Routledge, 1993), pp. 22–3.

67 "An al-Jami'a' [About the University], *al-Jami'a al-Islamiyya bi-al-Madina al-Munawwara*, official university website, http://iu.edu.sa/Page/index/20234,

accessed 12 June 2018. The English version of the website translates the
second term as 'affiliation'.

68 Cited in 'Call for Female Departments at Islamic University', *Arab News*,
8 February 2016, www.arabnews.com/saudi-arabia/news/877201, accessed
22 September 2018. He said: 'The Madinah University is Islamic in its
policies and directions, and Islam doesn't cut away the woman from
public and educational life.' He is a graduate of Imam Muhammad Ibn
Sa'ud University, which has long had a women's section.

69 See http://iu.edu.sa.

70 The quoted terms are Michael Farquhar's; see 'Saudi Petrodollars,
Spiritual Capital, and the Islamic University of Medina: A Wahhabi
Missionary Project in Transnational Perspective', *International Journal
of Middle East Studies* 47 (2015): 701–21 (p. 702).

71 Interview with Dr Hatem al-Marzoky, President of Islamic University of
Medina, Medina, 5 December 2017. He indicated that, in 2017–18, the
university served 18,000 meals, three times a day, every day. And suggested they were all free. But one student-operated website says: 'Students who first enter the University are provided a ticket which allows
them to eat for free for the first few days or for the first month. After this
period you are required to purchase monthly tickets for the mess-hall',
which are subsidised: Australian Students at The Islamic University in
Madinah, www.asmu.info/, accessed 21 July 2018.

72 The younger brother of Sayyid Qutb, Muhammad Qutb moderated
some of his ideas. The prominent *shaykh* Safar al-Hawali was his
student, and Usama Bin Ladin admired his writings, recommending,
for instance, his *Mafahim yanbaghi an tusahhah* [Concepts that Must
be Corrected]. See Bruce B. Lawrence, ed., *Messages to the World:
The Statements of Osama bin Laden* (London: Verso Books, 2005),
p. 229.

73 Farquhar, 'Saudi Petrodollars, Spiritual Capital, and the Islamic University of Medina', p. 701; he also insightfully points out the oversight role
of religious bureaucratisation. *Circuits of Faith: Migration, Education,
and the Wahhabi Mission* (Stanford University Press, 2017), pp. 64,
79–81, for example.

74 Al-Marzoky stressed that today the university is firmly committed to
'humanising' both its physical environment, with improved landscaping
and architecture, and its studies. Interview, 5 December 2017. Marko
Babić has argued, however, that, at least in the 1980s and 1990s,
students from Bosnia-Herzegovina were mobilised to Salafi causes as a
result of study at Medina. 'Two Faces of Islam in the Western Balkans:
Between Political Ideology and Islamist Radicalization', in *Perseverance*

of Terrorism: Focus on Leaders, ed. Marko Milosevic and Kacper Rekawek (Amsterdam and Berlin: IOS Press, 2014), p. 133.

75 Hamud ibn Salih al-'Uqayl, a Riyadh *imam*, cited in James Buchan,
'Secular and Religious Opposition in Saudi Arabia', in *State, Society
and Economy in Saudi Arabia*, ed. Tim Niblock (London: Croom Helm,
1982), p. 123.

76 Husayn Muhammad 'Abdullah ibn Qurash, *Fikr al-watan: mas'uliyyat
al-jami'* [The Idea of the Nation: Everyone's Responsibility] (Riyadh: Dar
al-Qabas li-al-Nashr wa al-Tawzi', 1437 A.H./2016), p. 120.

77 www.oic-oci.org/page/?p_id=52&p_ref=26&lan=en, accessed 2 February 2018. For an informed and balanced study of the organisation, under
its original name, and its relevance to the *umma*, see 'Abdullah al-Ahsan,
*OIC: The Organization of the Islamic Conference (An Introduction to
an Islamic Political Organization* (n.p. [Herndon, VA]: International
Institute of Islamic Thought, 1408 A.H./1988).

78 A self-described 'political' work extolling the Saudi contributions to the
OIC (then called the Organisation of the Islamic Conference) is Sulayman 'Abd al-Rahman al-Haqil, *al-Wataniyya wa mutatallabatha fi dau'
ta'alim al-Islam* [Nationalism and Its Requirement in Light of the Teachings of Islam], 3rd edn. (Riyadh: Jam'at al-Imam Muhammad ibn Sa'ud
al-Islamiyya, 1417 A.H./1996), pp. 192–9.

79 Figures are hard to come by, but the Saudi contribution is usually put at
10 per cent of the budget (with Iran providing around 5.5 per cent). See,
for example Marie Juul Petersen, 'Islamic or Universal Human Rights?
The OIC's Independent Permanent Human Rights Commission', DIIS
Report 2012/13, Copenhagen: Danish Institute for International Affairs,
2012, p. 47.

80 *Annual Report 2017* (Jeddah: Islamic Development Bank, 2018), p. 103.
The Saudi share has remained largely constant. In 2002, it was 24.56 per
cent: *Annual Report 1422 A.H. (2001–2002)* (Jeddah: Islamic Development Bank, 2002), p. 334.

81 The OIC Secretary-General credits Saudi Arabia, the United Arab Emirates, and Turkey with the major financial backing of the Fund: 'Islamic
Solidarity Fund Projects Financing Approvals Total US$249 million',
Reliefweb, 29 May 2017, https://reliefweb.int/report/occupied-palestin
ian-territory/islamic-solidarity-fund-projects-financing-approvals-total-us,
accessed 5 February 2018. In 2012, Saudi Arabia contributed over 77 per
cent of the 'voluntary contributions' to the *waqf* account of the Islamic
Solidarity fund: 'Draft 34th Report of the Finance Control Organ of the
Organisation of Islamic Cooperation on the Closing Accounts of the
OIC's General Secretariat and Its Specialised Organs for the Financial

Year 2012', OIC/FCO-34/2013/REP (Jeddah: Organisation of Islamic Cooperation, 2013), p. 23.

82 Interview with Maha Mostafa Akeel, Director of Information Department, Chief Editor of *OIC Journal*, Jidda, 6 December 2017.

83 *OIC Journal* 26 (January–March 2014) [in order of discussion] 'Madinah Governor Announces 13 Initiatives for Sustainable Cultural and Scientific Projects', p. 55; 'OIC Celebrates International Women's Day ... Under the Patronage of Princess Adela bint Abdulaziz Al Saud', p. 45; 'The New Secretary General Vows to Work for the Benefit of the Ummah', p. 28; 'OIC and Arab League to Coordinate in the Face of Common Dangers', p. 9; 'Ministers of Culture Adopt Implementation Plan for King Abdullah's Initiative for Inter-Faith and Inter-Cultural Dialogue', p. 54.

84 The *imam* was the representative of the Muslim World League in Belgium. Reuters identified the group as 'Soldiers of Truth', *The Independent*, 1 April 1989; whereas the *Washington Post* called it 'Soldiers of Justice', 30 March 1989.

85 For the text of the final resolution on *The Satanic Verses* of the 18th Foreign Ministers' Conference of the OIC, see *Mideast Mirror*, I7 March 1989, pp. 25–6. For the relevant paragraph in the final communiqué, see BBC, *Summary of World Broadcasts*, ME/04I3, 20 March 1989, p. A/6, para. no. 46.

86 For Ayatullah Muhammad Emami-Kashani's comments, from Tehran home service, I7 March 1989, see *Summary of World Broadcasts*, ME/ 0413, 20 March 1989, pp. A/9–10.

87 'Munazzamat al-Ta'awun al-Islami hatta 'am 2025: barnamaj al-'amal' [Organisation of Islamic Cooperation until the Year 2025: Programme of Action] (Istanbul: Munazzamat al-Ta'awun al-Islami, 15 April 2016), p. 11.

88 'Abdullah 'Abd al-Rahman 'Alam, 'Al-musalaha hi al-sabil al-wahid 'ilhalil al-salam fi Afghanistan' [Reconciliation Is the Only Way to Bring Peace in Afghanistan], *Majallat al-Munazzama* 36 [Arabic version of *OIC Journal*] (February–April 2017), p. 14; among other posts, 'Alam had been Saudi ambassador to Indonesia from 2003 to 2005', *al-Riyad*, issue 14757, 20 Dhu-al-Qa'da 1429 A.H./18 November 2008, www.alriyadh.com/388684; he was replaced by Muhammad al-Dhuba'yi of the Saudi Ministry of Foreign Affairs in May 2018. 'OIC Appoints New Assistant Secretaries General', *Saudi Press Agency*, 6 May 2018, www.spa.gov.sa/ viewfullstory.php?lang=en&newsid=1760141, both accessed 23 July 2018; and 'Jumhuriyyat Indonesia tamnah al-safir al-sa'udi 'Abdullah 'alim al-wasam al-taqdiri min al-daraja al-mumtaza' [The Indonesian Republic Awards Ambassador 'Abdullah an Award of Scholarly

Excellence], *al-Riyad*, issue 14757, 20 Dhu-al-Qa'da 1429 A.H./ 18 November 2008, www.alriyadh.com/388684, accessed 18 October 2018.

89 "Ilan al-mutamar al-'alami li-'ulama' al-muslimin hawl al-salam wa-al-aman fi 'Afghanistan' [Declaration of International 'Ulama Conference on Peace and Security in Afghanistan], *Sawt al-Hikma* (Voice of Wisdom), Organisation of Islamic Conference, 26–7 Shawwal 1429 A.H./10–11 July 2018, Mecca, www.oic-cdpu.org/ar/topic/?tID=5884, accessed 1 August 2018.

90 See for example Asma Alsharif, 'Organization of Islamic Cooperation Suspends Syria', *Reuters*, 16 August 2012, www.reuters.com/article/us-syria-crisis-islamic-summit/organization-of-islamic-cooperation-suspends-syria-idUSBRE87E19F20120816, accessed 5 February 2018.

91 'Nonintervention in the Affairs of the Kingdom of Bahrain', *OIC Journal* 33 (April–July 2016), p. 11.

92 'Tawahad sufuf al-'alam al-Islami did al-tatarruf wa-al-irhab' [Unite the Islamic World against Extremism and Terrorism], *Majallat al-Munazzama* 37 (May–September 2017), p. 11.

93 'Munazzamat al-Ta'wun al-Islami turahib bi-akhtiyar al-Amir Muhammad bin Salman Waliyan li-al-'Ahd [The Organisation of the Islamic Conference Welcomes Crown Prince Muhammad Bin Salman], *Majallat al-Munazzama* 37 (May–September 2017), p. 12.

94 'Al-Othaimeen Commends KSA and Arab Alliance Initiatives to Support Yemen', *OIC Journal* 39 (January–April 2018), p. 12.

95 Praise for WAMY support for the inter-faith initiative can be found in Samar Fatany, 'Let Us Unite against Radicals and Promote Peaceful Coexistence', *Saudi Gazette*, 26 July 2013, www.saudigazette.com.sa/article/54040/Let-us-unite-against-radicals-and-promote-peaceful-coexistence, accessed 24 February 2018; see also Pew Forum, 'Muslim World League and World Assembly of Muslim Youth', *Religion and Public Life*, Pew Research Center, 15 September 2010, www.pewforum.org/2010/09/15/muslim-networks-and-movements-in-western-europe-muslim-world-league-and-world-assembly-of-muslim-youth/#fnref-5859-24, accessed 15 January 2018. A WAMY publication is *Islam in Concept* (Kuwait: Dar Al Watan Publishing, 1980), but it has also been accused, for example, of distributing a book, *The Difference between the Shiites and the Majority of Muslim Scholars*, which argues that Shi'ism is a Jewish distortion of Islam. See Liyakat Nathani Takim, *Shi'ism in America* (New York University Press, 2009), p. 116.

96 Mohamed Abu Bakar, 'Regional Islamic Da'wa Council of Southeast Asia and the Pacific', *Islamicus*, 14 July 2017, http://islamicus.org/regional-islamic-dawah-council-southeast-asia-pacific/, accessed 15 July 2018.

97 *Maradika* [official publication of the Moro Islamic Liberation Front] 5,
     3 (March 1985/8 Jamadil Akhir–10 Rajab 1405), pp. 1, 4, 7.
 98 'Muhammad bin Salman: sanaqdi 'ala al-tatarruf … wa sana'ud ila
     al-Islam al-wasati' [Muhammad bin Salman: We Will Eliminate
     Extremism … We Will Return to Moderate Islam], *al-Sharq
     al-Awsat*, issue 14211, 5 Safar 1439 A.H./25 October 2017,
     https://aawsat.com/home/article/1062851/-محمد-بن-سلمان-سنقضي-على
     التطرف-وسنعود-إلى-الإسلام-الوسطي, accessed 25 September 2018.
 99 Quoted in John Irish, '"Wiping out" Extremist Ideology Is My Mission:
     Head of Saudi-Based Muslim Body', *Reuters*, 25 November 2017,
     www.reuters.com/article/us-saudi-islam/wiping-out-extremist-ideology-
     is-my-mission-head-of-saudi-based-muslim-body-idUSKBN1DO1JV,
     accessed 1 December 2017.
100 Dr Muhammad bin Abdul Karim al-Issa, 'Ideology', presentation at
     Inaugural Meeting of the IMCTC Ministers of Defense Council, Islamic
     Military Counter Terrorism Coalition, Riyadh, 26 November 2017,
     https://mod.imctc.org/Speakers/En/Dr.%20Mohammad%20Al-Issa.pdf,
     accessed 2 March 2018.
101 'Rabitat al-'Alam al-Islami tatalaqa 'istinkar al-hay'at al-Islamiyya wa
     ghayr al-Islamiyya li-mumarasat 'Iran bi-al-mintaqa' [The Muslim
     World League Receives Islamic and Non-Islamic Organisations' Con-
     demnation of Iran's Activities in the Region], *Majallat al-Rabita* 54,
     614 (Rabi' al-Awwal 1439/December 2017), p. 9.
102 'Bayan Rabitat al-'Alam al-Islami bi-shan majzara (al-Ghuta al-Shar-
     qiyaa) bi-Dimashq' [MWL Statement on the Massacre in Eastern Ghuta
     in Damascus], *Rabitat al-'Alam al-Islami/Muslim World League*,
     28 February 2018, www.themwl.org/web; 'Rabitat al-'Alam al-Islami
     tudin itlaq malishiyya Houthi sarwkhan balistiyyan 'ala al-Riyadh'
     [The MWL Condemns the Launching of Houthi Missiles on Riyadh],
     20 December 2017, www.themwl.org/web, both accessed 12 May
     2018.
103 To give an example, a Saudi newspaper reported that, during one
     month in 2012, the Complex distributed 329,766 copies of the Qur'an
     in Arabic and in translations, along with other religious books and
     audio-tapes of Qur'anic recitations. 'King Fahd Qur'an Printing Com-
     plex Distributes 329,766 Prints and Audio Materials', *Arab News*,
     6 August 2012, www.arabnews.com/king-fahd-quran-printing-complex-
     distributes-329766-prints-and-audio-materials, accessed 7 July 2014.
     The distribution of Qur'ans in translation as part of international *da'wa*
     (*bi-yada'u al-nas*) is validated by a *fatwa* from the Permanent Committee
     for Scholarly Research and Ifta': *Fatawa al-lajna al-da'ima li-al-buhuth
     al-'ilmiyya wa-al-ifta'*, vol. 4 (*Tafsir*), *fatwa* 833, pp. 162–3. The general

view is that Qur'anic translations are not the literal word of the Qur'an, but a translation of its meanings. See also *fatwa* 2882, p. 167.

104 Noorhaidi Hasan, 'The Salafi Movement in Indonesia: Transnational Dynamics and Local Development', *Comparative Studies of South Asia, Africa and the Middle East* 27, 1 (2007): 83–94 (pp. 87–90).

105 William Racimora, 'Salafist/Wahhabite Financial Support to Educational, Social and Religious Institutions', EXPO/B/AFET/FWC/2009-01/Lot4/22, PE 457.136, Directorate-General for External Policies, European Parliament, Policy Department, Brussels, June 2013, p. 14.

106 'Bangladesh Launches Billion Dollar "Model" Mosques to Counter Radicals', *Arab News*, 6 April 2018, www.arabnews.com/node/1280101/world, accessed 25 May 2018.

107 Pierre Conesa, a former French Ministry of Defence official, says that 30,000 have returned from Medina (presumably) to Mali, Niger, and the Central African Republic, but does not indicate the timeframe. Armin Arefi and Pauline Tissot, 'L'Arabie saoudite, pays géniteur du radicalisme' [Saudia Arabia, the Birthplace of Radicalism], *Le Point*, 12 September 2016, www.lepoint.fr/monde/l-arabie-saoudite-geniteur-du-radicalisme-12-09-2016-2067860_24.php, accessed 3 December 2017.

108 Noorhaidi Hasan, 'The Failure of the Wahhabi Campaign: Transnational Islam and the Salafi Madrasa in post-9/11 Indonesia', *South East Asia Research* 18, 4 (December 2010): 675–705 (p. 677).

109 Stéphane Lacroix, 'Islamic Dissent in an Islamic State: The Case of Saudi Arabia', *AUC Forum*, American University in Cairo, Cairo, December 2010, p. 1.

110 Hasan, 'The Salafi Movement in Indonesia', p. 92.

111 Mohd. Faizal Musa, 'The Riyal and Ringgit of Petro-Islam: Investing Salafism in Education', in *Islam in Southeast Asia: Negotiating Modernity*, ed. Norshahril Saat (Singapore: ISEAS–Yusof Ishak Institute, 2018), pp. 67–73, 78–9.

112 Vali Nasr refers to the encouragement of PERKIM by the 'secular' former Prime Minister, Tunku Abdul-Rahman. *Islamic Leviathan: Islam and the Making of State Power* (Oxford University Press, 2001), p. 89. Also see Joseph Chinyong Liow, 'Political Islam in Malaysia: Problematising Discourse and Practice in the UMNO–PAS "Islamisation Race"', *Commonwealth and Comparative Politics* 42, 2 (2004): 184–205 (pp. 195–6).

113 Joseph Kostiner and Joshua Teitelbaum, 'State-Formation and the Saudi Monarchy', in *Middle East Monarchies: The Challenge of Modernity*, ed. Joseph Kostiner (Boulder, CO and London: Lynne Reinner, 2000), pp. 135–7.

114 For example, 'Turkey President Reciting Quran/Tayyip Erdogan Real Sultan of Ummah', *The Voice of Deoband*, YouTube, 22 January 2017, www.youtube.com/watch?v=EWOTxfdzKCg, accessed 3 March 2018. Al-Qaradawi called him an 'invincible "sultan" who has become the sentinel of the Ummah'. Cited in Ali Mohamed and Kristin Smith-Diwan, 'Gulf Islamists Praise Erdogan Victory, Prophesy Revival of the Ummah', The Arab Gulf States Institute in Washington, 26 August 2016, www.agsiw.org/gulf-islamists-praise-erdogan-victory-prophesy-revival-of-the-ummah/, accessed 4 September 2016. In December 2017, a number of Saudi professionals expressed to one of this volume's co-authors disquiet about Turkey's new Sunni-world ascendancy, and thus its challenge to Saudi Arabia's supposed primacy as guardians of the Holy Places.

115 Salman al-Dussari, the former editor-in-chief of *al-Sharq al-Awsat*, a key Saudi newspaper, said attempts to exploit the murder – especially by Turkey – were unacceptably hostile, but also 'grotesque and opportunistic', amounting to 'trading in the blood' (*al-mutajara bi-dam*) of Khashoggi. 'Intiha' tasyis qadiyya Khashoqji' [The Politicisation of Khashoggi's Case Is Over], *al-Sharq al-Awsat*, issue 14599, 9 Rabi'al-Awwal 1440 A.H./17 November 2018, https://aawsat.com/home/article/1466101/انتهاء-تسييس-قضية-خاشقجي/سلمان-الدوسري, accessed 17 November 2018. For an overview of Turkish–Saudi relations, see Nader Habibi, 'How Turkey and Saudi Arabia Became Frenemies – and Why the Khashoggi Case Can Change That', *The Conversation*, 18 October 2018, https://theconversation.com/how-turkey-and-saudi-arabia-became-frenemies-and-why-the-khashoggi-case-could-change-that-105021, accessed 15 November 2018.

116 Gerry Shih, 'After Years of Silence, Turkey Rebukes China for Mass Detention of Muslim Uighurs', *The Washington Post*, 10 February 2019, www.washingtonpost.com/world/after-years-of-silence-turkey-rebukes-china-for-mass-detention-of-muslim-uighurs/2019/02/10/011c7dd6-2d44-11e9-ac6c-14eea99d5e24_story.html?utm_term=.52d11647b4c3, accessed 19 February 2019. In 2009, Erdoğan had called Chinese policy towards the Uighurs 'genocide', but the criticism were muted for a decade: Ayla Jean Yackley, 'Turkish Leader Calls Xinjiang Killings "Genocide"', *Reuters*, 11 July 2009, www.reuters.com/article/us-turkey-china-sb/turkish-leader-calls-xinjiang-killings-genocide-idUSTRE56957D20090710, accessed 19 February 2019.

117 Jeffrey Goldberg, 'Saudi Crown Prince: Iran's Supreme Leader "Makes Hitler Look Good"', *The Atlantic*, 2 April 2018, www.theatlantic.com/international/archive/2018/04/mohammed-bin-salman-iran-israel/557036/, accessed 15 May 2018.

118 Opposition to Saudi support for post-September 11 American military interventionism in the Middle East has been strongly expressed. For example Nasr ibn Hamad al-Fahd (b. 1968), *al-Tibyan fi kufr man a'ama al-Amrikan* [Demonstration of the Unbelief of Those Who Help the Americans] (n.p. Sha'ban 1422 A.H./October–November 2001). He says that the 'support for the infidels' (*muzaharat al-kuffar*) is 'apostasy' (*al-ridda*), https://archive.org/details/tr_45, accessed 13 March 2018, part 1, p. 58; also see part 2, pp. 23–7. Also see Madawi Al-Rasheed, *Contesting the Saudi State: Islamic Voices from a New Generation* (Cambridge University Press, 2007), pp. 141–8.
119 Madawi Al-Rasheed, 'Political Legitimacy and the Production of History: The Case of Saudi Arabia', in *New Frontiers in Middle East Security*, ed. Lenore G. Martin (New York: St. Martin's Press, 1999).

5 | *ISIS's Conception of the* Umma

The ideological roots and communicative strategy of the Sunni Islamic State of Iraq and Syria (ISIS; in Arabic, *al-Dawla al-Islamiyya fi-al-'Iraq wa-al-Sham* or *Da'ish*) – also known as the Islamic State of Iraq and the Levant (ISIL) – have received comprehensive scholarly and critical attention. The group, which succeeded in declaring an Islamic state (*al-dawla al-Islamiyya*)[1] or Caliphate (*khilafa*) over swathes of territory in Iraq and Syria in June 2014, only to arrive at its territorial demise by early 2018, has been vigorously studied and analysed from both Islamic and non-Islamic perspectives. In both camps, there has been disagreement over the interpretation of this 'Islamic' state; some have viewed it as an Islamic phenomenon and others have rejected it as such. An abundance of widely accessible literature about the group has been produced not only in English, but also in Arabic and many other major languages.

Whilst references to ISIS's structures, methods of operations, and political dispositions are made, this chapter focuses specifically on its conception of the *umma*, which must be understood with reference to five distinct variables in the group's ideology. First, the *umma* is grounded in ISIS's Salafist worldview, which is fundamentalist and inherently exclusionary, and which limits the definition of 'authentic' Islam to a narrow interpretation of a restricted canon of scriptural texts, as well as specific precedents established during the first three generations of Islamic history. Second, the *umma* is inherently political and based on an Islamist and jihadist approach that obliges the Muslim community to be in a state of perpetual war. Third, ISIS places a heavy emphasis on the internal purification of the *umma*, and demonstrates a hostility towards fellow Muslims who do not conform to its strict interpretation of Islam. This emphasis explains their extensive application of *takfir* (excommunication) and their use of violence against Muslims who deviate from their conception of authentic Islam. Fourth, the *umma* is intrinsically tied to the territoriality of the *khilafa*, and the practical and scriptural obligations associated with its defence and expansion. Fifth, the *umma* is an ideal state, reflecting ISIS's vision of a virtuous future that it seeks to establish in the present as its main ideological priority.

The *Umma* as Salafist

The most notable characteristic of ISIS's imagining of the *umma* is that membership within it is based on a Salafist interpretation of what constitutes authentic 'Islam' that is highly exclusionary. Salafism is a reformist ideological movement which argues that the Muslim world has fallen into malaise because it has strayed from the path of 'true' Islam, and that, in response, Muslims must look back to the time of the *salaf* or *al-salaf al-salih* (pious ancestors) of the first three generations of Muslims following the Prophet Muhammad to rediscover the right and proper path of their faith. It emerged in the mid-nineteenth century as a reaction to the immense social and political changes and challenges that were taking place in the Muslim world, especially in the context of the European powers' colonisation of many parts of the Muslim domain. In particular, the intrusion of foreign ideas, values, and practices – both secularist and religious – into the lives of Muslims, as a result of European domination, caused deep concerns amongst those who wanted their countries to develop as sovereign and independent societies, according to a pristine Islam.

There are two strands of Salafist thought. Its earliest scholars, the most notable of whom we have encountered earlier, were Jamal al-Din al-Afghani and Muhammad 'Abduh. They espoused 'Enlightened Salafism' (*al-salafiyya al-tanwiriyya*), which focuses on the *salaf* as a source of guidance and inspiration, but which acknowledges the role and importance of *ijtihad* as crucial to creating the philosophical and material tools needed to institute an Islamic revival that would address issues in the Muslim world and reverse its decline.[2] Importantly, Enlightened Salafism advocated the use of Western ideas and technologies, particularly its scientific achievements, to reach its goal. As such, it was not as literalist or fundamentalist as the contemporary movements that share its name.

By contrast, contemporary Salafists tend to diverge from this approach, adopting a strong scriptural focus that is hostile to all syncretic accretions. The movements that today claim the title of Salafi are heavily influenced by a second ideological tradition, which is largely synonymous with the Wahhabi brand of Islam or what can be called Wahhabism, a specific form of Salafism named after its founding figure, Muhammad ibn 'Abd al-Wahhab (1703–92), discussed in Chapter 4.[3] He argued that the decline of the Muslim world was caused by the negative influence of foreign innovations (*bid'a*). To return to an authentic, virtuous, and pious Islamic society, it was necessary for Muslims to confine their actions and interpretations within the scriptural boundaries of these sources. As a corollary of this, he not only rejected the possibility of synthesising Islamic and foreign ideas but contended that all foreign ideas and practices (including those Islamic ones that developed after the *salaf* and might conflict with their teachings) must be opposed and eradicated from the Muslim world.[4] Wahhabism, as we have seen in the prior chapter, is not monolithic, but, in its most rigid form, it is defined by several features: its literalist approach to religious texts; its emphasis on *tawhid* (monotheism or the unity of God); its willingness to apply *takfir* (the excommunication of apostates); and its division of the world into two warring sides along the lines of the classical Islamic distinction between *dar al-Islam* (the land of Islam) and *dar al-kufr* (the land of disbelief).[5]

ISIS espouses this highly literalist perspective of Wahhabism as well as its textual methodologies. While adhering to the Salafi principle of observing the precedents set during the time of the Prophet, it takes an extreme, literalist approach. This is evident in the group's communications and propaganda, where it typically justifies its actions with abundant references to specific passages from the Qur'an and the *hadith*. The primacy given to these two sources can be seen in this opening passage from an ISIS textbook:

Today [the Islamic State] proceeds along these steps, with its new methodology that spares nothing in following the way of the pious predecessors in its preparation, attentive to it in accordance with the Quran and the *sunna*, defining itself on the basis of these two sources and neither deviating from them nor changing them, during a time in which the corruptions of the corrupters has multiplied, [as have] the falsification of the falsifiers, the aversion of the deniers, and the excessiveness of the extremists.[6]

ISIS's literalist interpretation of Islamic texts and principles has been well-documented,[7] and relates to two key aspects of its ideology and approach. The first is that it is guaranteed success because its literalist faithfulness to the traditions and practices of the *salaf* are the work of Allah and therefore aided by *tamkin* (divine enabling). The second is that it has a binary worldview that is sharply divided between Muslim believers (*dar al-Islam*) and the infidels (*dar al-kufr*) and therefore inherently combative and expansionist. Here, like other Salafist groups, ISIS continually demonstrates its commitment to following and observing the millenarian precedents set during the period of the *salaf* through its frequent references to a 'prophetic methodology'.[8]

ISIS's Discourse of Divine Will

A major theme in ISIS's ideology is its firm belief that because it is following the 'true' path of Islam, its actions are divinely sanctioned (and therefore religiously legitimate and necessary). Furthermore, they insist that following what they see as God's work will guarantee them success because it is part of a broader, pre-destined, divine plan. This claim stems from their interpretation of *Surat al-nur* [Chapter of Light] in the Qur'an (24:55), which reads:

Allah has promised those who have believed among you and done righteous deeds that He will surely grant them succession [to authority] upon the earth just as He granted it to those before them and that He will surely establish for them [therein] their religion which He has preferred for them and that He will surely substitute for them, after their fear, security, [for] they worship Me, not associating anything with Me. But whoever disbelieves after that – then those are the defiantly disobedient.[9]

ISIS defends its actions as 'righteous deeds', which qualify and legitimise their claim to establish and lead the *khilafa*.

For example, the ISIS leader Abu Bakr al-Baghdadi (b. 1971),[10] whose real name is Ibrahim Awwad Ibrahim al-Badri, quotes the Prophet Muhammad as enjoining Muslims: 'So do not weaken and call for peace while you are superior; and Allah is with you and will never deprive you of [the reward of] your deeds.'[11] Similarly, he implicitly invokes the concept of *tamkin* when he calls on ISIS followers to fight despite the odds that are against them:

O soldiers of the Islamic State, do not be awestruck by the great numbers of your enemy, for Allah is with you. I do not fear for you the numbers of your opponents, nor do I fear your neediness and poverty, for Allah (the Exalted) has promised your Prophet (peace be upon him) that you will not be wiped out by famine, and your enemy will not himself conquer you and violate your land.[12]

He goes on to make a clear connection between ISIS and what he believes to be the Qur'anic prophecy invoking the fall of 'Rome', declaring: 'This is my advice to you. If you hold to it, you will conquer Rome and own the world, if Allah wills.'[13]

The *Umma* as Exclusionary

ISIS's purely literalist approach to Islamic texts has led it to adopt a binary and reductionist view of the world. As a result, its view of what constitutes 'authentic' Islam is extremely narrow and absolute. This was most clearly demonstrated in the sermon that al-Baghdadi delivered on 4 July 2014 in Mosul after his forces captured the Iraqi city, in which he declared the establishment of a *khilafa* and himself as *khalifa*. He stated:

O *umma* of Islam, indeed the world today has been divided into two camps and two trenches, with no third camp present: The camp of Islam and faith, and the camp of kufr [disbelief] and hypocrisy – the camp of the Muslims and the *mujahidin* everywhere, and the camp of the Jews, the crusaders, their allies, and with them the rest of the nations and religions of *kufr*, all being led by America and Russia, and being mobilized by the Jews.[14]

Similarly, ISIS's magazine publication, *Dabiq*, outlines this same logic:

As the world progresses towards al-Malhamah al-Kubra [the battle preceding Armageddon], the option to stand on the sidelines as a mere observer is being lost. As those with hearts diseased by hypocrisy and bid'ah are driven towards the camp of kufr, those with a mustard seed of sincerity and Sunnah are driven towards the camp of iman [faith].[15]

This binary division underpins the group's wholesale rejection of all other socio-political systems, ideologies, and beliefs, outside of its own narrow interpretation of Islam, as *jahiliyya* (state of ignorance). It influences the group's political, Islamist approach.

The *Umma* as Political

The second key feature of ISIS's conception of the *umma* is that it is inherently political. Most mainstream Salafis follow an apolitical tradition and prefer to spread their message and ideology through proselytisation, religious networks, and education. Muhammad Nasir al-Din al-Albani, for example, argued that Salafis should pursue a programme of 'purification and education' in order to create the foundations for an Islamic state.[16] These Salafis are known as 'quietists' because they reject political action and violence on the grounds that a leader who is not actively encouraging un-Islamic practice must be tolerated for the sake of the unity of the *umma*.[17]

By contrast, ISIS is an activist group whose political approach is influenced by two ideological strands: Islamism and *jihadi* Islam. Islamism emerged in the 1970s in response to the apparent failures of secular pan-Arabism, especially the comprehensive Arab defeat in the 1967 Six Day War with Israel.[18] It is a movement which argues that religion is essential to creating a virtuous Islamic society, and that as a result, political activism and engagement should be used to achieve this goal. The Muslim Brotherhood, founded by Islamic scholar Hasan al-Banna in Egypt in 1928,[19] and its ideologues were amongst the foremost leaders of this movement and have had widespread influence.[20] Although his views were not always consistent and he reconciled with a number of political realities, as Chapter 2 shows, al-Banna also wrote, for example, that 'Islam requires that the Muslim community unite around one leader or one head, the head of the Islamic State, and it forbids the Muslim community from being divided among states.'[21]

ISIS has presented itself not just as an Islamic group, but also as a political Islamist vanguard. This is evident in its publications and propaganda. *Dabiq*, for example, declares that:

[T]he *imamah* mentioned in the above verse isn't simply referring to *imamah* in religious affairs, as many would wish to interpret. Rather, it's inclusive of *imamah* in political affairs, which many religious people have shunned and avoided on account of the hardship it entails itself and on account of the hardship entailed in working to establish it.[22]

Much of ISIS's discourse reflects this rejection of the separation between religion and politics. In fact, it explicitly rejects what it sees as 'the weak-hearted methodology of *irja*' (political quietism and neutrality towards schisms within Islam).[23] In its view, *irja*' has contributed to the decline of the *umma*, which it portrays as being a victimised, persecuted, and downtrodden community that has been continually oppressed by secular powers. Abu Muhammad al-'Adani, a spokesperson for ISIS, stated in *Dabiq*:

> The time has come for the *Umma* of Muhammad ... to wake up from its sleep, remove the garments of dishonour, and shake off the dust of humiliation and disgrace, for the era of lamenting and moaning has gone, and the dawn of honour has emerged anew. The sun of *jihad* has risen. The glad tidings of good are shining. Triumph looms on the horizon. The signs of victory have appeared.[24]

Indeed, the positioning of the *umma* as the victim is a rhetorical strategy which set up ISIS's calls for an 'awakening', through its presentation of a competitive, superior alternative Islamic system.[25] Crucially, however, this awakening can only be achieved through *jihadi* tactics – that is, through the use of violence.

The *Umma* as Combative

Islamism is a term that refers to any application of political Islam, and thus describes a broad and fragmented movement. As Islamist activity exists on a spectrum, there are many Islamist groups participating within the extant political system. *Jihadi* Islamism, however, sits at the extreme end of this ideological spectrum, rejecting participation within the existing political system and legitimising the use of violence to achieve its overthrow and the installation of a new order. *Jihad*, which is mentioned in the Qur'an primarily in the sense of a 'sustained struggle',[26] has evolved to assume two dimensions: *jihad al-kabir* (greater *jihad*), which refers to an internal, personal struggle for self-improvement ('to be a selfless, decent and virtuous human being'), and *jihad al-saqhir* (lesser *jihad*), which refers to physical combat in defence of Islam.[27] Within the Qur'an, *jihad al-saqhir* describes the Prophet's experiences in defending and expanding Islam in its early formative years and is always secondary to *jihad al-kabir*.

A key influence in the development of a *jihadi* Islamist ideology was the Egyptian thinker and Muslim Brotherhood activist, Sayyid Qutb (1906–66), who argued for the use of force to achieve social and political change. Qutb was in favour of the revolutionary overthrow of secular regimes in order to establish an Islamic state, arguing, as we have seen, that Muslims living under non-Islamic governments existed in *jahiliyya*. He reconceptualised the concept of *jihad* to give greater emphasis to its combative form (lesser *jihad*), which he called 'offensive *jihad*' and which he argued was necessary to fight *jahiliyya*.[28] This call implied that Muslims had a duty not only to defend their religion against foreign forces, but also to promote it actively and fight un-Islamic practices wherever they may be.

Jihadi Islam initially emerged amongst Islamic militants who used violence to achieve localised goals of overthrowing Muslim governments, and targeted Western governments for their support of these regimes only as a secondary goal.[29] However, the Soviet invasion of Afghanistan, combined with the 1978/79 Iranian revolution, led to the development of a transnational *jihadi* movement which advocated an expanded campaign of violence against non-Muslim governments worldwide.[30] The rise of a de-territorialised *jihadi* ideology, and the subsequent terrorist attacks and acts of violence that its adherents have perpetrated, has shifted popular understandings of *jihad* (particularly within the West). As Saikal writes:

In modern times, especially since 9/11, physical *jihad* has gained wider currency and publicity over the more widely sanctioned concept of greater *jihad*. Many in the West and indeed in the Muslim domain itself have often seen *jihad* through the prism of smaller rather than greater *jihad*.[31]

Jihadi movements typically see themselves as engaged in a long and global war against non-believers, and see the use of violence and terrorism as legitimate strategies. ISIS, like most *jihadi* groups, draws its justification for this violence from Qur'an 9:5, which states: 'When the sacred months have passed, slay the idolaters wherever you find them, and take them, and confine them, and lie in wait for them at every place of ambush.'[32] While this passage was referring to non-Muslims in Mecca during the Prophet's lifetime, modern *jihadi* Islamists have since reinterpreted it to justify the expansion of *dar al-Islam* by violent means.[33]

ISIS undoubtedly follows this *jihadi* approach. Indeed, the group has openly espoused this ideology. Its leader, al-Baghdadi, stated in a 2015 audio message that:

Islam was never a religion of peace. Islam is the religion of fighting. No one should believe that the war that we are waging is the war of the Islamic State. It is the war of all Muslims, but the Islamic State is spearheading it. It is the war of Muslims against infidels.[34]

The group's notorious acts of violence and brutality are well-known and well-documented. Here, its application of violence is justified by its uncompromising, literalist interpretation of passages from the Qur'an, including those that mention the crucifixion of infidels, the stoning of adulterers, and the taking of slaves. Bernard Haykel argues that 'slavery, crucifixion, and beheadings are not something that freakish [jihadists] are cherry-picking from the medieval tradition', but rather, ISIS '[is] smack in the middle of the medieval tradition and [is] bringing it wholesale into the present day'.[35] Hassan, for example, notes how ISIS scholars cite the seventh-century beheading of Khalid ibn Sufyan al-Hadhli as a textual justification (and inspiration) for the group's own use of that method of execution.[36] Indeed, there is a self-reinforcing nexus between the group's Salafi worldview and its *jihadi* approach, as the former determines what is sinful and un-Islamic, while the latter gives it a political direction and the tool (violence) to 'right' or correct this apostasy.

The *Umma* as Expansionist

ISIS's *jihadi* roots underpin two key aspects of its position on violence: perpetual expansionism, and the treatment of apostates and non-Muslims. A major impetus behind its use of violence is its view of the *umma* as inherently combative and expansionist. This conception of the *umma* in line with the aforementioned concept of *tamkin* and the group's belief that they are carrying out the will of God, comes from a *jihadi* interpretation of Islamic law which argues that it is an obligation of all Muslims to establish a single, comprehensive, and global *umma*.

Islamic law enjoins Moslems to maintain a State of permanent belligerence with all non-believers, collectively encompassed in the dar al-harb the domain of war ... The Muslims are, therefore, under a legal obligation to reduce non-Muslim communities to Islamic rule in order to achieve Islam's ultimate objective, namely the enforcement of God's law (the Sharia) over the entire world.[37]

In this view, all Muslims are religiously and legally obligated to resist non-believers and to work to expand the world of Islam through combative means. Indeed, one of ISIS's main slogans was *baqiyya wa tatamaddad* (remaining and expanding).[38] This expansionist view is epitomised in the group's call to conquer Rome – a call that draws a connection to the fall of the Roman Empire, which facilitated the emergence of Islam, and to the Qur'anic prophecy predicting the fall of Rome.[39] In addition to its war against outsiders and non-Muslims, ISIS also directs its *jihadi* approach internally to Muslims that do not conform to its beliefs, which leads us to the third characteristic of the group.

The *Umma* as Focused on Internal Purification

ISIS's use of violence against Muslims (including Sunnis) demonstrates its extreme application of its Salafist-*jihadi* approach. At the same time, its liberal application of *takfir* and violence against other Muslims sets it apart from many other Salafist-*jihadi* groups. ISIS's willingness to use *takfir* stems from its extreme Wahhabi and Salafist view, while its extensive application of the concept distinguishes it from its predecessors. Because of its very narrow view of legitimate Islamic source materials and practices, Salafism would contend that most Muslims are practising *bid'a* and are therefore living in sin. The notable Salafi quietist al-Albani argued that 'the command with respect to devotional acts is to stop at what the Prophet Muhammad did and to follow him and not to rationally improve and innovate'.[40]

The deployment of *takfir* against fellow Muslims is a key differentiator between Salafist and *jihadi* groups. While Salafism's strict adherence to textual literalism defines the standards and boundaries of Islamic authenticity, there is no consensus among Salafis on how to eradicate *bid'a* and spread Islam.[41] Despite sharing a common view on the sinful existence of many Muslims, both the quietest and activist Salafis accept that this can be caused by a number of possible reasons, notably ignorance or miscommunication. By comparison, *jihadi* groups view this deviation as a clear and active rejection of Islam (regardless of the reason) that makes the practitioners of *bid'a* culpable to consequences – thus conflating sin with apostasy.[42] From a *jihadi* perspective, these same Muslims would therefore be considered heretics or *murtads* (apostates), whose execution is deemed permissible according to a dogmatic interpretation of Islamic law.[43] Here, ISIS's selective use of scriptural excerpts as justification has been an effective communicative and discursive strategy that it has deployed to improve its legitimacy. This problem is inherent in all scriptural texts because 'there is language that has been interpreted not only to permit killing, but where killing in the name of God becomes a sacred obligation'.[44] This makes ISIS's application of *takfir* wide-ranging, because in its eyes 'failure to rule in accordance with a narrow definition of God's law constitutes unbelief'.[45] The group employs *takfir* not only against typical targets (e.g. Shi'a and Sufis) but also against other conventional Sunni Muslims who do not conform to its version and application of Islam.

While ISIS's objection and animosity to non-Sunni sects is well-known and documented,[46] it has shown a particular enmity towards the followers of Shi'a Islam, whom it views as polytheists and a subversive 'fifth' column that seeks to spread the influence of predominantly Shi'i Iran throughout the Sunni-dominated Muslim domain. Most *jihadi* groups consider Shi'a to be heretics, but there is widespread disagreement about whether they are part of the *umma* and whether they can be 'reformed', as is the position of al-Qa'ida in Iraq.[47] Furthermore, there is even more disagreement about whether and under what circumstances it is acceptable to use violence against Shi'a, particularly civilians.[48] Despite the killing of Muslims being expressly forbidden in the Qur'an, the permissibility of killing Shi'a has been defended by one of ISIS's key ideological influences, Abu Mus'ab al-Zarqawi (1966–2006). The late al-Zarqawi, who fought the 2003 US-led invasion of Iraq, igniting a bloody Sunni–Shi'a conflict and declaring the al-Qa'ida linked Islamic State of Iraq (ISI, *al-Dawla al-Islamiyya fi-al-'Iraq*), the precursor of ISIS, before he was killed in an American bombing in 2006, wrote:

The Shi'a, have declared a secret war against the people of Islam. They are the proximate, dangerous enemy of the Sunnis, even if the Americans are also an archenemy. The danger from the Shi'a, however, is greater and their damage is worse and more destructive to the [Islamic] nation than the Americans, on whom you find a quasi-consensus about killing them as an assailing enemy.[49]

This view is echoed in ISIS publications. *Dabiq*, for example, declares that 'the fact that the Rāfidah [rejectionists] are apostates necessitates more severity when applying the sword of jihād to their filthy necks ... [they] are apostates who must be killed wherever they are to be found, until no Rafidi walks on the face of earth'.[50]

The targeting of Shi'a was a major point of contention that led to the split between ISI and al-Qa'ida. In a 2005 letter to al-Zarqawi, Ayman al-Zawahiri (b. 1951), then second-in-command in al-Qa'ida, criticised ISI's excessive use of violence against Shi'a. He wrote:

And if some of the operations were necessary for self-defense, were all of the operations necessary? Or, were there some operations that weren't called for? And is the opening of another front now in addition to the front against the Americans and the government a wise decision? Or, does this conflict with the Shia lift the burden from the Americans by diverting the mujahedeen to the Shia, while the Americans continue to control matters from afar? And if the attacks on Shia leaders were necessary to put a stop to their plans, then why were there attacks on ordinary Shia? Won't this lead to reinforcing false ideas in their minds, even as it is incumbent on us to preach the call of Islam to them and explain and communicate to guide them to the truth? And can the mujahedeen kill all of the Shia in Iraq? Has any Islamic state in history ever tried that? And why kill ordinary Shia considering that they are forgiven because of their ignorance?[51]

This excerpt perfectly represents the divergent priorities between the then-ISI and its parent organisation, al-Qa'ida. While the latter was more focused on strategic objectives (fighting the United States and winning popular support), al-Zarqawi and ISI privileged their fundamentalist ideological objectives first (although al-Zarqawi's actions also had a strategic dimension, as he aimed to trigger a civil war that would force Sunnis to see things from his point of view and take sides with his group's struggle).[52] ISIS's willingness to employ violence against non-Sunni Muslims therefore reflects an extreme application of *takfir* that goes beyond even that of al-Qa'ida.

More than just targeting non-Sunni groups, however, ISIS distinguishes itself from many other *jihadi* groups by its view on who is a legitimate target. Not only targeting Shi'a, it extends the label of *takfir* to any Muslim that it deems undesirable according to its Islamist ideology and makes him/her a legitimate target to be killed under its interpretation of the Islamic law. Jacob Olidort describes how ISIS's textbooks frequently label Muslims who collaborate with non-Muslims as 'hypocrites' (*al-munafiqin*) who must be resisted.[53] Indeed, the discourse of 'hypocrites' has been a major theme in ISIS propaganda and clearly reflects its particular focus on internal 'enemies' and its efforts to 'purify' Islam. *Dabiq* warns its followers of this subversive threat:

Yes, there is fear and anxiety, because the hypocrites lurk in ambush for the muwahhidīn [true believers in Islamic monotheism], but who is it that keeps people firm? Who keeps them secure? Who sends tranquillity [sic] down upon His weak slaves? It is Allah, the King of kings![54]

Samantha Mahood and Halim Rane outline this extreme logic: in the eyes of ISIS, 'those who oppose this vision are collaborators or hypocrites and should be targeted with violence'. Importantly, this underpins its use of violence against Muslim civilians because 'by extension, the citizens of the invading countries are seen as complicit and also legitimate targets'.[55]

ISIS's intolerance towards other Sunni Muslims is a defining (if not novel) feature of its extremist approach, reflecting its apocalyptic perspective that views violence as a necessary and virtuous obligation. Here, it has adopted what Eli Alshech calls a 'Neo-Takfiri' approach which 'consider[s] resolute confrontation as a required form of piety and thus as a goal in itself'.[56] He contrasts this to the more typical Salafist-*jihadi* groups such as al-Qa'ida, which 'view confrontation as a means to achieve the end goal of establishing an Islamic state that should be employed only under appropriate circumstances and subject to the restrictions of Islamic law'.[57]

The split between these groups is epitomised in the debate between al-Zarqawi and his mentor Abu Muhammad al-Maqdisi (b. 1959), who wrote:

I pray to Allah that [Abu Mus'ab, i.e., al-Zarqawi] will not cause himself [moral] harm through his choices in *jihad* and in fighting ... He must exercise the utmost care not to shed the blood of Muslims, even if they are sinners.[58]

He questions ISI's targeting of Muslim civilians, and writes:

It is forbidden to place the [unarmed] masses and the combatant leaders on the same level ... In any event, declaring war on these sects that are obedient to Islam and on Muslims [living] under the shadow of the criminal Crusader occupation ... has nothing to do with Islamic political thought (*laysa min al-siyāsa al-shar'iyya fī shay'*).[59]

By contrast, al-Zarqawi justified this use of violence by stating that 'the shedding of Muslim blood ... is allowed in order to avoid the greater evil of disrupting *jihad*'.[60] He further argued that 'the evil of heresy is greater than the evil of collateral killing of Muslims'.[61] ISIS's broad application of *takfir* and its willingness to use violence against civilians – especially fellow Muslims – has led to vigorous debates within Salafist-*jihadi* communities. Whether it was due to strategic or ideological motivations, al-Zarqawi's wholesale condemnation of Shi'a as apostates played a major role in the split between the two groups. In fact, ISIS's calls to violence sit within a broader framework of specific obligations and requirements that it demands all 'true' believers perform if they are to be legitimate Muslims – obligations that are largely shaped by its position on the *khilafa*.

The *Umma* as the Territorial *Khilafa*

The strict definitions of appropriate beliefs and behaviours and the corresponding obligations that these beliefs entail lead to the third feature of ISIS's conception of *umma*: that it is closely intertwined with the imperative of establishing the political and territorial state of the *khilafa*. Ever since the abolition of the Ottoman Caliphate by the founder of the modern Republic of Turkey, Mustafa Kemal Ataturk in 1924, the restoration of the *khilafa* has been a major, recurring objective across Islamist thought, particularly for *jihadi* groups.[62] However, so long as the likelihood of re-establishing the *khilafa* has remained low, the theory of the institution remained underdeveloped. Shmuel Bar notes how until the rise of ISIS, 'few Islamic movements had made any serious attempt to define a modern concept of how a Khilafat would be structured. Islamic scholars of all schools … accepted the medieval prescriptions and did not see any reason to update the concept.'[63]

Another reason for the underdevelopment of this theory is the view that *khilafa* is an inherently political institution whose shape and form, as we have seen in Chapter 2, is inextricably linked to broader ideational and normative debates within Islam. This has been a particular point of contention within *jihadi* groups on *how* to implement and restore the *khilafa*. ISIS's declaration of the *khilafa* was a major point of contention among Islamists. Indeed, one of the main points of difference between al-Qaʿida and ISIS was about when it was appropriate to declare the *Caliphate*. Whereas al-Qaʿida was more strategic and wanted to wait until the conditions were right, ISIS declared the *khilafa* because it gave precedence to its religious and ideological objectives. In this, it distinguished itself from the majority of Islamist groups, which consider the restoration of the *khilafa* as an ideal that exists in the future, rather than as an immediate objective.

ISIS's conception of the *umma* is heavily influenced by their 'medieval' inspiration and the historical precedents prescribing the

conditions for the *khilafa*. The group took significant measures to
ensure that the *khilafa* that it had declared, aligned with all the key
conditions outlined by venerable jurists such as al-Mawardi discussed
in Chapter 2, notably that the Caliph was a descendant of the Quraysh
tribe (to which Prophet Muhammad belonged) and that he possessed
'knowledge (*'ilm*) of Islamic tradition and law'.[64] In this, many of the
obligations that ISIS places on Muslims are the result of its conflation
of the obligations of religious and political spheres. Shmuel Bar states
that ISIS's ideology stems from ISI's more conservative ideology,
which 'became the ideological base for a project of state-building that
involved moving away from the Al Qaeda strategy of seeking a broad
base of legitimacy for global *jihad* towards a narrower goal of con-
quering land as the basis for a new *khilafa*'.[65] *Dabiq* writes '[T]he
Muslim *Umma* (nation) should strive to be united behind a single
imam (leader), fighting under his banner and empowering him to
guard the landmarks of this religion and implement the Shari'ah
(law) of Allah.'[66] Indeed, by insisting on the need for the Caliphate
to be rooted in particular lands and accentuating the territorial dimension in the understanding of the *umma*, ISIS distinguishes itself from
al-Qa'ida. The latter's ideology did not exclude territorial considerations but advocated a worldwide community and warned against a
hastily constructed political order based on a specific area. Al-Qa'ida
conceded that jihadists would need safe-havens, and railed against
existing territorial states, such as Saudi Arabia. But its primary
emphasis fell on liberating 'all lands of Islam' (*kul 'ard al-Islam*) from
Satanic forces, such as the American military,[67] and working to secure
the all-encompassing community of believers, rather than a territorially bounded and interim Caliphate. By way of contrast, ISIS recon-
ceptualises the purpose and focus of this community, from shared
belief in a future *khilafa* to an active duty to expand the territorial
Islamic state.

   Thus, according to ISIS, membership of the *umma* is not a right, but
a responsibility that requires specific political actions and not simply
belief in Allah or compliance with ritual prescriptions. There are
several key actions that ISIS calls on all 'true' Muslims to undertake
which are related to the requirements of the *khilafa*. The first is to
pledge loyalty to the Islamic state, which it identifies with the *khilafa*
declared by al-Zarqawi. Hussein Solomon notes that the purpose
behind declaring themselves as *the* Islamic State is to emphasise that

they are the 'one to which all 1.5 billion Muslims owe loyalty'.[68] *Dabiq* invokes a Prophetic *hadith* that declares, 'whoever dies without a pledge of allegiance, dies a death of jahiliyyah'.[69]

The second is to immediately undertake *hijra* to the new *khilafa*. This call stems from their conflation of the political and religious dimensions of the *umma* (to be discussed later), and the requirement that the *umma* be unified physically and territorially, as well as spiritually through belief. On justifying the call to migrate to ISIS territory, the group cites several *hadiths* as precedents, notably ones which state 'whoever gathers and lives with the *mushrik* [polytheist], then he is like him'; and also 'Allah does not accept any deed from a *mushrik* after he accepts Islam until he departs from the *mushrikin* and goes to the Muslims'.[70] Both these directives – pledging loyalty and committing *hijra* – stem from the group's precept that it is a religious and moral obligation to create a single, unified community in the territory of the *khilafa*.[71] ISIS especially emphasises these actions as incumbent on doctors, engineers, and those with technical knowledge, due to the special contributions these individuals can make to the group's goals.[72] Indeed, in his declaration of the *khilafa*, al-Baghdadi stated:

We make a special call to the scholars, fuqahā' (experts in Islamic jurisprudence), and callers, especially the judges, as well as people with military, administrative, and service expertise, and medical doctors and engineers of all different specializations and fields. We call them and remind them to fear Allah, for their emigration is wājib 'aynī (an individual obligation).

This call reflects how individual obligations (and therefore piety) are tied to the specific, territorially based, state-building priorities of ISIS's *khilafa* project.

The third requirement of Muslims is an active commitment to expanding the world of Islam. Specifically, this calls on all Muslims to engage in a global war against non-Muslims and infidels. This call is rooted in the group's millenarian and apocalyptic worldview, which sees conflict as both an obligation and a virtuous act. The most prominent examples are the very specific, brutal methods it employs against its opponents, including civilians. On justifying its use of violence, *Dabiq* references a collection of quotations from the Qur'an, including 8:39, enjoining fighting until there is no more *fitna* (dissent) and until 'the religion is completely for Allah'.[73] On their use of beheadings, *Dabiq* invokes 47:4, among other verses: 'So when you meet those who disbelieve, strike their necks until, when you have inflicted slaughter upon them, then secure their bonds ...'.[74]

However, more importantly, for those that are physically unable to undertake *hijra*, they are compelled to support ISIS by working to bring down the states that they currently live in. On the subject of a Muslim's obligations, *Dabiq* declares:

This is the order of the Khalifa ... Either one performs hijrah to the wilayat of the Khilafa or, if he is unable to do so, he must attack the crusaders, their allies, the Rafidah, the tawaghit, and their apostate forces, wherever he might be with any means available to him ... He should attack after declaring his bay'ah to the Khilafa, so as not to die a death in Jahiliyyah.[75]

This call underpins and has inspired the lone wolf attacks conducted by ISIS members and supporters residing in foreign countries. Here, IS's call to violence targets not only non-Muslims, but also those Muslims who cooperate or coexist with non-Muslims. Indeed, for IS, it is only through the 'purifying' nature of violence that its conception of the *umma* as an idealised future community can be realised.

The *Umma* as a Normative Concept

For ISIS, the *umma* is not just a descriptive, empirical state, as it is in mainstream Islam when referring to the current global community of Muslims. Instead, it is deployed as a normative vision through which it can convey its image of an ideal world (possible, partly due to its conflation with the *khilafa*) which is heavily imbued with themes of virtuosity, piety, and unity.[76] *Dabiq* states:

In the midst of a raging war with multiple fronts and numerous enemies, life goes on in the Islamic State. The soldiers of Allah do not liberate a village, town or city, only to abandon its residents and ignore their needs.[77]

Remy Low writes that 'the *Umma* that ISIS speaks of is not the empirical *Umma* of the global Muslim populace as they are, but an empty signifier that seeks to actively produce a collective identity according to its view of the world'.[78]

One notable characteristic of this idealised *umma* that is a recurring theme throughout ISIS's propaganda is that it is multi-ethnic. This is both an intentional propaganda strategy to attract disenfranchised minorities from Western countries, and a logical outgrowth of its strong focus on religious faith as the core (and only) criterion for membership of the *umma*. Al-Baghdadi epitomised this call to multi-ethnic unity, stating in his Mosul sermon that the Islamic state will be:

a state where the Arab and non-Arab, the white man and black man, the easterner and westerner are all brothers. It is a khilāfah that gathered the Caucasian, Indian, Chinese, Shāmī, Iraqi, Yemeni, Egyptian, Maghribī (North African), American, French, German, and Australian. Allah brought their hearts together, and thus, they became brothers by His grace, loving each other for the sake of Allah, standing in a single trench, defending and guarding each other, and sacrificing themselves for one another. Their blood mixed and became one, under a single flag and goal, in one pavilion, enjoying this blessing, the blessing of faithful brotherhood.[79]

The call to inclusivity, unity, and brotherhood is therefore a key theme in ISIS's conception of the *umma* that aligns with its strongly idealised and romanticised image of the *khilafa* under a single Caliph.

Conclusion

ISIS's conception of the *umma* is grounded in a highly fundamentalist, belligerent, and ultimately political interpretation of Islam. It views membership of this *umma* as being limited to those who adhere to its millenarian view of Islamic authenticity, and who are, as a result, willing to undertake the literalist scriptural obligations that it prescribes. Key to these ideas is the call to violence as a purifying and necessary method for protecting and expanding the territory of the *khilafa*. Those Muslims that do not fit into this narrow definition of 'Islam' are consequently labelled as apostates and designated as legitimate targets of violence.

However, despite its frequent exhortations to being religiously 'authentic', often supported by specific excerpts from Qur'anic and Prophetic texts and traditions, the religious legitimacy of ISIS's self-declared Islamic state and *khilafa* have rested on dubious grounds from the beginning. David Sorenson notes that there are two dimensions to a *khilafa*'s authority: one is its recognition of the sovereignty of God (its internal beliefs and structure), and the other is an extrinsic recognition of its right to enforce that authority, which is derived by the consensus of the *umma* – in line with the election of Muhammad's successors (the *Rashidun*) via *ijma'*. Within Sunni Islam, as elaborated in Chapter 2, this is a central and unavoidable requirement that many Islamist scholars, including notable Salafi ideologues, have debated.[80] A Sudanese Islamic scholar and activist, Hasan al-Turabi (1932–2016), writes that 'an Islamic state is not primordial; the primary institution is the [*umma*]. The phrase "Islamic state" itself is a misnomer. The state is only the political dimension of the collective endeavor of Muslims.'[81] Thus, unsurprisingly, while internally ISIS's declaration is consistent with some scriptural and traditional requirements, it is not recognised as a legitimate authority by most Muslims. This has constituted a central factor in ISIS's failure to ensure the continuity of its Islamic state or *khilafa*, and therefore to receive any measure of acceptability to enable it to play a leadership role within the *umma*.

Yet, the folding up of ISIS's territorial *khilafa* does not mean the end of ISIS's ideological and operational capability. The group, like al-Qa'ida, is now franchised. In addition to retaining a capacity to carry out terrorist operations in Iraq and Syria, ISIS has managed to establish niches, either on its own or in linkage with other extremist entities acting in the name of Islam, in other conflict zones, especially Afghanistan, Yemen, and Libya. Although these groups are currently too small to pose a strategic threat to any region, these niches are able to engage in similar actions as ISIS in other zones of conflict. In this respect, no country has borne as much of the brunt of its operations as Afghanistan. In 2015, ISIS set up what it calls its Khorasan branch, named after an ancient territorial entity comprised of parts of today's Afghanistan, Iran, Uzbekistan, and Turkmenistan. This branch, which has become known as ISIS-K, was soon able to take advantage of the conflict-ridden Afghanistan and some disaffected Afghan and Pakistani Taliban to secure a presence primarily in eastern Afghanistan. Whilst opposed by the mainstream Afghan Taliban, as well as the Afghan government and the US and allied forces in Afghanistan, and also the Pakistani government that has backed the Afghan Taliban, ISIS-K carried out a number of high profile attacks in Kabul and Afghanistan's eastern provinces bordering Pakistan at the cost of hundreds of lives in 2018.[82] ISIS has justified its operations over what it regards as a domain of the *umma* even though the latter, in the sense of the generality, but not the totality, of Muslims has rejected the group as repugnant.

Notes

1 Amin Saikal, 'How Islamic Has the "Islamic State" Been?' *Journal of Muslim Minority Affairs* 38, 2 (June 2018): 143–52.

2 Bernard Haykel, 'On the Nature of Salafi Thought and Action', in *Global Salafism: Islam's New Religious Movement*, ed. Roel Meijer (Oxford University Press, 2013), p. 45.

3 Ibid., pp. 38–9.

4 Haykel writes extensively about the specific core tenets of contemporary Salafism. See 'On the Nature of Salafi Thought and Action'.

5 For details, see Saikal, 'How Islamic Has the "Islamic State" Been?', pp. 144–5.

6 An Islamic State textbook, quoted in Jacob Olidort, *Inside the Caliphate's Classroom: Textbooks, Guidance Literature, and Indoctrination Methods of the Islamic State* (Washington, DC: The Washington Institute for Near East Policy, 2016), p.17.

7 John Esposito, for example, describes ISIS's ideology as a 'new and unique militant Salafi ideology/religious rationale' for violence. 'Islam and Political Violence', *Religions* 6 (2015): 1067–81.

8 William McCants, 'Islamic State Invokes Prophecy to Justify Its Claim to Khilafat', Brookings Institute, 5 November 2014, www.brookings.edu/blog/markaz/2014/11/05/islamic-state-invokes-prophecy-to-justify-its-claim-to-khilafat/, accessed 2 February 2015.

9 The English translation is taken from https://quran.com/24/55.

10 Abu Bakr al-Baghdadi, an Iraqi native, is unlike leaders of other violent extremist groups (such as Abu Mus'ab al-Zarqawi and Usama Bin Ladin). He is a trained scholar of Islamic studies, with a PhD from the Islamic University of Baghdad. He was reportedly radicalised during his imprisonment by the Americans in 2004 and followed al-Zarqawi's steps and cherished the later declaration of the 'Islamic State of Iraq'. US intelligence had gained insight into his extremist religious political leanings and activities, and on 16 October 2011 put him on the Special Designated Nationals List, with a reward of US$10 million for information leading to his capture or death. Following his June 2014 declaration of the Caliphate, the United States raised the bounty on his head to US$25 million. However, since September 2016, his whereabouts remain unknown, and he has not been heard or sighted. There have been conflicting reports about whether he is dead or alive. Whilst the ISIS media confirmed the death of his 18-year-old son, Hudhayfah al-Badri, in early July 2018, the general assumption is that his father may still be alive. For details, see 'IS leader Abu Bakr al-Baghdadi's Son "Killed in Syria"', *BBC News*, 4 July 2018, www.bbc.com/news/world-middle-east-44710004, accessed 5 July

2018; Alissa J. Rubin, 'Militant Leader in Rare Appearance in Iraq', *The New York Times*, 5 July 2014, www.nytimes.com/2014/07/06/world/asia/iraq-abu-bakr-al-baghdadi-sermon-video.html, accessed 5 July 2018; Andrew Hosken, *Empire of Fear: Inside the Islamic State* (London: Oneworld Publications, 2015).

11 English translation taken from https://quran.com/47/31-38?translations=20.

12 Abu Bakr al-Baghdadi, Mosul speech, quoted in Amaryllis Maria Georges, 'ISIS Rhetoric for the Creation of the Ummah', in *Political Discourse in Emergent, Fragile, and Failed Democracies*, ed. Daniel Ochieng Orwenjo, Omondi Oketch, and Asiru Hameed Tunde (Hershey: IGI Global, 2016), p. 196.

13 Ibid. However, *sura* 30 notes an initial defeat and later victory of the Byzantines ('Rum').

14 Remy Low, 'Making up the *Ummah*: The Rhetoric of ISIS as Public Pedagogy', *Review of Education, Pedagogy, and Cultural Studies* 38, 4 (2016): 297–316 (p. 306).

15 'Two Camps with No Third in Between' section of 'The Extinction of the Greyzone', *Dabiq*, issue 7, Rabi' al-Akhir 1436 A.H./ January–February 2015, p. 66, https://azelin.files.wordpress.com/2015/02/the-islamic-state-e2809cdc481biq-magazine-722.pd, accessed 16 August 2018.

16 Muhammad Nasir-ur Din al-Albani, quoted in Jacob Olidort, 'The Politics of "Quietist" Salafism' (analysis paper 18 , Brookings Project on U.S. Relations with the Islamic World, Washington, DC, February 2015), www.brookings.edu/wp-content/uploads/2016/07/Brookings-Analysis-Paper_Jacob-Olidort-Inside_Final_Web.pdf, accessed 18 November 2018, p. 16.

17 While quietist Salafis do not actively participate in political activity, they do of course contribute to political discourse.

18 The strong advocate of pan-Arabism was Egyptian President Gamal Abdul Nasser (1954–70) who wanted to generate unity among Arab states against 'colonialism, imperialism, and Zionism', and in support of liberation of the Israeli occupied Palestinian lands. However, ultimately, he could not achieve his goal, given Israel's defeat of the Egyptian, Syrian, and Jordanian armies in the 1967 War, and deep-seated ideological and political differences between Arab states. For details, see Albert Hourani, *A History of the Arab Peoples* (New York: Warner Books, 1992), chapters 24–6; Eugene Rogan, *The Arabs: A History* (London: Penguin Books, 2011), chapters 10–11; Peter Woodward, *Nasser* (London: Longman, 1992).

19 The Muslim Brotherhood emerged as a popular organisation, with supporters in Egypt and throughout the Arab world, despite being officially banned from the early 1950s, only to win Egypt's general elections in

2012 following the so-called Arab Spring popular uprising, that ended the three-decade long dictatorial rule of President Husni Mubarak in February. However, Its government was overthrown by the military a year later. For a detailed discussion, see Amin Saikal, 'The Third Arab Awakening and Its Geopolitical Implications', in *The Contemporary Middle East: Revolution or Reform?* ed. Adel Abdel Ghafar, Brenton Clark, and Jessie Moritz (Melbourne University Press, 2014), pp. 21–39.

20 It is important to note that the Muslim Brotherhood, at least in its early years, did not advocate violence or the overthrow of the state, but prioritised educational and other social reforms along the lines of the quietist Salafi tradition.

21 Hassan al-Banna, quoted in Cole Bunzel, 'From Paper State to Khilafat', (analysis paper 19, Brookings Project on U.S. Relations with the Islamic World, March 2015), www.brookings.edu/wp-content/uploads/2016/06/The-ideology-of-the-Islamic-State.pdf, accessed 12 November 2018, p. 8.

22 'The Concept of Imamah is from the Millah of Ibrahim', *Dabiq*, issue 1, Ramadan 1435 A.H./June–July 2014, p. 25, https://jihadology.net/2014/07/05/al-%E1%B8%A5ayat-media-center-presents-a-new-issue-of-the-islamic-states-magazine-dabiq-1/, accessed 16 November 2018.

23 'From Hijrah to Khalifa', *Dabiq*, issue 1, Ramadan 1435 A.H./July 2014, p. 39, https://jihadology.net/2014/07/05/al-%E1%B8%A5ayat-media-center-presents-a-new-issue-of-the-islamic-states-magazine-dabiq-1/, accessed 16 November 2018.

24 'A New Era Has Arrived of Might and Dignity for the Muslims', *Dabiq*, issue 1, Ramadan 1435 A.H./July 2014, p. 9, https://jihadology.net/2014/07/05/al-%E1%B8%A5ayat-media-center-presents-a-new-issue-of-the-islamic-states-magazine-dabiq-1/, accessed 16 November 2018.

25 Ibid.

26 Ziauddin Sardar, *Reading the Qur'an: The Contemporary Relevance of the Sacred Text of Islam* (London: Hurst & Company, 2011), p. 285.

27 See David Cook, *Understanding Jihad* (Berkeley: University of California Press, 2005).

28 Michael Bonner, *Jihad in Islamic History: Doctrines and Practice* (Princeton University Press, 2006), p. 162.

29 There were some exceptions, for example the 1993 bombing of the World Trade Center and the 1995 Paris bombings. Esposito, 'Islam and Political Violence', p. 1072.

30 Ibid., p. 1070.

31 Amin Saikal, 'Women and *Jihad*: Combating Violent Extremism and Developing New Approaches to Conflict Resolution in the Greater Middle East', *Journal of Muslim Minority Affairs* 36, 3 (2016): 313–22 (p. 315).

32 Quoted in Esposito, 'Islam and Political Violence', p. 1070.

33 Ibid.

34 'Islamic State Releases "al-Baghdadi Message"', *BBC News*, 14 May 2015, www.bbc.com/news/world-middle-east-32744070, accessed 17 November 2018.

35 Graeme Wood, 'What ISIS Really Wants', *The Atlantic*, March 2015, www.theatlantic.com/magazine/archive/2015/03/what-isis-really-wants/384980/, accessed 12 November 2018.

36 Hassan Hassan, 'The Sectarianism of the Islamic State: Ideological Roots and Political Context' (Washington, DC: Carnegie Endowment for International Peace, 13 June 2016), http://carnegieendowment.org/2016/06/13/sectarianism-of-islamic-state-ideological-roots-and-political-context-pub-63746, accessed 14 November 2018, p. 17.

37 Roda Mushkat, 'Is War Ever Justifiable? A Comparative Survey', *Loyola of Los Angeles International and Comparative Law Journal* 9, 2 (1987): 227–317 (p. 302).

38 Aaron Y. Zelin, 'The Islamic State's Model', *The Washington Post*, 28 January 2015, www.washingtonpost.com/news/monkey-cage/wp/2015/01/28/the-islamic-states-model/?noredirect=on&utm_term=.c7636fe93ebc, accessed 17 November 2018.

39 Georges, 'ISIS Rhetoric for the Creation of the Ummah', p. 194.

40 Olidort, 'The Politics of "Quietist" Salafism', p. 8.

41 Here, there are three general approaches to the issue. The first is quietist Salafism, which forgoes political involvement in favour of educating Muslims on the error of their ways. Second is activist Salafism, which aims to pursue change and reform to society through participation within political structures and institutions. The third is *jihadism*, which rejects the legitimacy of the current nation-state system and advocates the use of violence to achieve revolutionary change. Quintan Wiktorowicz labelled these groups purists, politicos and *jihadis* respectively. See Shiraz Maher, *Salafi-Jihadism: The History of an Idea* (Oxford: Oxford University Press, 2016), p. 9.

42 Olidort, *Inside the Caliphate's Classroom*, p. 11.

43 John Esposito, ed., *The Oxford Dictionary of Islam* (Oxford University Press, 2003), p. 312.

44 Jerrold M. Post, *The Mind of the Terrorist: The Psychology of Terrorism from the IRA to al-Qaeda* (New York: Palgrave Macmillan, 2007), p. 160.

45 'ISIS (Islamic State of Iraq and Syria): Origins, Ideology, and Reponses by Mainstream Muslim Scholars' (National Centre of Excellence for Islamic Studies, The University of Melbourne, Melbourne, 2016), p. 9.

46 Islamic State has also notably targeted Sufis, whom they view as heretics for their veneration of saints, which they view as *shirk* (polytheism). See, for example, Rukmini Callimachi, 'To the World, They Are Muslims. To ISIS, Sufis Are Heretics', *The New York Times*, 25 November 2017, www.nytimes.com/2017/11/25/world/middleeast/sufi-muslims-isis-sinai.html, accessed 16 November 2018.

47 Brian Fishman, *The Master Plan: ISIS, Al Qaeda, and the Jihadi Strategy for Final Victory* (New Haven: Yale University Press, 2016), p. 63.

48 Ibid.

49 Al Zarqawi, 'Zarqawi Letter', trans. Coalition Provisional Authority, *U.S. Department of State*, released online from 20 January 2001 to 20 January 2009 at https://2001–2009.state.gov/p/nea/rls/31694.htm.

50 'The Rafidah: From Ibn Saba' to the Dajjal', *Dabiq*, issue 13, Rabi' al-Akhir 1437 A.H. /January–February 2016, pp. 43, 45, https://jihadology.net/2016/01/19/new-issue-of-the-islamic-states-magazine-dabiq-13/, accessed 30 July 2018.

51 Ayman al-Zawahiri, quoted in Fawaz A. Gerges, *A History of ISIS* (Princeton University Press, 2016), p. 79.

52 Ibid., p. 82.

53 Olidort, *Inside the Caliphate's Classroom*, p. 14.

54 Umm Sumayyah Al-Muhajirah, 'The Twin Halves of the Muhajirin', by Umm Sumayyah Al-Muhajirah, *Dabiq*, issue 8, Jumada al-Akhira 1436 A.H./March–April 2015, p. 35, https://azelin.files.wordpress.com/2015/03/the-islamic-state-e2809cdc481biq-magazine-8e280b3.pdf, accessed 15 August 2018.

55 Samantha Mahood and Halim Rane, 'Islamist Narratives in ISIS Recruitment Propaganda', *The Journal of International Communications* 23, 1 (2017): 15–35 (p. 24).

56 Eli Alshech, 'The Doctrinal Crisis within the Salafi-Jihadi Ranks and the Emergence of Neo-Takfirism: A Historical and Doctrinal Analysis', *Islamic Law and Society* 21, 4 (2014): 419–52 (p. 431).

57 Ibid.

58 Although this is a clear break from Salafist thought, which views Muslims who do not follow their strict interpretation of Islam as living in error, they would not designate Sunni Muslims as apostates. Abu Muhammad al-Maqdisi, quoted in Alshech, 'The Doctrinal Crisis within the Salafi-Jihadi Ranks', p. 426.

59 Ibid., p. 427.

60 Zarqawi, quoted in David Aaron, *In Their Own Words: Voices of Jihad* (Santa Monica: RAND, 2008), p. 103.

61 Ibid.

62 Paul B. Rich, 'How Revolutionary Are Jihadist Insurgencies?' (Working Paper 4/2015, Trends Research & Advisory, Abu Dhabi, 2015), p. 4.

63 Shmuel Bar, 'The Implications of the Khilafat', *Comparative Strategy* 35, 1 (2016): 1–14 (p. 4).

64 Joas Wagemakers, 'The Concept of Bay'a in Islamic State Ideology', *Perspectives on Terrorism* 9, 4 (2015), www.terrorismanalysts.com/pt/index.php/pot/article/view/448, p. 98.

65 Rich, 'How Revolutionary Are Jihadist Insurgencies?', p. 4.

66 'The Concept of Imamah', p. 24.

67 'Fatwa al-Jabha al-Islamiyya al-'Alamiyaa li-al-Jihad dad al-Yahud wa-al-Salibin' (Fatwa of the Islamic World Front against the Jews and Crusaders), dated 24 February 1998, reproduced in "An "al-Jabha al-Islamiyya al-'Alamiyya" li-qatl al-Amrikan' [From the "Islamic World Front" for Killing the Americans], *al-Hayat*, 10 March 1998, www.alhayat.com/article/948657, accessed 15 February 2019.

68 Hussein Solomon, 'The Particular Role of Religion in Islamic State', *South African Journal of International Affairs* 23, 4 (2016): 437–56 (p. 441).

69 'A Fatwa for Khurasan', *Dabiq*, issue 10, Ramadan 1436 A.H./June–July 2015, p. 23, https://archive.org/details/Dabiq10_20150714, accessed 20 September 2018.

70 'Abandon the Lands of Shirk ... and Come to the Land of Islam', *Dabiq*, issue 8, Jumada al-Akhira 1436 A.H./March–April 2015, pp. 28–9, https://azelin.files.wordpress.com/2015/03/the-islamic-state-e2809cdc481biq-magazine-8e280b3.pdf, accessed 22 September 2018.

71 Alex P. Schmid, 'Challenging the Narrative of the "Islamic State"' (International Centre for Counter-Terrorism, The Hague, June 2015), p. 9.

72 Ahmed A. Hashim, *The Khilafat at War: Operational Realities and Innovations of the Islamic State* (Oxford University Press, 2018), p. 257.

73 'And Allah Is the Best of Plotters', *Dabiq*, issue 9, Sha'ban 1436 A.H./May–June 2015, p. 51, https://azelin.files.wordpress.com/2015/05/the-islamic-state-e2809cdc481biq-magazine-9e280b3.pdf, accessed 12 September 2018.

74 'Islam Is the Religion of the Sword, not Pacifisim', *Dabiq*, issue 7, Rabi' al-Akhir 1436 A.H./January–February 2015, p. 21, https://azelin.files.wordpress.com/2015/02/the-islamic-state-e2809cdc481biq-magazine-722.pdf, accessed 16 August 2018.

75 'And Allah Is the Best of Plotters', *Dabiq*, issue 9, p. 54.

76 This juxtaposition of the present and future is a common rhetorical tactic amongst revolutionary groups.

77 'A Window into the Islamic State', *Dabiq*, issue 4, Dhul-Hijjah 1435/ September–October 2014, p. 27, https://azelin.files.wordpress.com/ 2015/02/the-islamic-state-e2809cdc481biq-magazine-422.pdf, accessed 19 September 2018.

78 Low, 'Making up the *Ummah*', p. 11.

79 Al-Baghdadi, quoted in Georges, 'ISIS Rhetoric for the Creation of the Ummah', p. 195.

80 David S. Sorenson, 'Priming Strategic Communications: Countering the Appeal of ISIS', *Parameters* 44, 3 (2014): 25–36 (p. 33).

81 Ibid.

82 For some details, see Ben Brimelow, 'ISIS Wants to Be as Dangerous as the Taliban – But It's Not Even Close', *Business Insider*, 12 February 2018, www.businessinsider.com.au/isis-taliban-afghanistan-terrorism-2018-2?r= US&IR=T, accessed 5 July 2018; Thomas Joscelyn, 'Taliban and Islamic State Target Religious Opponents in Afghanistan', *FDD's Long War Journal*, 31 May 2018, www.longwarjournal.org/archives/2018/05/taliban-and-islamic-state-target-religious-opponents-in-afghanistan.php, accessed 5 July 2018.

6 | Conclusion

The issue of unity has long featured in political assessments of Islam, and it has generally been overstated. Western imperialists routinely saw it as a threat to their interests, while enthusiastic Muslims have found it a natural expression of the principle of oneness that underpins Islamic belief. Pan-Islamic sentiment is rarely regarded as neutral, however, and, especially in the era of Islamic radicalisation, it has caused considerable concern.

The chapters of this volume present a more nuanced view – one that illuminates three points: the meaning of the *umma* has varied considerably across theological, sectarian, and political lines; despite the differences of interpretation, it remains a powerful pull on Muslim identities; and, in large part because of its symbolic and emotional power, it is a useful tool for a variety of social and political actors.

The first general theme that emerges relates to the fact that the *umma* is the fundamental community of the faith for Sunnis and Shi'a, both of whom have routinely and consistently invoked it throughout the centuries. While in both traditions, the grand doctrinal position has been what might be summarised as 'no *umma* without leadership', the conceptual and political trajectories have differed – and clashed. As seen in Chapters 2 and 5, the Sunni Caliphate was abolished in 1924 and, despite the claims of the Islamic State of Iraq and Syria (ISIS), its revival has foundered on political rivalries. Chapter 3 demonstrates that the extraordinary Imamate of the Twelver Shi'a is in a kind of abeyance, the Occultation, until the last Imam's return. For many Sunnis, this need for the Hidden Imam to return to complete the revolution started by the Prophet undermines the idea of Muhammad's final prophecy.

However, the lack of a present Caliph and Imam has posed a pressing theological as well as pragmatic quandary: who rightly wields communal authority in their absence? The *'ulama*, or religious officials, have acquired over time a kind of proximate legitimacy in both

160

traditions, although some have charged the traditional religious class with stale and rigid thinking and sought inspiration in early figures considered pioneers of Islamic reform.[1] But the *'ulama* have been a fixed feature of the religious and political landscape, even as they have taken on variant concrete form. In the contemporary period, the bureaucratisation of the religious establishment in Saudi Arabia has made the *'ulama* an integral, and generally compliant, part of a monarchical regime, whereas in revolutionary Iran they function as the governing class itself.

As seen throughout, differences have also evolved with regard to membership in the *umma*. While there is a common belief in its universality, some have questioned whether Muslims who live as a minority under non-Muslim rule, such as in Europe or the Americas, are in a special jurisprudential category from those living as a majority under Muslim rule. In addition, some argue that the *umma* extends to monotheists (*hunafa'*) generally, but others regard this as a 'Muslim'-only enterprise. By general agreement, 'unbelievers' (*kuffar*) are excluded, but debate has swirled over the precise nature of 'unbelief'. Practitioners of idolatry or polytheism (*shirk*) are thought by all to have committed the gravest capital sin against Islam, given that it violates the core principle of God's Oneness, but how inclusive must the *umma* be of 'people of the Book' (*ahl al-kitab*) and of other Muslims of varying beliefs? The latter debate has been especially virulent in our time. Even when the community is regarded as reserved for Muslims, sharp disputes have emerged over who constitutes a 'proper' Muslim. Although attempts have been made to bridge such disagreements, Muslim beliefs and movements continue to be routinely anathematised as committing 'rejectionism' (*taraffud*), 'innovation' (*bid'a*), or 'transgression' (*taghut*), among other ostensible deviations.

The second general theme is the pull of *umma* sentiment. Although our focus has been on intellectual and political elites, grassroots sentiment is a notable feature of the modern experience – and one that the elites recognise and sometimes acknowledge. Forms of interaction and solidarity already exist to a considerable extent. Pilgrimages, educational travel, and humanitarian assistance are just part of the story. Sufi groups exemplify populist movements that have had far-reaching effects. Orders such as the Tijaniyya, Qadiriyya, and Naqshbandiyya have had extensive links throughout North and sub-Saharan Africa, the Middle East, and Central Asia, and have often wielded significant political influence. Colonial intelligence officers overstated the organisation of these orders as monolithic conspiracies, but the translocal linkages they have forged have created important channels of communication across frontiers. Often new, broader communities have resulted. By crossing existing ethnic and social identities, for example, the Khatmiyya helped to inspire the Sudanese national movement around the Mahdi.

Issues that seem to encapsulate injustice against Muslims, such as the Palestinian question and the plight of endangered minorities, are also galvanising. Street demonstrations have occurred in India, Chechnya, Malaysia, and other societies demanding action in support of the Rohingyas, who have suffered severe oppression in Myanmar and have been described by the United Nations as the world's most persecuted minority.[2] Protesters in Penang in Malaysia carried signs that read 'Stop Killing our Rohingya Brothers and Sisters'. Referencing a popular *hadith* noted in Chapter 1, a leader of the Malaysian Consultative Council of Islamic Organisation (Mapim), a non-governmental organisation (NGO), said the suffering of the Rohingyas was naturally felt in Malaysia: 'When one part of the body is hurt, the whole body feels hurt. As a Muslim, we must help wherever possible.'[3] Turkish NGOs, such as the International Refugee Rights Association (UMHD) and Sadakatasi, have provided assistance to Rohingyas who have sought refuge in Bangladesh, and the Canadian branch of the Organization of North American Shia Ithna-asheri Muslim Communities (NASIMCO) raised funds as part of its Rohingya Emergency Appeal.[4]

Afghanistan, Iraq, and Syria became bywords for crisis in the Muslim world, and the lure of *jihad*, in these cases, had a popular base broader than just formalised jihadist groups. The Saudi religious establishment, for example, had difficulty in dissuading volunteer enlistments. Muslim identities exist on several registers simultaneously – family, ethnic, national, and religious – and while their salience needs to be calibrated against context, the sense of belonging to a great and cosmopolitan Muslim enterprise is, for most Muslims, a constant, if not always paramount, defining characteristic. While differences are accepted, the belief that deep structures underpin and link Muslim societies is also broadly granted.

The third theme that emerges from our analysis is that the *umma* has been instrumentalised in the modern period. The concept's utility flows from both the affective pulls on identity noted above and the need for legitimacy in political circles in Muslim societies. If the conventional view of the *umma* can be summarised as 'no *umma* without leadership', the instrumental approach can be summarised as the obverse: 'no leadership without the *umma*'. In other words, invocation of the *umma* provides an authentication of governance. As noted in both the cases of Saudi Arabia and Iran, 'Islam' is central to regime validation, even regime security. Both propose themselves as leaders of the *umma* to enhance their influence abroad and to solidify acquiescence at home. The Saudis have showcased their management and expansion of the *hajj*, even grandly referring to the millions of pilgrims each year as the 'guests of God' (*duyuf al-Rahman*). Considerable deference accrues to the Saudi monarch through his role as 'guardian' or 'servant' (*khadim*) of the Holy Places and ostensible philanthropic patronage.

Ayatullah Khomeini argued that Muslims must unite around God's sovereignty and oppose blasphemy, the anti-Islamic position taken by Western powers. Muslims should form a political union that overrides prior national divisions and serves as the prototype for a world state. There was, however, a political sub-text: Iran, locked in battle with the secular Arab nationalist and dictatorial Iraq of Saddam Hussein in the 1980s, projected itself as its alternative – that is, both Muslim and enlightened. As the vanguard of the *umma*, Iran bore a special responsibility to propagate Islam to the world and thus needed to be protected. The 'rays' of Islam spread from Iran: 'We should safeguard this source; we should protect the centre of these rays.'[5]

To this end, both the Saudi and Iranian regimes have overseen the expansion of an elaborate network of institutions, groups, and media ostensibly in the cause of pan-Islam – a 'push' to the *umma*. Indeed, a kind of 'vertical' transnationalism has evolved, sponsored and funded by state or non-state actors but intended to serve as linking others: 'hierarchical linkages through which local actors are connected to broader or extra-local levels of the larger society, culture, economy and polity'.[6] One rather staid and conservative trend is that intergovernmental organisations have developed by the agreement of existing Muslim states. The most important of these are the Organisation of the Islamic Conference (OIC) and the Islamic Development Bank (IDB). But the OIC, which some regard as the most concrete contemporary institutionalisation of pan-Islam, is in practice an inter-state organisation based on the principles of respect for the members' sovereignty and, as we have seen, is Saudi-influenced.

A notable feature of the contemporary period, especially with regard to non-state movements, is vigorous 'marketing' and social media activity. Through the standardisation of language and the formal presentation of issues of concern to believers worldwide, outlets such as periodical and book publications, videos, and blogging seek to expand a broad consciousness among Muslims that does not neatly overlap with state, or other communal, borders. Today virtually every Muslim periodical, for example, has a section devoted to the problems and prospects of Muslim minority communities throughout the world. Jihadist groups have found the framing of their message through regular media to be mobilising of support. These include *Inspire* in English and *Sada al-Malahim* (Echo of the Fierce Battles) in Arabic for al-Qaʿida, and *Dabiq* and *Rumiyah* (Rome) in multiple languages such as English, French, German, Russian, Uighur, and Bahasa Indonesian for ISIS.

The first issue of the *International Journal of Muslim Unity* in 2003 offered a kind of *ijmaʿ*, arguing that the spiritual kinship of Islam is a given. The drawing power of the *umma* ideal is understood as substantial, but the need for a directed Muslim revival is required today in order to ward off the twin evils of external intervention and internal division. The underlying spiritual ties are not enough, in this perspective, and, just as the Prophet and his immediate successors accomplished, the *umma* needs to take on concrete form. But the sponsoring centre of the journal equates the restoration of the *umma* with the *unity* of the believers. It reaffirms that 'Muslims are enjoined by Islam to be united so to provide the leadership and moral direction for humanity' and 'to achieve their religious and civilisational goals'. Moreover, it undertakes 'to create awareness on the importance and necessity of UNITY [sic]' and 'to forge linkages and networks' to this effect. The self-professed goal of unity, as distinct from 'solidarity', 'cooperation', or 'fraternity', has, upon the reflection of its sponsors, seemed a goal too far: the journal's name has been changed to the *International Journal of Muslim World Studies*.[7]

But the sponsors of these transnational institutions and publications have also had the goal of advancing their own state interests, as seen in our two case studies, and, to some extent, in the foreign policies of other would-be Islamic patrons such as Malaysia[8] or Turkey.[9] Yet, despite the pan-Islamic intent, limitations have come in several forms. One is the inherently sectarian nature of their appeals. Saudi-

Wahhabist hostility towards the Shi'a and the Iranian clerical regime's distinctive ideology, such as *velayat-e faqih*, have proven constraining, as sectarianised differences have been intensely politicised throughout the Middle East and broader Muslim world. Another limitation occurs when patrons appear to fail their own high standards, bringing into question the role of Islam in their legitimacy formulas. Yet another constraint occurs when patrons, despite having made generous expenditures beyond their borders, may well have stimulated religious sentiment but not necessarily extended their political influence. Saudi support for groups and causes has stimulated conservative, even Salafist, orientations; and Iranian support for groups and militias has mobilised Shi'i-defined postures. But, at times, limited influence, even resentment, has resulted from such external involvement, as with Saudi involvement in Indonesia,[10] or Iranian in Lebanon.[11]

The case of jihadist groups such as ISIS is particularly striking. Reacting against the nationalisation of Islam and its appropriation by regimes that have seemed corrupt, irreligious, or in the service of Western hegemony, the pan-Islamic field has seemed open to 'radicals', who seek, in their view, to reclaim the *umma* from the nation-state and dynastic regimes. They seek to reconstruct modern Islam along the lines of an alternative interpretation, one that places the community of faith above individual states and governments. At the funeral, in early November 2018, of the Pakistani religious leader Sami-ul-Haq (1937–2018), whose *madrasa* (school) exerted considerable transnational influence across the Pakistan–Afghan border, his death was lamented by the Afghan Taliban as 'a great loss for the entire Islamic ummah'.[12]

What the jihadists lack in coherence they make up in fervour. Examples include Hizb al-Tahrir al-Islami (the Islamic Liberation Party), a transnational Sunni group that espouses the restoration of the Caliphate along traditional lines,[13] al-Qa'ida, ISIS, and myriad smaller, affiliated groups. Many of these speak in the name of a fictive *umma* and deploy, in Homi Bhabha's words, the 'language of archaic belonging'.[14] In the process, they might even be described as weaponising the *umma*.

There is appeal in presenting a clear alternative to current troubles, particularly as they stretch across the globe. Afghanistan, Kashmir, Bosnia, Chechnya, Iraq, Yemen, Libya, and Syria have loomed large in Muslim opinion generally, but especially so in the worldview of jihadist groups. The common view has been that Muslim victimhood needs to be avenged, but how this is to be achieved and what kind of Muslim solidarity would follow have remained open questions. The ideology of ISIS, as we saw in Chapter 5, is a mixture of contested perspectives and, by its very Sunni nature, restricted in impact. The utility of co-opting leadership of the *umma* has been further reduced by disputes among the jihadists themselves. Al-Qa'ida and ISIS, as we have seen, have differed on both the modern understanding of the Caliphate and the means to achieve it. Because the very idea of an 'Islamic state' remains a touchstone of authenticity for many, Islamic radicalism is not likely to disappear even with the military and territorial defeat of ISIS. But what precisely such a state would entail, let alone a strategy to realise it, eludes a clear or agreed answer.

It is not surprising that pan-Islam has very often been misconstrued, seen as either more powerful, or more manipulable, than it in fact could be. Some trace Western apprehensions to early Islamic history, when the Umayyads advanced on Western Europe, or to the Ottomans who twice threatened, but ultimately failed to capture, Vienna. In the nineteenth century, pan-Islam was seen as eluding centralised imperial control, and in the context of the twentieth-century Cold War, was often viewed as the bulwark to an intractable pan-Arabism. In the late 1940s and early 1950s, for instance, the British Foreign Office saw that pan-Islam was not the exaggerated threat it had been thought to be in earlier periods, but, if properly 'guided', it could be of use to Western policy.[15] The burning of the al-Aqsa mosque in 1969, by a deranged tourist, alarmed diplomats, but the Islamic summit that followed was recognised in Washington as at least a temporary success for the 'moderates' such as Saudi Arabia and a useful counterweight to the 'radical Arab states' such as Egypt, Iraq, and Syria.[16]

The advent of the Iranian revolution in 1978/79 precipitated widespread negative views of Islam generally and Shi'ism specifically.[17] Pondering on how to rescue American diplomats who were being held as hostages, then US Secretary of State, Cyrus Vance, warned: 'Khomeini and his followers, with a Shi'ite affinity for martyrdom, actually might welcome American military action as a way of uniting the Moslem world against the West.'[18] Following 11 September 2001 and especially since ISIS's successes on the ground, Muslims as well as Westerners have often referred to Islamic radicalisation as posing a core danger to our very existence. A government official from the United Arab Emirates said, 'radical Islam is an existential threat to those of us who believe in the true nature of Islam as a religion of peace'.[19] The Foreign Minister of Australia characterised ISIS as 'the most significant threat to the global rules based order to emerge in the past 70 years – and included in my considerations is the rise of communism and the Cold War'.[20] In effect, the reaction has at times amounted to 'moral panic'.[21]

While exaggeration is a hallmark of discussions on pan-Islam, this volume has sought to provide a tempering perspective. The great majority of Muslims routinely affirm that Islam is a complete way of life, affecting all spheres of activity – ritual, personal, social, economic, and political. An understandable by-product of this conceptualisation is to see Islam as so all-encompassing and comprehensive that a unified community is imperative, and unable to avoid an inherently antagonistic relationship with other universalist visions. Hence, the common – and distorted – motif of 'Islam' versus the 'West'. What we have shown is that viewing the subject of the *umma* through the prism of monoliths overstates both the cohesion of the community of the faith itself and the degree of antipathy with the Other.

In reality, it must be said that ambivalence is embedded in Muslim self-understandings of solidarity. On the one hand, as we have seen, the political unity of all Muslims acquires the force of dogma in some circles, even though it is not clear how to attain or organise it. On the other hand, the political mission of pan-Islam, at least from the twentieth century, has been represented in state, or would-be state, enterprises, even though they routinely invoke a cosmopolitan standard of legitimacy. Muslims, at least at the elite level, have in general adapted to the Westphalian concept of the nation-state. Multiple fault-lines exist in fact, and the imagining of the *umma* as the unity of the believers has emerged before the material conditions to sustain it have evolved. But to ignore the symbolic impact of the *umma* and its integral place in the formation of Muslim identities is to understate the constancy of its presence in the life of Muslims. Unity may be an elusive aspiration, but forms of solidarity have already emerged, however much state and non-state patrons seek to manipulate and control them. To the extent it looms large in the contest over identity, authority, and influence, the *umma* is an inescapable – and fluid – dimension of Muslim politics today.

Notes

1 'Ali Shariati admired Abu Dhar – an early companion of the Prophet – and 'Ali, the Prophet's cousin and son-in-law and fourth Caliph. He saw their moral character embodied in other stirring figures of the modern age, such as Jamal al-Din al-Afghani and Muhammad Iqbal. 'Mohammad Iqbal, A Manifestation of Self-reconstruction and Reformation', Dr Ali Shariati (website), www.shariati.com/english/iqbal.html, accessed 1 October 2017.

2 Statement of Pramila Patten, Special Representative of the Secretary-General on Sexual Violence in Conflict, 'Human Rights Council Opens Special Session on the Situation of Human Rights of the Rohingya and Other Minorities in Rakhine State in Myanmar', United Nations, Office of the High Commissioner for Human Rights, news, 5 December 2017, www.ohchr.org/EN/NewsEvents/Pages/DisplayNews.aspx?NewsID=224 91&LangID=E, accessed 9 November 2018.

3 Predeep Nambiar, 'Malaysian NGOs Rouse Muslims to Defend Rohingyas', *FMT*, 8 September 2017, www.freemalaysiatoday.com/category/nation/2017/09/08/malaysian-ngos-rouse-muslims-to-defend-rohingyas/, accessed 10 December 2017.

4 'Turkish NGOs Begin Aid Campaign for Rohingya Muslims', *Yeni Şafak*, 20 July 2018, www.yenisafak.com/en/world/turkish-ngos-begin-aid-campaign-for-rohingya-muslims-3436881, accessed 9 November 2018; Nadine Osman, 'Muslim NGO Raises $500,000 for Rohingya Crisis', *The Muslim News*, 28 December 2017, http://muslimnews.co.uk/newspaper/world-news/muslim-ngo-raises-500000-rohingya-crisis/, accessed 9 November 2018; the Canadian government provided a matching amount of the raised CAD$250,000. Malaysian NGOs, such as Liga Muslim Pulau Pinang, have called on their government to be more assertive internationally on this issue. Mohamed Basyir, 'Penang-based Muslim NGOs Call for Urgent Action on Rohingya Crisis', *New Straits Times*, 7 September 2017.

5 Ayatullah Khomeini's speech at the Guards' Day celebration as reported by Tehran home service, 24 April 1985. *Foreign Broadcast Information Service*, SAS-85-080, 25 April 1985, p. 12; the 'path' references are quoted in FBIS, 12 February 1985, p. 11; with regard to Iran's mission, Khomeini also said: 'Islam is a sacred trust from God to ourselves, and the Iranian nation must grow in power and resolution until it has vouchsafed Islam to the entire world'. Cited in R. K. Ramazani, 'Khumayni's Islam in Iran's Foreign Policy', in *Islam in Foreign Policy*, ed. Adeed Dawisha (Cambridge University Press, 1983), p. 18.

6 Steven Vertovec, 'Migration and Other Modes of Transnationalism: Towards Conceptual Cross-Fertilization', *The International Migration Review* 37, 3 (Fall 2003): 641–65 (p. 649), referencing Thomas

Schweizer's 'Embeddedness of Ethnographic Cases: A Social Networks Perspective', *Current Anthropology* 38, 5 (December 1997): 739–60.

7 'About IJMWS', http://ijmws.net/about-ijmws/, accessed 5 March 2018. The International Institute for Muslim Unity, which was established in 2001, continues under this name credited to then-Prime Minister Mahathir Mohamad.

8 Suzalie Mohamad Antang, 'Islamic Dimension in Malaysian Foreign Policy Towards the Muslim World', *IKIM Journal of Islam and International Affairs* 1, 4 (2005): 63–81; David Delfolie, 'Malaysian Extraversion towards the Muslim World: Ideological Positioning for a "Mirror Effect"', *Journal of Current Southeast Asian Affairs* 31, 4 (2013): 3–29; a variation on pan-Islamic policy is Malaysia's policy to become a hub for 'Islamic tourism' by catering to Muslim social, financial, and other needs. Fatemeh Shafaei and Badaruddin Mohamed, 'Malaysia's Branding as an Islamic Tourism Hub: An Assessment', *GEOGRAFIA: Malaysia Journal of Society and Space* 11, 1 (2015): 97–106.

9 For instance: Faisal Edroos, 'Erdogan Calls on Muslim Countries to Unite and Confront Israel', *al Jazeera*, 19 May 2018, www.aljazeera.com/news/2018/05/erdogan-calls-muslim-countries-unite-confront-israel-180518185258629.html, accessed 10 June 2018.

10 Hasan, 'The Failure of the Wahhabi Campaign'.

11 For resistance to Iranian cultural policies in southern Lebanon, see Shaery-Eisenlohr, 'Iran, the Vatican of Shi'ism?'.

12 'Pakistan: "Father of Taliban" Cleric Buried after Attack', *BBC News*, 3 November 2018, www.bbc.com/news/world-asia-46084410, accessed 3 November 2018.

13 Suhi Taji-Farouki, *A Fundamental Quest: Hizb al-Tahrir and the Search for the Islamic Caliphate* (London: Grey Seal, 1996).

14 Homi K. Bhabha, 'DissemiNation: Time, Narrative, and the Margins of the Modern Nation', in *Nation and Narration*, ed. Homi K. Bhabha (London: Routledge, 1990), p. 317.

15 See, for example, FO371/75120 (1949), 'Foreign Office Minutes' and 'Pan-Islam', both in October 1949, in Anita L. P. Burdett, ed., *Islamic Movements in the Arab World, 1913–1966*, vol. 4: *1949–1966* (Chippenham: Archive Editions, 1998), pp. 42–3, 48.

16 Protests from around the Muslim world were lodged with the United Nations. King Faysal of Saudi Arabia wrote: 'We Moslems look forward, very shortly, to the day when we will meet on the soil of Jerusalem to liberate our usurped land, to save our holy shrines from the claws of treacherous Zionism and to win one of two deeds, either victory or martyrdom.' United Nations, Security Council, S/9447, 12 September 1969. The response to the fire, as we saw in Chapter 4, was not a military

one, but a diplomatic convocation and founding of the OIC. The Director of the Bureau of Intelligence and Research in the Department of State noted the positive development of a 'moderate consensus', but also that 'it is virtually certain that the radical Arab states will continue to agitate for a more extreme political posture in the Islamic forum'. 'Intelligence Note 693 from the Director of the Bureau of Intelligence and Research (Denney) to the Acting Secretary of State (Richardson), Washington, September 29, 1969', in *Foreign Relations of the United States, 1969–1976*, ed. Monica L. Belmonte, vol. E-5, part 2, Documents on North Africa, 1969–1972, chapter 1, document 2 (Washington, DC: United States Government Printing Office, 2007), pp. 40–1.

17 See, for example, Edward Said, *Covering Islam: How the Media and the Experts Determine How We See the Rest of the World*, revised edn. (New York: Vintage Books, 1997).

18 Cyrus R. Vance, *Hard Choices: Critical Years in America's Foreign Policy* (New York: Simon & Schuster, 1983), p. 408.

19 Yousef Al Otaiba, 'Our Nations Must Work Together to Stop This Cancer in All Its Forms', *The Telegraph*, 20 September 2014.

20 Hon. Julie Bishop, MP, Minister of Foreign Affairs, 'Address to the 2015 Annual Dinner, Sydney Institute', 27 April 2015, https://foreignminister.gov.au/speeches/Pages/2015/jb_sp_150427.aspx?ministerid=4, accessed 7 November 2018.

21 Scott Burchill, 'Radical Islam and the West: The Moral Panic behind the Threat', *The Conversation*, 16 June 2015, https://theconversation.com/radical-islam-and-the-west-the-moral-panic-behind-the-threat-43113, accessed 17 November 2017.

Glossary

'Abbasid	the third Islamic Caliphate, ruling an empire from the capital Baghdad between 750 and 1258.
Ahl al-bayt	the Prophet's household; immediate relations of Muhammad to the second generation and, in Shi'ism, extending to the twelve Imams.
Ahl al-Kitab	People of the Book; monotheistic faiths with a scriptural tradition; Jews, Christians, and Sabeans.
'Alam al-Islami	Islamic world.
'Alim	learned one; pl. *'ulama*
Al-Qa'ida	a militant Sunni organisation founded in the 1980s by Usama Bin Ladin.
Amir	commander; leader.
Amir al-mu'minin	Commander of the Faithful; in Sunni Islam traditionally a title by which the Caliph may be addressed, in Shi'a Islam it is reserved for 'Ali; today used to designate the Moroccan king.
Amman Message	statement by King 'Abdullah of Jordan in November 2004 calling for tolerance and unity and identifying valid schools of thought in Islam.
Ansar	helpers; the residents of Medina who supported and assisted the Prophet and his followers when they migrated from Mecca in 622.
'Aql	reason.
'Asabiyya	kin partisanship; solidarity.
Ash'arite	of the dominant al-Ash'ari Sunni theological school.
'Ashura	tenth day of the month of Muharram in the Islamic calendar; in Shi'a tradition a day of

	commemoration for the death of the Imam Husayn, grandson of Muhammad.
'Awlama	globalisation.
Ayatullah	sign of God; high ranking Twelver Shi'i cleric.
Bab	gateway; deputy; intermediaries between the twelfth Imam and his Shi'i followers.
Bid'a	unacceptable innovation.
Buyid	Iranian Shi'a dynasty ruling from 934 to 1062.
Companions of the Prophet	Arabic *sahaba*; Muslim contemporaries of Muhammad.
Copts	a Christian ethnic group in North Africa, primarily Egypt.
Da'ish	acronym for al-Dawla al-Islamiyya fi-al-'Iraq wa-al-Sham; ISIS.
Dar al-harb	the realm or abode of war; a territorial concept referring to places where Islamic law is not in force.
Dar al-Islam	the abode of Islam; a territorial concept often, but not exclusively, referring to places where Islamic law is applied.
Dar al-kufr	the abode of disbelief; where Islamic law is not in force; synonymous with *dar al-harb*.
Da'wa	proselytising.
DDII	Dewan Dakwah Islamiyah Indonesia; Indonesian Council for Islamic Propagation.
Din	religion.
Duyuf al-Rahman	guests of God; a term applied to pilgrims to Mecca.
Fatimid	an Isma'ili Shi'i Caliphate ruling from Egypt between 909 and 1171.
Fatwa	an authoritative (but not binding) religious opinion.
Fiqh	Islamic jurisprudence.
Fiqh al-aqalliyat	jurisprudence of the minorities; the legal theory relating to Muslims living in minority situations.
Fitna	disorder; crisis.
Furu'	branches; used in the context of *furu'al-fiqh*; branches of jurisprudence, as distinct from its 'roots' (*usul*).

Ghayba	Occultation; the period during which the twelfth Imam remains hidden.
Greater Occultation	the period from 940 onwards, during which the twelfth Imam has remained hidden and made no contact with his followers.
Hakimiyya	sovereignty.
Hashimites	ruling dynasty of Mecca and the Hijaz region of western Arabia until its conquest by 'Abd al-'Aziz Ibn Sa'ud in the 1920s; currently, the ruling family of Jordan
Hijaz	the western province of Saudi Arabia and the location of Mecca and Medina.
Hijra	migration, especially of the Prophet from Mecca to Medina in 622; migration undertaken by Muslims for religious purposes.
Hizb al-Tahrir al-Islami	the Islamic Liberation Party; a transnational Islamic political organisation committed to establishment of a Caliphate, founded in Jerusalem in 1953 by Taqi al-Din al-Nabhani.
Hizbullah	Party of God; Shi'a political party and militant movement founded in 1982 in Lebanon.
Houthi	militant Shi'a movement founded in Yemen in the 1990s.
Hujjat	proof.
Ibadi	Islamic school of thought based mainly in Oman.
IDB	Islamic Development Bank; founded in 1973 and located in Saudi Arabia.
Ijma'	consensus.
Ijtihad	expert, independent reasoning on matters of ambiguity in the Sunna.
Ikhwatun	brothers.
'Ilm	knowledge.
Imam	in Shi'i thought one of the infallible leaders of the Islamic community following Muhammad; in Sunnism a leader of formal prayers or a religious scholar.
Imam Mahdi	Guided One; the twelfth and last of the Imams in Twelver Shi'ism, remains in Occultation until just before the Day of Judgement.

Imama	Imamate; leadership; the Shi'i version of the Caliphate.
Irja'	political quietism.
ISI	al-Dawla al-Islamiyya fi-al-'Iraq; Islamic State of Iraq; a precursor to ISIS.
ISIS	Islamic State of Iraq and Syria; also known as Islamic State of Iraq and the Levant, or Islamic State of Iraq and al-Shams; a militant jihadist group and, between 2014 and 2017, a proto-state.
'Isma	infallibility.
Isma'ili	a branch of Shi'ism.
Ithna 'Ashari	Twelver Shi'ism; the dominant branch of Shi'ism.
Ittihad-i Islam	pan-Islamic union; also name of an 1873 publication by Esad Efendi.
Jahiliyya	ignorance; a reference to the era before the Prophet's revelation; today used as a negative description of un-Islamic practices.
JCPOA	Joint Comprehensive Plan of Action; 2015 nuclear agreement between Iran and the five permanent members of the United Nations Security Council, plus Germany (P5+1).
Jihad al-kabir	greater jihad; an inner struggle against sin.
Jihad al-saqhir	lesser jihad; a struggle or fight against the enemies of Islam.
Jinn	supernatural beings; demons and spirits.
Khadim al-haramayn al-sharifayn	Servant of the Two Holy Places; title applied to the Saudi King.
Khalifa	Caliph.
Khawarij	also Kharajite; a movement that revolted against the leadership of the fourth Caliph, 'Ali.
Khilafa	Caliphate; a political community under the control of a Sunni Muslim Caliph.
Khums	one fifth; religious tax.
Küçuk Kaynarca treaty	1774 treaty between the Russian and Ottoman Empires.

Kuffar	*kafir*, sing. unbelievers.
Lesser Occultation	the seventy years of the Imamate of the twelfth Imam, during which he contacted his followers through one of four successive deputies.
LIPIA	Lembaga Ilmu Pengetahuan Islam dan Bahasa Arab; Institute for the Study of Islam and Arabic, in Indonesia.
Madhhab	legal school.
Madrasa	school; educational institution.
Maliki	one of four major schools of jurisprudence in Sunni Islam.
Mapim	Malaysian Consultative Council of Islamic Organization.
Marja' al-taqlid	source of emulation; the highest ranking positions in the Shi'i hierarchy.
Mostakbareen	the haves; the oppressors.
Mostazafeen	the have nots; the oppressed.
Mufti	an expert in Islamic law.
Muhajirun	migrants, especially referring to those who travelled with the Prophet from Mecca to Medina in 622.
Mujahidin	*mujahid* in; those who engage in jihad.
Mujtahid	one who performs *ijtihad*; an original authority on Islamic law.
Mulk	kingship.
Murtads	apostates.
Mushrikun	polytheists.
Muslim Brotherhood	in Arabic al-Ikhwan al-Muslimun, a transnational Islamic political organisation founded in Egypt in 1928 by Hasan al-Banna.
Mu'tazilite	a rationalist school of Islamic thought, viewed by some as heretical.
Najdi	people of Najd, a vast central region of Saudi Arabia.
NASIMCO	Organization of North American Shia Ithna-asheri Muslim Communities.
Nifaq	hypocrisy.
OIC	Organisation of Islamic Cooperation; founded after the 1969 al-Aqsa mosque fire as 'the

	collective voice of the Muslim World', it currently has fifty-seven members, mostly Muslim-majority states.
PERKIM	Pertubuhan Kabajikan Islam Se-Malaysia; Muslim Welfare Organisation of Malaysia.
Pesantren	Indonesian Islamic school.
Qajar	Iranian dynasty ruling from 1794 to 1925.
Qawm	people.
Quds Day	instituted by Khomeini in 1979 as an international day of solidarity with the Palestinians.
Rafidun	rejectionists; a disparaging term applied by some Salafist groups to Shi'a and other sects.
Rashidun	refers to first four 'Rightly-Guided Caliphs'.
Rihla	travel for knowledge.
Safavid	an Iranian dynasty that ruled from 1501 to 1736 and established Shi'ism as the official religion of the empire.
Salaf	pious ancestors.
Salafi	a reform movement of the nineteenth century with links to Wahhabism, it advocated a return to the traditions of the *salaf*, the first three generations of Muslims.
Sayyid	descendant of the Prophet's grandsons, Hasan or Husayn.
Shari'a	law derived from Islamic texts.
Shaykh	a title; often referring to the leader of a tribe; used as a sign of respect, a religious scholar such as in Saudi Arabia today.
Shura	consultation.
Siyasa shari'iyya	Islamic-based governance.
Sunna	traditions of Islamic law.
Takfir	excommunication; its applicability is contested by Islamic scholars.
Taqiyya	prudent dissimulation; an important practice of Shi'a Islam, the followers of which have historically formed a persecuted minority.
Taqrib	'bringing closer', as in reconciliation of legal schools.

Tartars	Turkic-speaking people living in Russia and Central Asia.
Tashdid	excess.
Tawhid	oneness; the central concept of Islamic belief.
Twelver Shi 'ism	a minority branch of Islam that accepts twelve infallible leaders descending from the Prophet.
'Ulama	*'alim* reglious scholars and officials.
UMHD	International Refugee Rights Association.
Umma wahida	united *umma*; a singular community of faith.
Ummat al-da'wa	the *umma* of the call; the community of those called to submission to Allah.
Ummat al-ijaba	the *umma* of the response; the community of Muslims.
Ümmet	Turkish for *umma*; religious community.
Usul	roots; used in the context of *usul al-fiqh*, roots of jurisprudence; the fundamentals of Islamic law.
Velayat	guardianship; the faculty that enables a person to assume authority and exact obedience.
Velayat-e faqih	the rule of supreme jurist; also *wilayat al-faqih* in Arabic.
Vision 2030	plan, instituted by Crown Prince Muhammad ibn Salman, to diversify Saudi Arabia's economy.
Wahhabism	a puritanical reform movement founded by Muhammad ibn 'Abd al-Wahhab, during the eighteenth century, in the Najd region of modern-day Saudi Arabia.
Wali	lord.
WAMY	World Assembly of Muslim Youth; al-Nadwa al-'Alamiyya li-al-Shabab al-Islami, a Saudi-sponsored international organisation.
Wasatiyya	middle way; used today to describe a 'moderate' Islam.
Wataniyya	patriotism.
Wilayat al-faqih	the rule of supreme jurist; also *velayat-e faqih*.
Zahiri	school that privileges textual authority over other legal sources.
Zakat	a form of Islamic tithing; a religious obligation.
Zaydi	a branch of Shi'ism.
Ziyarat	*ziyara*; minor pilgrimages, as to Sufi shrines.

Bibliography

Books

Aaron, David. *In Their Own Words: Voices of Jihad*. Santa Monica: RAND, 2008.

'Abd al-Raziq, 'Ali. *al-Islam wa Usul al-Hukm: Bahth fi-l Khilafa wa-l Hukuma fi-l Islam* [Islam and the Roots of Governance: Study on the Caliphate and Government in Islam], 3rd printing, ed. Ammar 'Ali Hasan. Cairo: Dar al-Kitab al-Misri/Beirut: Dar al-Kitab al-Lubnani, 1433 A.H./2012; originally published 1344 A.H./1925.

Abir, Mordechai. *Saudi Arabia: Government, Society and the Gulf Crisis*. London: Routledge, 1993.

Abrahamian, Ervand. *Khomeinism: Essays on the Islamic Republic*. London: I. B. Tauris, 1993.

Ahmed, Manzooruddin. *Islamic Political System in the Modern Age: Theory and Practice*. Karachi: Saad Publications, 1983.

al-Ahsan, 'Abdullah. *OIC: The Organization of the Islamic Conference (An Introduction to an Islamic Political Organization*. N.p. [Herndon, VA]: International Institute of Islamic Thought, 1408 A.H./1988.

Ummah or Nation? Identity Crisis in Contemporary Muslim Society. Leicester: Islamic Foundation, 1992.

Aldamer, Shafi. *The Visit of HRH Princess Alice, Countess of Athlone and the Earl of Athlone to the Kingdom of Saudi Arabia, 25 February–17 March 1938*, trans. Richard Mortel. Riyadh: King Abdulaziz Public Library, 2007.

al-Alwani, Taha Jabir. *Fi fiqh al-aqalliyyat al-Muslima* [On the Jurisprudence of Muslim Minorities]. Cairo: Nahdat Misr, 2000.

Maqasid al-shari'a [The Foundational Goals of *Shari'a*]. Beirut: Dar al-Hadi, 2001.

Anderson, Benedict. *Imagined Communities: Reflections on the Origin and Spread of Nationalism*, rev. edn. London: Verso, 2006; originally published 1983.

Anjum, Ovamir. *Politics, Law, and Community in Islamic Thought: The Taymiyyan Moment*. Cambridge University Press, 2012.

Arnold, Thomas W. *The Caliphate*. Oxford: Clarendon Press, 1924.

Asad, Muhammad. *The Principles of State and Government in Islam*. Kuala Lumpur: Islamic Book Trust, 1999; originally published 1961.
The Road to Mecca, 4th and rev. edn. Gibraltar: Dar al-Andalus, 1980.

Aydin, Cemil. *The Idea of the Muslim World: A Global Intellectual History*. Cambridge, MA: Harvard University Press, 2017.

al-Banna, Hasan. *Mudhakkirat al-da'wa wa-al-da'iya* [Memoirs of the Call and the Preacher]. First published 1950. Cited version edited by Abu'l-Hasan 'Ali al-Nadvi [online]. www.kutub-pdf.net/book/2243. Accessed 22 July 2017.

Belmonte, Monica L., ed. *Foreign Relations of the United States, 1969–1976*. Washington, DC: United States Government Printing Office, 2007.

Bonner, Michael. *Jihad in Islamic History: Doctrines and Practice*. Princeton University Press, 2006.

Brown, L. Carl. *Religion and State: The Muslim Approach to Politics*. New York: Columbia University Press, 2000.

Burdett, Anita L. P., ed. *Islamic Movements in the Arab World, 1913–1966*, vol. 4: *1949–1966*. Chippenham: Archive Editions, 1998.

Commins, David. *The Wahhabi Mission and Saudi Arabia*. London and New York: I. B. Tauris, 2009.

Cook, David. *Understanding Jihad*. Berkeley: University of California Press, 2005.

Corboz, Elvire. *Guardians of Shi'ism: Sacred Authority and Transnational Family Networks*. Edinburgh University Press, 2015.

Dakake, Maria Massi. *The Charismatic Community: Shi'ite Identity in Early Islam*. Albany: State University of New York Press, 2007.

Eickelman, Dale F. and Jon W. Anderson. *New Media in the Muslim World: The Emerging Public Sphere*, 2nd edn. Bloomington: Indiana University Press, 2003.

Esposito, John, ed. *The Oxford Dictionary of Islam*. Oxford University Press, 2003.

al-Fahd, Nasr ibn Hamad. *al-Tibyan fi kufr man a'ama al-Amrikan* [Demonstration of the Unbelief of Those who Help the Americans]. N.p. Sha'ban 1422 A.H./October–November 2001. https://archive.org/details/tr_45. Accessed 13 March 2018.

Farquhar, Michael. *Circuits of Faith: Migration, Education, and the Wahhabi Mission*. Stanford University Press, 2017.

al-Fawzan, Salih ibn 'Abdullah. *al-Wala' wa-al-bara'* [Loyalty and Disavowal]. Cairo: Dar al-Imam Ahmad, 1434 A.H./2013.

Fishman, Brian. *The Master Plan: ISIS, Al Qaeda, and the Jihadi Strategy for Final Victory*. New Haven: Yale University Press, 2016.

Gerges, Fawaz A. *A History of ISIS*. Princeton University Press, 2016.

al-Ghannushi, Rashid. *al-Hurriyyat al-'amma fi-al dawla al-islamiyya* [Public Liberties in the Islamic State]. Beirut: Markaz Dirasat al-Wahda al-'Arabiyya, 1993.

    Muqarabat fi-al 'ilmaniyya wa-al-mujtama'al-madani [Approaches on Secularism and Civil Society]. London: al-Markaz al-Maghribi li-al-Buhuth wa-al-Tarjama, 1999.

al-Ghazali, Muhammad. *Qadha'if al-haq* [Bombshells of Truth], 2nd edn. Damascus: Dar al-Qalam, 1418 A.H./1997.

Gheissari, Ali and Vali Nasr. *Democracy in Iran: History and the Quest for Liberty*. Oxford University Press, 2006.

Ghobadzadeh, Naser. *Religious Secularity: A Theological Challenge to the Islamic State*. Oxford University Press, 2015.

Gibb, H. A. R. *Modern Trends in Islam*. University of Chicago Press, 1947.

Hamidullah, Muhammad. *The First Written Constitution in the World: An Important Document of the Time of the Holy Prophet*, 3rd edn. Lahore: Ashraf Press, 1975.

al-Haqil, Sulayman 'Abd al-Rahman. *al-Wataniyya wa mutatallabatha fi dau' ta'alim al-Islam* [Nationalism and Its Requirement in Light of the Teachings of Islam], 3rd edn. Riyadh: Jam'at al-Imam Muhammad ibn Sa'ud al-Islamiyya, 1417 A.H./1996.

Hashim, Ahmed A. *The Khilafat at War: Operational Realities and Innovations of the Islamic State*. Oxford University Press, 2018.

al-Hawali, Safar. *Kashf al-ghumma 'an 'ulama' al-umma* [Revealing the Sorrow to the Umma's Scholars]. N.p.: Dar al-Hikma, 1991.

Hebron, Lui and John F. Stack, Jr. *Globalization: Debunking the Myths*, 3rd edn. London: Rowman & Littlefield, 2017.

Heern, Zackery M. *The Emergence of Modern Shi'ism: Islamic Reform in Iraq and Iran*. London: Oneworld Publications, 2015.

Hodgson, Marshall G. S. *The Venture of Islam*, vol. 1: *The Classical Age of Islam*. University of Chicago Press, 1974.

Hosken, Andrew. *Empire of Fear: Inside the Islamic State*. London: Oneworld Publications, 2015.

Hourani, Albert. *A History of the Arab Peoples*. New York: Warner Books, 1992.

Ibn Baaz, 'Abdul Azeez. *Majmu'fatawa wa maqalat mutanawwi'a* [Collection of Fatwas and Miscellaneous Articles]. Vol. 2. Riyadh: Maktabat al-Ma'arif li-al-Nashr wa-al-Tawzi', 1992.

Ibn Jamil Zaynu, Muhammad. *Majmu'at risa'il al-tawjihat al-Islamiyya li-aslah al-fard wa-al-mujtama'* [Collection of Letters on Islamic Guidance for Reform of the Individual and Society], 9th edn. Riyadh: Dar al-Sami'i li-al-Nashr wa-al-Tawzi', 1417 A.H./1997.

Ibn Kathir, Ismail. *Tafsir al-Qur'an al-'Azim* [Exegesis of the Glorious Qur'an], 2nd edn. Riyadh: Dar Tiba li-l-Nashr wa-al-Tawzi', 1420 A.H./1999.

Ibn Khaldun, 'Abd al-Rahman. *The Muqaddimah: An Introduction to History*, trans. Frantz Rosenthal. Princeton University Press, 1958.

Ibn Qurash, Husayn Muhammad 'Abdullah. *Fikr al-watan: mas'uliyyat al-jami'* [The Idea of the Nation: Everyone's Responsibility]. Riyadh: Dar al-Qabas li-al-Nashr wa al-Tawzi', 1437 A.H./2016.

Ibn Taymiyya, Taqi al-Din Ahmad. *al-Siyasa al-shar'iyya* [Legitimate Governance]. Cairo: Dar al-Sha'b, 1971.

Imarah, Muhammad. *al-Amal al-Kamila: Jamal al-Din al-Afghani* [The Complete Works: Jamal al-Din al-Afghani]. Beirut: al-Mu'assasa al-'Arabiyya li-l-Dirasat wa-al-Nashr, 1981.

International Hajj Seminar. *Hajj: A Ritual or the Heart of the Islamic Movement*. London: The Open Press, 1983.

Ismail, Raihan. *Saudi Clerics and Shi'a Islam*. Oxford University Press, 2016.

Izutsu, Toshihiko. *God and Man in the Qur'an*. Petaling Jaya: Islamic Book Trust, 2002; originally published 1964.

Jadhakhan, Haroon M., ed. *The Thieves of Riyadh: Lives and Crimes of the Al Sauds*. London: The Muslim Chronicle, 1990.

Jami'at al-Tirmidhi *(Arabic–English)*. Supervised by Abdul Malik Mujahid. Riyadh: Maktaba Dar-us-Salam, 2007.

Kane, Ousmane. *The Homeland Is the Arena: Religion, Transnationalism, and the Integration of Senegalese in America*. Oxford University Press, 2011.

Kayali, Hasan. *Arabs and Young Turks: Ottomanism, Arabism and Islamism in the Ottoman Empire, 1908–18*. Berkeley: University of California Press, 1997.

Keddie, Nikki. *An Islamic Response to Imperialism: Political and Religious Writings of Sayyid Jamal Ad-Din 'al-Afghani'*. Berkeley: University of California Press, 1968.

Kerr, Malcolm. *Islamic Reform: The Political and Legal Theories of Muhammad 'Abduh and Rashid Rida*. Berkeley: University of California Press.

Khomeini, Ruhollah. *Islam and Revolution I: Writings and Declarations of Imam Khomeini (1941–1980)*, trans. and ed. Hamid Algar. Berkeley: Mizan Press, 1981.

Islamic Government: Governance of the Jurist, trans. and ed. Hamid Algar. Tehran: Institute for Compilation and Publication of Imam Khomeini's Work, 2002; originally published as *Velayet-e Faqih*, 1970.

Kingdom of Saudi Arabia. *Fatawa al-lajna al-da'ima li'l-buhuth al-'ilmiyya wa-al-ifta'* [Fatwas of the Higher Committee for Research and Guidance], vol. 2 (*al-'Aqida*), 3rd edn. Riyadh: Dar al-Mu'ayyad, 1421 A.H./2000.

Kostiner, Joseph. *The Making of Saudi Arabia, 1916–1936: From Chieftaincy to Monarchical State.* Oxford University Press, 1993.

Kramer, Martin. *Islam Assembled: The Advent of the Muslim Congresses.* New York: Columbia University Press, 1986.

Lacroix, Stéphane. *Awakening Islam: The Politics of Religious Dissent in Contemporary Saudi Arabia.* Cambridge, MA: Harvard University Press, 2011.

Lambton, A. K. S. *State and Government in Medieval Islam: An Introduction to the Study of Islamic Political Theory – The Jurists.* Oxford University Press, 1981.

Lane, Edward William. *An Arabic–English Lexicon.* Beirut: Librairie du Liban, 1968; originally published 1863.

Laoust, Henri. *Essai sur les doctrines sociales et politiques de Taḳī-d-Dīn Aḥmad b. Taimïya* [Essay on the Social and Political Doctrines of Taqi al-Din Ahmad Ibn Taymiyya]. Cairo: Imprimerie de l'Institut Français d'Archéologie Orientale, 1939.

   Le Traité de droit publique d'Ibn Taymiyya: Traduction annotée de la Siyasa shar'iyya [Ibn Taymiyya's Public Law Treaty: Annotated Translation of *Siyasa Shar'iyya*]. Beirut: Institut Français de Damas, 1948.

Lapidus, Ira. *A History of Islamic Societies.* Cambridge University Press, 2002.

Lauzière, Henri. *The Making of Salafism: Islamic Reform in the Twentieth Century.* New York: Columbia University Press, 2016.

Lawrence, Bruce B., ed. *Messages to the World: The Statements of Osama bin Laden.* London: Verso Books, 2005.

Lecker, Michael. *The Constitution of Medina: Muḥammad's First Legal Document.* Princeton, NJ: Darwin, 2004.

Machlis, Elisheva. *Shi'i Sectarianism in the Middle East: Modernisation and the Quest for Islamic Universalism.* London: I. B. Tauris, 2014.

Maher, Shiraz. *Salafi-Jihadism: The History of an Idea.* Oxford University Press, 2016.

Mandaville, Peter. *Islam and Politics*, 2nd edn. London and New York: Routledge, 2014.

   Transnational Muslim Politics: Reimagining the Umma, revised edn. Abingdon: Routledge, 2003.

Manne, Robert. *The Mind of the Islamic State.* Carlton: Redback Quarterly, 2016.

Marcinowski, Christoph. *Twelver Shi'ite Islam: Conceptual and Practical Aspects.* Singapore: Institute of Defence and Strategic Studies, 2006.

Matthiesen, Toby. *Sectarian Gulf: Bahrain, Saudi Arabia and the Arab Spring that Wasn't*. Stanford University Press, 2013.

Mawdudi, Sayyid Abu A'la [Maudoodi, Syed Abul 'Ala Maulana]. *Khutabat* [Sermons], 2nd edn. Chicago: Kazi Publications, 1977.

  Towards Understanding the Qur'an. Volume 1. Abridged version of *Tafhim al-Qur'an*, trans. and ed. Zafar Ishaq Ansari. Leicester: The Islamic Foundation, 1408 A.H./1988.

  [Maududi, Siyyid Abul A'la]. *Unity of the Muslim World*, ed. Khurshid Ahmad. Lahore: Islamic Publications, 1967.

  Witnesses unto Mankind: The Purpose and Duty of the Muslim Ummah, trans. and ed. Khurram Murad. Leicester: The Islamic Foundation, 1406 A.H./1986.

Mellor, Noha. *Voice of the Muslim Brotherhood: Da'wa, Discourse, and Political Communication*. Abingdon: Routledge, 2018.

Milani, Abbas. *Eminent Persians: The Men and Women Who Made Modern Iran, 1941–1979*. New York: Syracuse University Press/Persian World Press, 2008.

Momen, Moojan. *An Introduction to Shi'i Islam: The History and Doctrines of Twelver Shi'ism*. New Haven: Yale University Press, 1985.

Mouline, Nabil. *Les clercs de l'Islam: Autorité religieuse et pouvoir politique en Arabie Saoudite, XVIIIᵉ–XXIᵉ siècles* [The Clerics of Islam: Religious Authority and Political Power in Saudi Arabia, 18th–21st Centuries]. Paris: Presses Universitaires de France, 2011.

Muhammad b. Qasim, 'Abd al-Rahman b. and Muhammad b. 'Abd al-Rahman b. Muhammad. *Majmu'Fatawa Shaykh al-Islam Ahmad b. Taymiyya* [Collection of the Fatwas of Ibn Taymiyya]. Cairo: Dar al-Rahma, n.d.

al-Mutayri, 'Abd al-Rahman. *al-Ghulu fi-l-din fi hayat al-muslimin al-mu'asara* [Extremism in the Life of Today's Muslims]. Riyadh: Kulliyat al-Shari'a, Jami'at Imam Muhammad Ibn Sa'ud University, 1990.

Nakash, Yitzhak. *Reaching for Power: The Shi'a in the Modern Arab World*. Princeton University Press, 2006.

Nasr, Vali. *Islamic Leviathan: Islam and the Making of State Power*. Oxford University Press, 2001.

al-Nawawi, Muhy al-Din. *al-Minhaj fi Sharh Sahih Muslim ibn al-Hajjaj* [Commentary on *Sahih Muslim*], ed. Muhammad Fu'ad al-Baqi. Beirut: Dar Ibn Hazm, n.d.

al-Nimla, 'Abd al-'Aziz. *al-Tansir fi-l-adabiyyat al-'arabiyya* [Evangelisation in Arabic Literature]. Riyadh: Jama'at al-Imam ibn Sa'ud al-Islamiyya, 1415 A.H./1994.

Olidort, Jacob. *Inside the Caliphate's Classroom: Textbooks, Guidance Literature, and Indoctrination Methods of the Islamic State*. Washington, DC: The Washington Institute for Near East Policy, 2016.

Post, Jerrold M. *The Mind of the Terrorist: The Psychology of Terrorism from the IRA to al-Qaeda.* New York: Palgrave Macmillan, 2007.

al-Qaradawi, Yusuf. *Dars al-nakba al-thaniyya: li-madha hazamna wa-kayfa nantasir* [Lesson of the Second *Nakba* (Disaster): Why We Lost and How We Win]. Cairo: Maktabat Wahba, 1993.

Fi fiqh al-aqalliyyat al-Muslima [On Islamic Minority Jurisprudence]. Cairo: Dar al-Shuruq, 2001.

Fiqh al-wasatiyya al-Islamiyya: ma'alim wa manarat [Islamic Jurisprudence of the 'Middle Way': Milestones and Lighthouses]. Cairo: Dar al-Shuruq, 2010.

Ummatna bayna qarnayn [Our *Umma* between Two Centuries]. Cairo: Dar al-Shuruq, 2000.

Qureshi, M. Naeem. *Pan-Islam in British Indian Politics: A Study of the Khilafat Movement, 1918–1924.* Leiden: Brill, 1999.

Qutb, Sayyid. *Hadha al-din* [This Religion]. Beirut and Cairo: Dar al-Shuruq, 1995.

Ma'alim fi-al-tariq [Signposts on the Road]. Beirut and Cairo: Dar al-Shuruq, 1399 A.H./1979.

Rabi', Muhammad Mahmoud. *The Political Theory of Ibn Khaldun.* Leiden: E. J. Brill, 1967.

Rajaee, Farhang. *Islamism and Modernism: The Changing Discourse in Iran.* Austin: University of Texas Press, 2007.

Rakel, Eva Patricia. *Power, Islam, and Political Elite: A Study on the Iranian Political Elite from Khomeini to Ahmadinejad.* Leiden: Brill, 2009.

al-Rasheed, Madawi. *Contesting the Saudi State: Islamic Voices from a New Generation.* Cambridge University Press, 2007.

Rida, Muhammad Rashid. *al-Khilafa aw'l-imama al-'uzma* [The Caliphate or Great Imamate]. Cairo: Matba'at al-Manar, 1923.

al-Wahda al-Islamiyya wa-al-ukhuwa al-Islamiyya [Islamic Unity and Islamic Brotherhood]. Cairo: Matba'at al-Manar, 1925.

al-Wahhabiyyun wa-al-Hijaz [The Wahhabis and the Hijaz]. Cairo: Matba'at al-Manar, 1344 A.H./1925.

Rogan, Eugene. *The Arabs: A History.* London: Penguin Books, 2011.

Rosenthal, E. I. J. *Political Thought in Medieval Islam: An Introductory Outline.* Cambridge University Press, 1962.

Roy, Olivier. *Globalised Islam: The Search for a New Ummah.* New York: Columbia University Press, 2004.

Sachedina, Abdulaziz Abdulhussein. The Just Ruler *(al-Sultan al-'adil) in* Shi'ite Islam: The Comprehensive Authority of the Jurist in Imamite Jurisprudence. Oxford University Press, 1988.

Sahih Al-Bukhari *(Arabic–English).* Trans. Muhammad Muhsin Khan. Riyadh: Maktaba Dar-us-Salam, 1997.

Sahih Muslim *(Arabic–English)*. Ed. Hafiz Abu Tahir Zubair Ali Za'i. Riyadh: Maktaba Dar-us-Salam, 2007.

Said, Edward. *Covering Islam: How the Media and the Experts Determine How We See the Rest of the World*, revised edn. New York: Vintage Books, 1997.

al-Samrani, Qasim. *al-Fihris al-wasfi li-makhutat al-sira al-nabawi wa muta'laqatuha* [Index of Manuscripts of the Prophet's Biography and Addenda]. Riyadh: Jama'at al-Imam Muhammad ibn Sa'ud al-Islamiyya, 1416 A.H./1995.

al-Sanhuri, 'Abd al-Razzaq [Sanhoury, A.]. *Le Califat: Son évolution vers une société des nations orientales* [The Caliphate: Its Evolution Towards a Society of Eastern Nations]. Paris: Librairie Orientaliste Paul Geuthner, 1926.

Sardar, Ziauddin. *Reading the Qur'an: The Contemporary Relevance of the Sacred Text of Islam*. London: Hurst & Company, 2011.

Shaheen, Saifuddin H. *Unification of Saudi Arabia: A Historical Perspective*, 2nd edn. Riyadh: Dar al-Utuq, 1414 A.H./1993.

Sixta Rinehart, Christine. *Volatile Social Movements and the Origins of Terrorism: The Radicalization of Change*. Lanham, MD: Lexington Books, 2013.

Sunan Abu Dawud *(Arabic–English)*. Ed. Hafiz Abu Tahir Zubair 'Ali Za'i. Riyadh: Maktaba Dar us-Salam, 2008.

Sunan Ibn Majah *(Arabic–English)*. Ed. Hafiz Abu Tahir Zubair 'Ali Za'i. Riyadh: Maktaba Dar us-Salam, 2007.

Taji-Farouki, Suhi. *A Fundamental Quest: Hizb al-Tahrir and the Search for the Islamic Caliphate*. London: Grey Seal, 1996.

Takim, Liyakat Nathani. *Shi'ism in America*. New York University Press, 2009.

Tamimi, Azzam S. *Rachid Ghannouchi: A Democrat within Islamism*. Oxford University Press, 2001.

Turnaoğlu, Banu. *The Formation of Turkish Republicanism*. Princeton University Press, 2017.

al-'Umar, Nasir ibn Sulayman. *al-Rafida fi bilad al-tawhid* [The Rejectionists in the Land of Tawhid (Oneness)], n.p., n.d. https://ar.islamway.net/book/3165. Accessed 2 June 2018.

Vaezi, Ahmad. *Shi'a Political Thought*. London: Islamic Centre of England, 2004.

Vance, Cyrus R. *Hard Choices: Critical Years in America's Foreign Policy*. New York: Simon & Schuster, 1983.

Voegelin, Eric. Modernity without Restraint. *Vol. 5 of* The Collected Works of Eric Voegelin, ed. Manfred Henningsen. Columbia: University of Missouri Press, 2000.

al-Wahhab, Muhammad Ibn. *Risala fi-al-radd 'ala al-rafida* [A Response to the Rejectionists]. Riyadh: Dar Ṭayyiba, n.d.

al-Wahhab, Sulayman Ibn. *Taysir al-'Aziz al-Hamid fi sharh Kitab al-Tawhid* [Facilitating the Explanation of *Kitab al-Tawhid* (Book on Oneness)]. Riyadh: Dar al-Sumai'i li-al-Nashr wa-al-Tawzi', 2007.

Watt, W. Montgomery. *Islamic Political Thought: The Basic Concepts.* Edinburgh University Press, 1968.

   Muhammad at Medina. Oxford University Press, 1956.

Wolfe, Michael. *The Hadj: An American's Pilgrimage to Mecca.* New York: Grove Press, 1993.

Woodward, Peter. *Nasser.* London: Longman, 1992.

Book Chapters

Adam, Volker. 'Why Do They Cry? Criticisms of Muharram Celebrations in Tsarist and Socialist Azerbaijan'. In *The Twelver Shia in Modern Times: Religious Culture and Political History*, ed. Rainer Brunner and Werner Ende. Leiden: Brill, 2001, pp. 114–34.

Arjomand, Said Amir. 'Introduction: Shi'ism, Authority and Political Culture'. In *Authority and Political Culture in Shi'ism*, ed. Said Amir Arjomand. Albany: State University of New York Press, 1988, pp. 1–22.

Arjomand, Said Amir. 'Revolution in Shi'ism'. In *Islam and the Political Economy of Meaning*, ed. William R. Roff. Sydney: Croom Helm, 1987, pp. 111–31.

Babić, Marko. 'Two Faces of Islam in the Western Balkans: Between Political Ideology and Islamist Radicalization'. In *Perseverance of Terrorism: Focus on Leaders*, ed. Marko Milosevic and Kacper Rekawek. Amsterdam and Berlin: IOS Press, 2014, pp. 126–37.

al-Banna, Hasan. 'Risalat al-mu'tamar al-khamis' [Message of the Fifth Congress]. In *Majmu'at al-Risa'il li-l-Imam al-Shahid Hasan al-Banna* [Collected Statements of the Martyred Imam Hasan al-Banna]. Cairo: Dar al-Tawzi', 1992, pp. 142–44.

Bhabha, Homi K. 'DissemiNation: Time, Narrative, and the Margins of the Modern Nation'. In *Nation and Narration*, ed. Homi K. Bhabha. London: Routledge, 1990, pp. 291–322.

Buchan, James. 'Secular and Religious Opposition in Saudi Arabia'. In *State, Society and Economy in Saudi Arabia*, ed. Tim Niblock. London: Croom Helm, 1982, pp. 106–24.

Georges, Amaryllis Maria. 'ISIS Rhetoric for the Creation of the Ummah'. In *Political Discourse in Emergent, Fragile, and Failed Democracies*, ed. Daniel Ochieng Orwenjo, Omondi Oketch, and Asiru Hameed Tunde. Hershey: IGI Global, 2016, pp. 178–99.

Ghobadzadeh, Naser and Lily Zubaidah Rahim. 'Islamic Reformation Discourses: Popular Sovereignty and Religious Secularisation in Iran'. In *Religion and Political Change in the Modern World*, ed. Jeffrey Haynes. London: Routledge, 2014, pp. 141–58.

Hassan, Mona. 'Modern Interpretations and Misinterpretations of a Medieval Scholar: Apprehending the Political Thought of Ibn Taymiyya'. In *Ibn Taymiyya and His Times*, ed. Yossef Rapoport and Shahab Ahmed. Oxford University Press, 2010, pp. 338–66.

Haykel, Bernard. 'On the Nature of Salafi Thought and Action'. In *Global Salafism: Islam's New Religious Movement*, ed. Roel Meijer. Oxford University Press, 2013, pp. 33–57.

Ibn Baaz, 'Abdul Azeez. 'The Importance of Muslim Minorities Adhering to Islaam'. In *Muslim Minorities: Fatawa Regarding Muslims Living as Minorities*, ed. 'Abdul Azeez b. Baaz and Muhammad b. Saalih al-'Uthaymeen. Hounslow: Message of Islam, 1988, pp. 4–42.

Ismail, Raihan. 'The Saudi 'Ulama and the Syrian Civil War'. In *The Arab World and Iran: A Turbulent Region in Transition*, ed. Amin Saikal. New York: Palgrave Macmillan, 2016, pp. 83–102.

Kostiner, Joseph and Joshua Teitelbaum. 'State-Formation and the Saudi Monarchy'. In *Middle East Monarchies: The Challenge of Modernity*, ed. Joseph Kostiner. Boulder, CO and London: Lynne Rienner, 2000, pp. 131–49.

Lecker, Michael. 'Constitution of Medina'. In *The Encyclopedia of Ancient History*, ed. Roger S. Bagnall, Kai Brodersen, Craige B. Champion, Andrew Erskine, and Sabine R. Huebner. Oxford: Blackwell Publishing, 2013, pp. 1748–9.

Mahdavi, Mojtaba. 'The Rise of Khomeinism: Problematizing the Politics of Resistance in Pre-Revolutionary Iran'. In *A Critical Introduction to Khomeini*, ed. Arshin Adib-Moghaddam. Cambridge University Press, 2014, pp. 43–68.

Malkawi, Banan and Tamara Sonn. 'Ibn Taymiyya on Islamic Governance'. In *Islam, the State, and Political Authority: Medieval Issues and Modern Concerns, Middle East Today*, ed. Asma Afsaruddin. New York: Palgrave Macmillan, 2011, pp. 111–27.

Milani, Mohsen. 'Shiism and the State in the Constitution of the Islamic Republic of Iran'. In *Iran: Political Culture in the Islamic Republic*, ed. Samih K. Fasoun and Mehrdad Mashayekhi. London: Routledge, 1992, pp. 133–59.

Musa, Mohd. Faizal. 'The Riyal and Ringgit of Petro-Islam: Investing Salafism in Education'. In *Islam in Southeast Asia: Negotiating Modernity*, ed. Norshahril Saat. Singapore: ISEAS–Yusof Ishak Institute, 2018, pp. 63–88.

Ramazani, R. K. 'Khumayni's Islam in Iran's Foreign Policy'. In *Islam in Foreign Policy*, ed. Adeed Dawisha. Cambridge University Press, 1983, pp. 9–32.

al-Rasheed, Madawi. 'Political Legitimacy and the Production of History: The Case of Saudi Arabia'. In *New Frontiers in Middle East Security*, ed. Lenore G. Martin. New York: St. Martin's Press, 1999, pp. 25–46.

Robinson, Francis. 'Islam and the Impact of Print in South Asia'. In *The Transmission of Knowledge in South Asia; Essays on Education, Religion, History and Politics*, ed. Nigel Crook. Oxford University Press, 1996, pp. 52–97.

Saikal, Amin. 'The Third Arab Awakening and its Geopolitical Implications'. In *The Contemporary Middle East: Revolution or Reform?*, ed. Adel Abdel Ghafar, Brenton Clark, and Jessie Moritz. Melbourne University Press, 2014, pp. 21–39.

Sayyid, Salman. 'The Islamist Impasse?' In *Political Islam: A Critical Reader*, ed. Frédéric Volpi. Abingdon: Routledge, 2011, pp. 126–34.

Seifzadeh, Hosssein. 'Ayatollah Khomeini's Concept of Rightful Governance: The Velayat-e-Faqih'. In *Islam, Muslims, and the Modern State*, ed. Hussin Mutalib and Taj ul-Islam Hashmi. London: Macmillan, 1994, pp. 197–210.

Sheikholeslami, Ali Reza. 'From Religious Accommodation to Religious Revolution: The Transformation of Shi'ism in Iran'. In *The State, Religion, and Ethnic Politics: Afghanistan, Iran, and Pakistan*, ed. Ali Banuazizi and Myron Weiner. Syracuse: Syracuse University Press, 1986, pp. 227–56.

al-'Uthaymeen, Muhammad b. Saalih. 'Inviting to Allah in Communities Where There Are Muslim Minorities'. In *Muslim Minorities: Fatawa Regarding Muslims Living as Minorities*, ed. 'Abdul Azeez b. Baaz and Muhammad b. Saalih al-'Uthaymeen. Hounslow: Message of Islam, 1988, pp. 43–88.

Journal Articles

Akhavi, Shahrough. 'Contending Discourses in Shi'i Law on the Doctrine of Wilāyat al-Faqīh'. *Iranian Studies* 29, 3/4 (1996): 229–68.

Alshech, Eli. 'The Doctrinal Crisis within the Salafi-Jihadi Ranks and the Emergence of Neo-Takfirism: A Historical and Doctrinal Analysis'. *Islamic Law and Society* 21, 4 (2014): 419–52.

Angeles, Vivienne S. M. 'The Development of the Shi'a Concept of the Imamate'. *Asian Studies* 21 (1983): 145–60.

Arjomand, Said Amir. 'The Constitution of Medina: A Sociolegal Interpretation of Muhammad's Acts of Foundation of the *Umma*'. *International Journal of Middle East Studies* 41, 4 (2009): 555–75.

'The Crisis of the Imamate and the Institution of Occultation in Twelver Shiism: A Sociohistorical Perspective'. *International Journal of Middle East Studies* 28, 4 (1996): 491–515.

Bar, Shmuel. 'The Implications of the Khilafat'. *Comparative Strategy* 35, 1 (2016): 1–14.

Baylocq, Cédric and Aziz Hlaoua. 'Diffuser un "Islam du juste milieu"?' [Spread of 'a Middle-Ground Islam'?]. *Afrique contemporaine* 257 (2016): 113–28.

Caeiro, Alexandre. 'The Power of European Fatwas: The Minority Fiqh Project and the Making of an Islamic Counterpublic'. *International Journal of Middle East Studies* 42, 3 (2010): 435–49.

Chinyong Liow, Joseph. 'Political Islam in Malaysia: Problematising Discourse and Practice in the UMNO–PAS "Islamisation Race"'. *Commonwealth and Comparative Politics* 42, 2 (2004): 184–205.

Delfolie, David. 'Malaysian Extraversion towards the Muslim World: Ideological Positioning for a "Mirror Effect"'. *Journal of Current Southeast Asian Affairs* 31, 4 (2013): 3–29.

Denny, Frederick Mathewson. 'The Meaning of "Ummah" in the Qur'an'. *History of Religions* 15, 1 (1975): 34–70.

'Ummah in the Constitution of Medina'. *Journal of Near Eastern Studies* 36, 1 (1977): 39–47.

Doumato, Eleanor Abdella. 'Manning the Barricades: Islam According to Saudi Arabia's School Texts'. *Middle East Journal* 57, 2 (Spring 2003): 230–47.

Esposito, John. 'Islam and Political Violence'. *Religions* 6 (2015): 1067–81.

Farquhar, Michael. 'Saudi Petrodollars, Spiritual Capital, and the Islamic University of Medina: A Wahhabi Missionary Project in Transnational Perspective'. *International Journal of Middle East Studies* 47, 4 (2015): 701–21.

Fleischer, Cornell. 'Royal Authority, Dynastic Cyclism and Ibn Khaldunism in Sixteenth Century Ottoman Letters'. *Journal of Asian and African Studies* 18, 3–4 (1983): 198–220.

Fleischmann, Fenella, Karen Phalet, and Olivier Klein. 'Religious Identification and Politicization in the Face of Discrimination'. *British Journal of Social Psychology* 50, 4 (2011): 628–48.

Gallie, W. B. 'Essentially Contested Concepts'. *Proceedings of the Aristotelian Society*, New Series 56 (1955–6): 167–98.

Guida, Michelangelo. 'Seyyid Bey and the Abolition of the Caliphate'. *Middle Eastern Studies* 44, 2 (2008): 275–89.

Haddad, Mahmoud. 'Arab Religious Nationalism in the Colonial Era: Rereading Rashid Rida's Ideas on the Caliphate'. *Journal of the American Oriental Society* 117, 2 (1997): 253–77.

Hasan, Noorhaidi. 'The Failure of the Wahhabi Campaign: Transnational Islam and the Salafi Madrasa in post-9/11 Indonesia'. *South East Asia Research* 18, 4 (December 2010): 675–705.

'The Salafi Movement in Indonesia: Transnational Dynamics and Local Development'. *Comparative Studies of South Asia, Africa and the Middle East* 27, 1 (2007): 83–94.

Hashemi-Najafabadi, Adel. 'Imamate and Leadership: The Case of the Shi'a Fundamentalists in Modern Iran'. *Canadian Social Science* 6, 6 (2010): 192–205.

'The Shi'i Concept of Imamate and Leadership in Contemporary Iran: The Case of Religious Modernists'. *Studies in Religion* 40, 4 (2011): 479–96.

Hegghammer, Thomas. 'Saudis in Iraq: Patterns of Radicalization and Recruitment/Combattants saoudiens en Irak: modes de radicalisation et de recrutement'. *Cultures & Conflits*, 12 June 2008. file:///C:/Users/u4442428/Downloads/conflits-10042.pdf. Accessed 23 September 2017.

Ingram, Haroro. 'An Analysis of Inspire and Dabiq: Lessons from AQAP and Islamic State's Propaganda War'. *Studies in Conflict & Terrorism* 40, 5 (2017): 357–75.

'An Analysis of Islamic State's *Dabiq* Magazine'. *Australian Journal of Political Science* 51, 3 (2016): 458–77.

Jones, Toby. 'Saudi Arabia's Not So New Anti-Shi'ism'. *Middle East Report* 242 (Spring 2007): 29–32.

Joscelyn, Thomas. 'Taliban and Islamic State Target Religious Opponents in Afghanistan'. *FDD's Long War Journal*, 31 May 2018. www.longwarjournal.org/archives/2018/05/taliban-and-islamic-state-target-religious-opponents-in-afghanistan.php. Accessed 5 July 2018.

Juneau, Thomas. 'Iran's Policy Towards the Houthis in Yemen: A Limited Return on a Modest Investment'. *International Affairs* 92, 3 (May 2016): 647–63.

Kibble, David G. '*Dabiq*, the Islamic State's Magazine: A Critical Analysis'. *Middle East Policy* 23, 3 (2016): 133–43.

Low, Remy. 'Making up the *Ummah*: The Rhetoric of ISIS as Public Pedagogy'. *Review of Education, Pedagogy, and Cultural Studies* 38, 4 (2016): 297–316.

Lynch, Orla. 'British Muslim Youth: Radicalisation, Terrorism and the Construction of the "Other"'. *Critical Studies on Terrorism* 6, 2 (2013): 241–61.

Mahood, Samantha and Halim Rane. 'Islamist Narratives in ISIS Recruitment Propaganda'. *The Journal of International Communications* 23, 1 (2017): 15–35.

Majallat al-Munazzama. 'Abdullah 'Abd al-Rahman 'Alam, 'Al-musalaha hi al-sabil al-wahid 'ilhalil al-salam fi Afghanistan' [Reconciliation is the Only Way to Bring Peace in Afghanistan]. Issue 36 (February–April 2017), p. 14.

'Munazzamat al-Ta'wun al-Islami turahib bi-akhtiyar al-Amir Muham-mad bin Salman Waliyan li-al-'Ahd' [The Organisation of the Islamic Conference Welcomes Crown Prince Muhammad Bin Salman]. Issue 37 (May–September 2017), p. 12.

Majallat al-Rabita. 'Rabitat al-'Alam al-Islami tatalaqa 'istinkar al-hay'at al-Islamiyya wa ghayr al-Islamiyya li-mumarasat 'Iran bi-al-mintaqa' [The Muslim World League Receives Islamic and Non-Islamic Organisations' Condemnation of Iran's Activities in the Region]. Issue 54, 614 (Rabi' al-Awwal 1439/December 2017), p. 9.

'Tawahad sufuf al-'alam al-Islami did al-tatarruf wa-al-irhab' (Unite the Islamic World against Extremism and Terrorism). Issue 37 (May–September 2017), p. 11.

Mandaville, Peter. 'Muslim Transnational Identity and State Responses in Europe and the UK after 9/11: Political Community, Ideology and Authority'. *Journal of Ethnic and Migration Studies* 35, 3 (March 1990): 491–506.

'Transnational Muslim Solidarities and Everyday Life'. *Nations and Nationalism* 17, 1 (2011): 7–24.

Massignon, Louis. 'L'Umma et ses synonymes: Notion de "communauté sociale" en Islam' [The Umma and Its Synonyms: Notion of 'Social Community' in Islam]. *Revue des études islamiques 1941–46* (1947): 151–6.

Mavani, Hamid. 'Khomeini's Concept of Governance of the Jurisconsult (*Wilayat al-Faqih*) Revisited: The Aftermath of Iran's 2009 Presidential Election'. *The Middle East Journal* 67, 2 (2013): 207–28.

Meisami, Sayeh. 'Mullā Ṣadrā's Philosophical Arguments for the Necessity of the Imamate'. *Religion Compass* 10, 10 (2016): 247–56.

Mohamad Antang, Suzalie. 'Islamic Dimension in Malaysian Foreign Policy Towards the Muslim World'. *IKIM Journal of Islam and International Affairs* 1, 4 (2005): 63–81.

Mushkat, Roda. 'Is War Ever Justifiable? A Comparative Survey'. *Loyola of Los Angeles International and Comparative Law Journal* 9, 2 (1987): 227–317.

OIC Journal. [Full journal]. Issue no. 26 (January–March 2014).

'Al-Othaimeen Commends KSA and Arab Alliance Initiatives to Support Yemen'. Issue 39 (January–April 2018), p. 12.

Roy, Olivier. 'La communauté virtuelle: L'internet et la déterritorialisation de l'islam' [The Virtual Community: The Internet and the

Deterritorialisation of Islam]. *Réseaux: Communication, Technologie, Société* 18, 99 (2000): 219–37.

Rubin, Uri. 'The "Constitution of Medina": Some Notes'. *Studia Islamica* 62 (1985): 5–23.

Sachedina, Abdulaziz. 'A Treatise on the Occultation of the Twelfth Imamite Imam'. *Studia Islamica* 48 (1978): 109–24.

Saffari, Said. 'The Legitimation of the Clergy's Right to Rule in the Iranian Constitution of 1979'. *British Journal of Middle Eastern Studies* 20, 1 (1993): 64–82.

Saikal, Amin. 'How Islamic Has the "Islamic State" Been?' *Journal of Muslim Minority Affairs* 38, 2 (June 2018): 143–52.

'Women and *Jihad*: Combating Violent Extremism and Developing New Approaches to Conflict Resolution in the Greater Middle East'. *Journal of Muslim Minority Affairs* 36, 3 (2016): 313–22.

Schweizer, Thomas. 'Embeddedness of Ethnographic Cases: A Social Networks Perspective'. *Current Anthropology* 38, 5 (December 1997): 739–60.

Serjeant, R. B. 'The Constitution of Medina'. *Islamic Quarterly* 8 (1964): 3–16.

Shaery-Eisenlohr, Roschanack. 'Iran, the Vatican of Shi'ism?' *Middle East Report* 233 (Winter 2004): 40–3.

Shafaei, Fatemeh and Badaruddin Mohamed. 'Malaysia's Branding as an Islamic Tourism Hub: An Assessment'. *GEOGRAFIA: Malaysia Journal of Society and Space* 11, 1 (2015): 97–106.

Shimamoto, Takamitsu. 'Leadership in Twelver Imami Shi'ism: Mortaza Motahhari's Ideas on the Imamate and the Role of Religious Scholars'. *JISMOR* 2 (2006): 37–57.

Solomon, Hussein. 'The Particular Role of Religion in Islamic State'. *South African Journal of International Affairs* 23, 4 (2016): 437–56.

Sorenson, David S. 'Priming Strategic Communications: Countering the Appeal of ISIS'. *Parameters* 44, 3 (2014): 25–36.

Stewart, Iain. 'The Critical Legal Science of Hans Kelsen'. *Journal of Law and Society* 17, 3 (1990): 273–308.

Thompson, Mark. 'Assessing the Impact of Saudi Arabia's National Dialogue: The Controversial Case of the Cultural Discourse'. *Journal of Arabian Studies* 1, 2 (2011): 163–81.

Vertovec, Steven. 'Migration and Other Modes of Transnationalism: Towards Conceptual Cross-Fertilization'. *The International Migration Review* 37, 3 (Fall 2003): 641–65.

Wagemakers, Joas. 'The Concept of Bay'a in Islamic State Ideology'. *Perspectives on Terrorism* 9, 4 (2015). www.terrorismanalysts.com/pt/index.php/pot/article/view/448.

'The Enduring Legacy of the Second Saudi State: Quietist and Radical Wahhabi Contestations of *al-Wala' wa-l-Bara'*. *International Journal of Middle East Studies* 44, 1 (2012): 93–110.

Zolondek, Leon. 'Ash-Sha'b in Arabic Political Literature of the 19th Century'. *Die Welt des Islams*, New Series 10, 1/2 (1965): 1–16.

'The Language of the Muslim Reformers of the Late 19th Century'. *Islamic Culture* 37, 3 (July 1963): 155–62.

News Articles

Alsharif, Asma. 'Organization of Islamic Cooperation Suspends Syria'. *Reuters*, 16 August 2012. www.reuters.com/article/us-syria-crisis-islamic-summit/organization-of-islamic-cooperation-suspends-syria-idUSBRE87 E19F20120816. Accessed 5 February 2018.

al-Ansari, Jubayr. 'Fatwa "ghariba" li-al-Qaradawi hawl al-hajj tuthir ghadban [Al-Qaradawi's "Strange" Fatwa on the Hajj Raises Anger]. *al-Sharq al-Awsat*, 11 Dhu al-Hijja 1439 A.H./22 August 2018. https://aawsat.com/home/article/1370436/-فتوى-«غريبة»-للقرضاوي-حول-الحج-تثير غضباً. Accessed 18 October 2018.

Arab News. 'Bangladesh Launches Billion Dollar "Model" Mosques to Counter Radicals', 6 April 2018. www.arabnews.com/node/1280101/world. Accessed 25 May 2018.

'Call for Female Departments at Islamic University', 8 February 2016. www.arabnews.com/saudi-arabia/news/877201. Accessed 22 September 2018.

'King Fahd Qur'an Printing Complex Distributes 329,766 Prints and Audio Materials', 6 August 2012. www.arabnews.com/king-fahd-quran-printing-complex-distributes-329766-prints-and-audio-materials. Accessed 7 July 2014.

Arefi, Armin and Pauline Tissot. 'L'Arabie saoudite, pays géniteur du radicalisme' [Saudia Arabia, the Birthplace of Radicalism]. *Le Pointe*, 12 September 2016. www.lepoint.fr/monde/l-arabie-saoudite-geniteur-du-radicalisme-12-09-2016-2067860_24.php. Accessed 3 December 2017.

Basyir, Mohamed. 'Penang-based Muslim NGOs Call for Urgent Action on Rohingya Crisis'. *New Straits Times*, 7 September 2017.

BBC News. 'Ayatollah Sentences Author to Death', 14 February 1989. http://news.bbc.co.uk/onthisday/hi/dates/stories/february/14/newsid_25 41000/2541149.stm. Accessed 16 November 2018.

'IS leader Abu Bakr al-Baghdadi's Son "Killed in Syria"', 4 July 2018. www.bbc.com/news/world-middle-east-44710004. Accessed 5 July 2018.

'Islamic State Releases "al-Baghdadi Message"', 14 May 2015. www.bbc
.com/news/world-middle-east-32744070. Accessed 17 November 2018.

'Pakistan: "Father of Taliban" Cleric Buried after Attack', 3 November 2018.
www.bbc.com/news/world-asia-46084410. Accessed 3 November 2018.

Brimelow, Ben. 'ISIS Wants to Be as Dangerous as the Taliban – But It's Not
Even Close'. *Business Insider*, 12 February 2018. www.business
insider.com.au/isis-taliban-afghanistan-terrorism-2018-2?r=US&IR=T.
Accessed 5 July 2018.

Bunglawala, Inayat. 'Bringing Back the Caliphate'. *The Guardian*, 16 July
2007. www.theguardian.com/commentisfree/2007/jul/16/bringingback
thecaliphate?CMP=Share_iOSApp_Other. Accessed 3 November 2018.

Burchill, Scott. 'Radical Islam and the West: The Moral Panic behind the
Threat'. *The Conversation*, 16 June 2015. https://theconversation.com/
radical-islam-and-the-west-the-moral-panic-behind-the-threat-43113.
Accessed 17 November 2017.

Callimachi, Rukmini. 'To the World, They Are Muslims. To ISIS, Sufis Are
Heretics'. *The New York Times*, 25 November 2017. www.nytimes
.com/2017/11/25/world/middleeast/sufi-muslims-isis-sinai.html. Accessed
16 November 2018.

Cheng Wee, Teo. 'More Malays Say They Are Muslim First: Malaysian Poll'.
Straits Times, 12 August 2015. www.straitstimes.com/asia/se-asia/more-
malays-say-they-are-muslim-first-malaysian-poll. Accessed 3 November
2018.

Coca, Nithin. 'Islamic Leaders Have Nothing to Say about China's Internment Camps for Muslims'. *Foreign Policy*, 24 July 2018. https://foreign
policy.com/2018/07/24/islamic-leaders-have-nothing-to-say-about-chinas-
internment-camps-for-muslims/. Accessed 18 December 2018.

Crescent International. 'Hajj Beyond Rituals', 27 Dhu-al-Qa'da–12 Dhu-al-
Hijja 1416 A.H./16–30 April 1996.

Dabiq. 'Abandon the Lands of Shirk … and Come to the Land of Islam',
Issue 8, Jumada al-Akhira 1436 A.H./March–April 2015, pp. 28–9.
https://azelin.files.wordpress.com/2015/03/the-islamic-state-e2809cdc48
1biq-magazine-8e280b3.pdf. Accessed 22 September 2018.

'And Allah Is the Best of Plotters', Issue 9, Sha'ban 1436 A.H./May–June
2015, pp. 50–9. https://azelin.files.wordpress.com/2015/05/the-islamic-
state-e2809cdc481biq-magazine-9e280b3.pdf. Accessed 12 September
2018.

'The Concept of Imamah Is from the Millah of Ibrahim', Issue 1, Ramadan
1435 A.H./June–July 2014 A.H./July 2014, pp. 24–5. https://jihadology
.net/2014/07/05/al-%E1%B8%A5ayat-media-center-presents-a-new-issue-
of-the-islamic-states-magazine-dabiq-1/. Accessed 16 November 2018.

'The Extinction of the Greyzone', Issue 7, Rabi' al-Akhir 1436 A.H./ January–February 2015, pp. 54–66. https://archive.org/stream/Dabiq Magazine_07/DabiqMagazine_07. Accessed 16 August 2018.

'A Fatwa for Khurasan', Issue 10, Ramadan 1436 A.H./June–July 2015, pp. 18–24. https://archive.org/details/Dabiq10_20150714. Accessed 20 September 2018.

'From Hijrah to Khalifa', Issue 1, Ramadan 1435 A.H./July 2014, pp. 35–40. https://jihadology.net/2014/07/05/al-%E1%B8%A5ayat-media-center-presents-a-new-issue-of-the-islamic-states-magazine-dabiq-1/. Accessed 16 November 2018.

'Islam Is the Religion of the Sword, Not Pacifism', Issue 7, Rabi' al-Akhir 1436 A.H./January–February 2015, pp. 20–4. https://azelin.files.word press.com/2015/02/the-islamic-state-e2809cdc481biq-magazine-722.pdf. Accessed 16 August 2018.

'A New Era Has Arrived of Might and Dignity for the Muslims', Issue 1, Ramadan 1435 A.H./July 2014, p. 9. https://jihadology.net/2014/07/05/al-%E1%B8%A5ayat-media-center-presents-a-new-issue-of-the-islamic-states-magazine-dabiq-1/. Accessed 16 November 2018.

'The Rafidah: From Ibn Saba' to the Dajjal', Issue 13, Rabi' al-Akhir 1437 A.H./January–February 2016, pp. 32–45. https://jihadology.net/2016/01/19/new-issue-of-the-islamic-states-magazine-dabiq-13/. Accessed 30 July 2018.

'The Twin Halves of the Muhajirin', by Umm Sumayyah Al-Muhajirah, Issue 8, Jumada al-Akhira 1436 A.H./March–April 2015, pp. 32–7. https://azelin.files.wordpress.com/2015/03/the-islamic-state-e2809cdc 481biq-magazine-8e280b3.pdf. Accessed 15 August 2018.

'Two Camps with No Third in Between', section of 'The Extinction of the Greyzone', Issue 7, Rabi' al-Akhir 1436 A.H./January–February 2015, p. 66. https://azelin.files.wordpress.com/2015/02/the-islamic-state-e2809 cdc481biq-magazine-722.pdf. Accessed 16 August 2018.

'A Window into the Islamic State', Issue 4, Dhul-Hijjah 1435 A.H./September–October 2014, p. 27. https://azelin.files.wordpress.com/2015/02/the-islamic-state-e2809cdc481biq-magazine-422.pdf. Accessed 19 September 2018.

al-Dhakil, Khalid. 'Al-'Ubaykan bayna rafad al-jihad wa-al-ta'yush ma'al-ihtilal' ['Ubaykan between the Rejection of Jihad and Coexistence with the Occupation]. *al-Ittihad*, 24 November 2004. www.alittihad.ae/wajhatdetails.php?id=8261. Accessed 16 October 2017.

al-Dhayadi, Mashari. 'Hal intahat 'al-Sahwa' fi al-Sa'udiyya?' [Has the Sahwa Ended in Saudi Arabia?]. *Al-Sharq al-Awsat*, Issue 14220, 13 Safar 1439 A.H./3 November 2017. https://

مشاري-الذايدي/هل-انتهت-"الصحوة"-في-«الصحوة»-في-هل-انتهت/الذايدي-مشاري
السعودية؟. Accessed 23 August 2018.

al-Dussari, Salman. 'Intiha' tasyis qadiyya Khashoqji' [The Politicisation of Khashoggi's Case Is Over]. *al-Sharq al-Awsat*, Issue 14599, 9 Rabi'al-Awwal 1440 A.H./17 November 2018. https://aawsat.com/home/article/1466101/قضية-تسييس-انتهاء/الدوسري-سلمان خاشقجي. Accessed 17 November 2018.

Edroos, Faisal. 'Erdogan Calls on Muslim Countries to Unite and Confront Israel'. *al Jazeera*, 19 May 2018. www.aljazeera.com/news/2018/05/ erdogan-calls-muslim-countries-unite-confront-israel-180518185258629 .html. Accessed 10 June 2018.

Fandy, Mamoun. 'The Hawali Tapes'. *The New York Times*, 24 November 1990.

Fatany, Samar. 'Let Us Unite against Radicals and Promote Peaceful Coexistence'. *Saudi Gazette*, 26 July 2013. www.saudigazette.com.sa/article/ 54040/Let-us-unite-against-radicals-and-promote-peaceful-coexistence. Accessed 24 February 2018.

Goldberg, Jeffrey. 'Saudi Crown Prince: Iran's Supreme Leader "Makes Hitler Look Good"'. *The Atlantic*, 2 April 2018. www.theatlantic .com/international/archive/2018/04/mohammed-bin-salman-iran-israel/ 557036/. Accessed 15 May 2018.

Habibi, Nader. 'How Turkey and Saudi Arabia Became Frenemies – and Why the Khashoggi Case Can Change That'. *The Conversation*, 18 October 2018. https://theconversation.com/how-turkey-and-saudi-arabia-became-frenemies-and-why-the-khashoggi-case-could-change-that-105021. Accessed 15 November 2018.

Hatayta, Abd al-Sattar. '"Layihat al-irhab" tabruz "wahdat al-hadaf" bayn al-mutatarifin [The "Terrorist List" Highlights "Unity of Purpose" among Extremists]. *al-Sharq al-Awsat*, Issue 14074, 15 Ramadan 1438 A.H/ 10 June 2017. https://aawsat.com/home/article/947911/تبرز-«الإرهاب-لائحة» «الهدف-وحدة»-بين-المتطرفين. Accessed 7 August 2018.

al-Hayat. "An "al-Jabha al-Islamiyya al-'Alamiyya" li-qatl al-Amrikan' [From the "Islamic World Front" for Killing the Americans], 10 March 1998. www.alhayat.com/article/948657. Accessed 15 February 2019.

Irish, John. '"Wiping out" Extremist Ideology Is My Mission: Head of Saudi-based Muslim Body'. *Reuters*, 25 November 2017. www.reuters.com/article/us-saudi-islam/wiping-out-extremist-ideology-is-my-mission-head-of-saudi-based-muslim-body-idUSKBN1DO1JV. Accessed 1 December 2017.

Khashoqji [Khashoggi], Jamal. 'Lam ya'ud hilalan shi' [Is No Longer a Shi'ite Crescent]. *Al-Hayat*, 15 June 2013. www.alhayat.com/article/ 436712/. Accessed 22 July 2018.

Le Monde. 'Après la catastrophe de La Mecque, Téhéran invite le monde islamique à retirer la garde des lieux saints à l'Arabie saoudite' [After the Catastrophe at Mecca, Tehran Asks the Islamic World to Take Custody of the Holy Places in Saudi Arabia], 6 July 1990.

Ma, Alexandra. 'Why the Muslim World Isn't Saying Anything about China's Repression and "Cultural Cleansing" of Its Downtrodden Muslim Minority'. *Business Insider Australia*, 27 August 2018. www .businessinsider.com.au/why-muslim-countries-arent-criticizing-china-uighur-repression-2018-8?r=US&IR=T. Accessed 5 September 2018.

al-Marsad. 'Bi-al-Fidyu: al-daʿia ʿAbd al-ʿAziz al-Fawzan yukshaf ʿan bidʿa-tayn ibtalayat bi-hima al-umma al-islamiyya bi-yawm ʿAshura' [Video: Caller ʿAbd al-ʿAziz al-Fawzan Reveals Two Innovations Plagued the Islamic *umma* on the Day of ʿAshura], 1 October 2017. https://al-marsd .com/160501.html. Accessed 22 November 2017.

Miller, Judith. 'War in the Gulf: Muslims; Saudis Decree Holy War on Hussein'. *The New York Times*, 20 January 1991, p. 18.

Nambiar, Predeep. 'Malaysian NGOs Rouse Muslims to Defend Rohingyas'. *FMT*, 8 September 2017. www.freemalaysiatoday.com/category/nation/ 2017/09/08/malaysian-ngos-rouse-muslims-to-defend-rohingyas/. Accessed 10 December 2017.

Osman, Nadine. 'Muslim NGO Raises $500,000 for Rohingya Crisis'. *The Muslim News*, 28 December 2017. http://muslimnews.co.uk/newspaper/ world-news/muslim-ngo-raises-500000-rohingya-crisis/. Accessed 9 November 2018.

al-Otaiba, Yousef. 'Our Nations Must Work Together to Stop This Cancer in All Its Forms'. *The Telegraph*, 20 September 2014.

Reuters. 'Iran, Saudi Spar over Running of Haj Pilgrimage', 5 September 2016. www.reuters.com/article/us-saudi-haj-iran-idUSKCN11B0Y0. Accessed 2 July 2018.

al-Riyad. 'Jumhuriyyat Indonesia tamnah al-safir al-saʿudi ʿAbdullah ʿalim al-wasam al-taqdiri min al-daraja al-mumtaza' [The Indonesian Repub-lic Awards Ambassador ʿAbdullah an Award of Scholarly Excellence]. Issue 14757, 20 Dhu-al-Qaʿda 1429 A.H./18 November 2008. www.alriyadh.com/388684, accessed 18 October 2018.

Rubin, Alissa J. 'Militant Leader in Rare Appearance in Iraq'. *The New York Times*, 5 July 2014. www.nytimes.com/2014/07/06/world/asia/iraq-abu-bakr-al-baghdadi-sermon-video.html. Accessed 5 July 2018.

al-Salim, Hamza. 'Al-Qaradawi!' *al-Jazira*, 16324, 13 Ramadan 1438 A.H./ 8 June 2017. www.al-jazirah.com/2017/20170608/lp3.htm. Accessed 19 August 2018.

al-Sari', Zayid. 'Mufti al-Saʿudiyya li-al-Qaradawi: mawqifik yadhkaruna bi-kibar al-ʿulama' ʿabr al-tarikh' [Saudi Mufti on al-Qaradawi: Your

Attitude Reminds Us of the Great Scholars of History]. *Elaph*, 6 June 2013. http://elaph.com/Web/news/2013/6/816758.html. Accessed 2 June 2018.

Saudi Press Agency. 'OIC Appoints New Assistant Secretaries General', 6 May 2018. www.spa.gov.sa/viewfullstory.php?lang=en&newsid= 1760141. Accessed 18 November 2018.

al-Sharq al-Awsat. 'Al-Jubayr: talab Qatar tadwil al-masha'ir al-muqadasa 'udwani wa i'lan harb dad al-Sa'udiyya' [Al-Jubayr: Qatar's Request to Internationalise the Holy Places Is Aggressive and a Declaration of War against Saudi Arabia], 6 Dhu-al-Qa'da 1438 A.H./30 July 2017. https:// aawsat.com/home/article/986271/. Accessed 20 July 2018.

'Mufti al-Sa'udiyya li-*al-Sharq al-Awsat*: da'wat tadwil al-haramayn 'haqida wa dala' [The Saudi Mufti to *al-Sharq al-Awsat*: Calls for the Internationalisation of the Holy Places Are Spiteful and Aberrant]. Issue 14126, 9 Dhu-al-Qa'da 1438 A.H./1 August 2017. https://aawsat.com/home/article/987646/دعوات-«الشرق-الأوسط»-لـ-مفتي-السعودية تدويل-الحرمين-«حاقدة-و-ضالة». Accessed 25 August 2018.

'Muhammad bin Salman: sanaqdi 'ala al-tatarruf . . . wa sana'ud ila al-Islam al-wasati' [Muhammad bin Salman: We Will Eliminate Extremism . . . We Will Return to Moderate Islam]. Issue 14211, 5 Safar 1439 A.H./25 October 2017. https://aawsat.com/home/article/1062851/محمد-بن-سلمان-سنقضي-على-التطرف وسنعود-إلى-الإسلام-الوسطي. Accessed 25 September 2018.

Shih, Gerry. 'After Years of Silence, Turkey Rebukes China for Mass Detention of Muslim Uighurs'. *The Washington Post*, 10 February 2019. www.washingtonpost.com/world/after-years-of-silence-turkey-rebukes-china-for-mass-detention-of-muslim-uighurs/2019/02/10/011 c7dd6-2d44-11e9-ac6c-14eea99d5e24_story.html?utm_term=.52d11 647b4c3. Accessed 19 February 2019.

al-'Ubaykan, Salih. 'Ma yajri fi-al-Iraq laysa jihadan' [What Is Going on in Iraq Is Not Jihad]. *al-Sharq al-Awsat*, Issue 9473, 20 Ramadan 1325 A.H./4 November 2004. http://archive.aawsat.com/leader.asp?article= 263861&issueno=9473#.W1k56FUzaUk. Accessed 16 October 2017.

al-Watan. 'Al-Shaykh al-Fawzan yu'qib 'ala iqtirahat al-Hiwar al-Watani . . .' [Shaykh al-Fawzan Follows the Proposals of the National Dialogue . . .], 30 June 2005. www.awbd.net/article.php?a=34. Accessed 17 February 2018.

Wood, Graeme. 'What ISIS Really Wants'. *The Atlantic*, March 2015. www.theatlantic.com/magazine/archive/2015/03/what-isis-really-wants/ 384980/. Accessed 12 November 2018.

Yackley, Ayal Jean. 'Turkish Leader Calls Xinjiang Killings "Genocide"'. *Reuters*, 11 July 2009. www.reuters.com/article/us-turkey-china-sb/turk

ish-leader-calls-xinjiang-killings-genocide-idUSTRE56957D20090710. Accessed 19 February 2019.

Yeni Şafak. 'Turkish NGOs Begin Aid Campaign for Rohingya Muslims', 20 July 2018. www.yenisafak.com/en/world/turkish-ngos-begin-aid-campaign-for-rohingya-muslims-3436881. Accessed 9 November 2018.

Zelin, Aaron Y. 'The Islamic State's Model'. *The Washington Post*, 28 January 2015. www.washingtonpost.com/news/monkey-cage/wp/2015/01/28/the-islamic-states-model/?noredirect=on&utm_term=.c7636fe93ebc. Accessed 17 November 2018.

Reports, Working Papers, and Policy Briefs

Amman Message. Amman: Royal Aal al-Bayt Institute for Islamic Thought, 2009.

Bunzel, Cole. 'From Paper State to Khilafat'. Analysis paper 19. Brookings Project on U.S. Relations with the Islamic World, March 2015. www.brookings.edu/wp-content/uploads/2016/06/The-ideology-of-the-Islamic-State.pdf. Accessed 12 November 2018.

Constitution of the Islamic Republic of Iran. Reproduced at Iran Chamber Society, *Iranian Laws and Government*. www.iranchamber.com/govern ment/laws/constitution_ch08.php. Accessed 4 June 2018.

Foreign Broadcast Information Service. '[Khomeini's] Speech at the Guards' Day Celebration'. Reported by Tehran Home Service, 24 April 1985. SAS-85-080, 25 April 1985.

Fradkin, Hillel. 'The Paradoxes of Shiism'. Report. Hudson Institute, Washington, DC, 29 May 2009. www.hudson.org/research/9885-the-para doxes-of-shiism. Accessed 20 July 2017.

Hassan, Hassan. 'The Sectarianism of the Islamic State: Ideological Roots and Political Context'. Carnegie Endowment for International Peace, Washington, DC, 13 June 2016. http://carnegieendowment.org/2016/06/13/sectarianism-of-islamic-state-ideological-roots-and-political-con text-pub-63746. Accessed 14 November 2018.

Kaur-Ballagan, Kully, Roger Mortimer, and Glenn Gottfried. 'A Review of Survey Research on Muslims in Britain'. Social Research Institute of Ipsos MORI, London, February 2018.

Kingdom of Saudi Arabia, *The March of Progress*. Riyadh: Ministry of Information, n.d., 2000 [?].

Kull, Steven. 'Muslim Public Opinion on US Policy, Attacks on Civilians and al Qaeda'. Report. WorldPublicOpinion.org, University of Maryland, College Park, 24 April 2007.

Lacroix, Stéphane. 'Islamic Dissent in an Islamic State: The Case of Saudi Arabia'. *AUC Forum*, American University in Cairo, Cairo, December 2010.

Levitt, Matthew. 'Charitable Organizations and Terrorist Financing: A War on Terror Status-Check'. *Policy Analysis*. Washington Institute for Near East Policy, Washington, DC, 19 March 2004.

Masbah, Mohammed, 'The Limits of Morocco's Attempt to Comprehensively Counter Violent Extremism'. Briefing paper. *Middle East Brief* 118. Crown Center for Middle East Studies, Brandeis University, Waltham, MA, May 2018.

MEMRI. 'Reactions and Counter-Reactions to the Saudi Clerics' Communiqué Calling for Jihad in Iraq'. Special Dispatch No. 896, 21 April 2005. www.memri.org/reports/reactions-and-counter-reactions-saudi-clerics-communiqu%C3%A9-calling-jihad-iraq#_ednref4. Accessed 2 November 2017.

  'Saudi Cleric Who Taught in U.S. on Al-Majd TV: "Allah Be Praised, America Is Collapsing..."'. Special Dispatch No. 2097, 30 October 2008. www.memri.org/reports/saudi-cleric-who-taught-us-al-majd-tv-allah-be-praised-america-collapsing-will-wes. Accessed 22 June 2018.

Mohamed, Ali and Kristin Smith-Diwan. 'Gulf Islamists Praise Erdogan Victory, Prophesy Revival of the Ummah'. The Arab Gulf States Institute in Washington, Washington, DC, 26 August 2016. www.agsiw.org/gulf-islamists-praise-erdogan-victory-prophesy-revival-of-the-ummah/. Accessed 4 September 2016.

Muslim World League. 'Bayan Rabitat al-'Alam al-Islami bi-shan majzara (al-Ghuta al-Sharqiyaa) bi-Dimashq' [MWL Statement on the Massacre in Eastern Ghuta in Damascus]. Report. 28 February 2018. www.themwl .org/web. Accessed 12 May 2018.

  'Rabitat al-'Alam al-Islami tudin itlaq malishiyya Houthi sarwkhan balis-tiyyan 'ala al-Riyadh' [The MWL Condemns the Launching of Houthi Missiles on Riyadh]. Report. 20 December 2017. www.themwl.org/web. Accessed 12 May 2018.

National Centre of Excellence for Islamic Studies. 'ISIS (Islamic State of Iraq and Syria): Origins, Ideology, and Reponses by Mainstream Muslim Scholars'. National Centre of Excellence for Islamic Studies, The University of Melbourne, Melbourne, 2016.

Olidort, Jacob. 'The Politics of "Quietist" Salafism'. Analysis paper 18. The Brookings Project on U.S. Relations with the Islamic World, February 2015. www.brookings.edu/wp-content/uploads/2016/07/Brookings-Analysis-Paper_Jacob-Olidort-Inside_Final_Web.pdf. Accessed 18 November 2018.

Organisation of Islamic Cooperation. 'Draft 34th Report of the Finance Control Organ of the Organisation of Islamic Cooperation on the Closing Accounts of the OIC's General Secretariat and its Specialised Organs for the Financial Year 2012'. OIC/FCO-34/2013/REP. Jeddah: Organisation of Islamic Cooperation, 2013.

Patten, Pramila. 'Human Rights Council Opens Special Session on the Situation of Human Rights of the Rohingya and Other Minorities in Rakhine State in Myanmar'. News brief. United Nations, Office of the High Commissioner for Human Rights, 5 December 2017. www.ohchr .org/EN/NewsEvents/Pages/DisplayNews.aspx?NewsID=22491&Lang ID=E. Accessed 9 November 2018.

Petersen, Marie Juul. 'Islamic or Universal Human Rights? The OIC's Independent Permanent Human Rights Commission'. DIIS Report 2012/13. Copenhagen: Danish Institute for International Affairs, 2012.

Pew Forum. 'Muslim World League and World Assembly of Muslim Youth'. *Religion and Public Life.* Pew Research Center, Washington, DC, 15 September 2010. www.pewforum.org/2010/09/15/muslim-networks-and-movements-in-western-europe-muslim-world-league-and-world-assembly-of-muslim-youth/#fnref-5859-24. Accessed 15 January 2018.

Pew Global Attitudes Project. 'Support for Terror Wanes Among Muslim Public. Islamic Extremism: Common Concern for Muslim and Western Publics'. Pew Research Center, Washington, DC, 14 July 2005.

Racimora, William. 'Salafist/Wahhabite Financial Support to Educational, Social and Religious Institutions'. Policy paper. Policy Department, Directorate-General for External Policies, European Parliament, Brussels, June 2013.

Rich, Paul B. 'How Revolutionary Are Jihadist Insurgencies?' Working paper 4/2015. Trends Research & Advisory, Abu Dhabi, 2015.

Rosset, Uri. 'Hizballah and Wilayat al-Faqih'. Working paper. The Eleventh Annual Herzliya Conference, The Interdisciplinary Center, Herzliya, Israel, 6–9 February 2011.

Schmid, Alex P. 'Challenging the Narrative of the "Islamic State"'. International Centre for Counter-Terrorism, The Hague, June 2015.

USCIFR. 'Study Revealed Numerous Passages in Saudi Textbooks Advocating Intolerance and Violence'. Report. United States Commission on International Religious Freedom, Washington, DC, May 2018.

Websites, Social Media, and Blogs

Abu Bakar, Mohamed. 'Regional Islamic Da'wa Council of Southeast Asia and the Pacific'. *Islamicus*, 14 July 2017. http://islamicus.org/regional-islamic-dawah-council-southeast-asia-pacific/. Accessed 15 July 2018.

al-'Awda, Salman. 'Asbab suqut al-duwal' [Causes of the Fall of Sates]. *islamweb.net*, 7 Safar 1411 A.H./28 August 1990. http://audio.islam web.net/audio/index.php?page=FullContent&audioid=13759#119704. Accessed 12 March 2018.

al-Banna, Hasan. 'Bayna al-qawmiyya wa-al-Islamiyya' [Between Regional Nationalism and Islam]. *Ikhwan Wiki*. https://translate.google.com.au/ translate?hl=en&sl=ar&tl=en&u=http%3A%2F%2Fwww.ikhwanwiki .com%2F&anno=2. Accessed 20 August 2017.

'Ila al-umma al-nahida' [To the Rising *Umma*]. *Ikhwan Wiki*. https:// translate.google.com.au/translate?hl=en&sl=ar&tl=en&u=http%3A% 2F%2Fwww.ikhwanwiki.com%2F&anno=2. Accessed 18 August 2017.

'Ila al-umma al-nahida 2' [To the Rising *Umma* 2]. *Ikhwan Wiki*. www.ikhwanwiki.com/index.php?title=الناهضة_الأمة_إلى_2. Accessed 18 August 2017.

'Mawqif al-Imam al-Banna min al-qawmiyya wa-al-wataniyya' [Position of Imam al-Banna on Regional Nationalism and Patriotism]. *Ikhwan Wiki*. www.ikhwanwiki.com/index.php?title=الوطنية_و_القومية_من_البنا_الإمام_موقف. Accessed 18 August 2017.

Dallal, Ahmad S., Yoginder Sikand, and Abdul Rashid Moten. 'Ummah'. *The Oxford Encyclopedia of the Islamic World*. Islamic Studies Online. www.oxfordislamicstudies.com/article/opr/t236/e0818?_hi=0&_pos=3#. Accessed 17 August 2017.

Fernandez, Alberto M. '"Kufr" and the Language of Hate'. *MEMRI Daily Brief* 98, 25 July 2016. www.memri.org/reports/kufr-and-language-hate. Accessed 12 February 2018.

al-Ghannushi, Rashid. 'Secularism and the Relation between Religion and the State from the Perspective of the en-Nahdah Party'. Transcript of speech made at the Center for the Study of Islam and Democracy, Tunisia, 2 March 2012. *Demi Rakyat*, Anwar Ibrahim Blog, 19 March 2012. http://anwaribrahimblog.com/2012/03/19/transcript-of-rachid-ghannouchis-speech-at-csid-tunisia-on-2-march-2012-on-secularism-and-relation-between-religion-and-the-state-from-the-perspective-of-the-en-nahdah-party/. Accessed 28 September 2017.

Gray, Shaykha Tamara. 'Who Belongs in the Ummah of the Prophet Muhammad?' YouTube video, 8 March 2016. www.youtube.com/ watch?v=zNeVsJeb_Gk. Accessed 5 November 2016.

al-Hawali, Safar. 'Jawab al-Shaykh Safar al-Hawali 'ama qadamathu al-ta'ifa al-Shi'a min matalib li-wali al-'ahd' [Shaykh Safar al-Hawali's Response to the Demands Made by the Shi'i Sect to the Crown Prince]. *DD-Sunnah.Net*. www.dd-sunnah.net/forum/showthread.php?t=16329. Accessed 14 July 2018.

Ibn Baaz, 'Abdul Azeez. 'al-Raja' min fadilatikum tawdih al-wala' wa-al-bara' li-man yakuna?' [Your Excellency, Please Clarify to Whom Does *al-Wala' wa-al-Bara'* Apply?]. *al-Imam Ibn Baz* [official website of Shaykh Ibn Baz]. https://binbaz.org.sa/old/37631. Accessed 24 March 2018.

'Ibn Baaz, 'Abdul Azeez. 'Ma haya al-wasa'il alati yastakhdimuhi al-Gharb li-tarwij afkarhu?' [What Are the Means Used by the West to Promote Its Ideas?]. *al-Riyasa al-'amma li-idarat al-buhuth al-'ilmiyya wa-al-ifta'*. www.alifta.gov.sa/Ar/IftaContents/Pages/IbnBazSubjects.aspx?language name=ar&View=Page&HajjEntryID=0&HajjEntryName=&Ramadan EntryID=0&RamadanEntryName=&NodeID=11094&PageID=246 &SectionID=4&SubjectPageTitlesID=38375&MarkIndex=0&0# الوسائلالتييستخدمهاالغربلترويجأفكاره؟. Accessed 22 February 2018.

Ibn Jibrin, 'Abdullah. 'Radd 'ala man qal 'ana 'awam al-rafida muslimun' [Answer to Those Who Say the Shi'a Are Muslims]. *DD-Sunnah.Net*, 26 July 2010. www.dd-sunnah.net/forum/showthread.php?t=104067. Accessed 18 January 2018.

Juma 'a, 'Ali. 'Mafhum al-Umma' [Understanding the *Umma*]. *al-Ahram*, 14 July 2014. Reproduced on his website. www.draligomaa.com/index المكتبة/مقالات/الأهرام/php.item/358-الأمة-وم——مفهـ. Accessed 8 March 2017.

al-Kittani, Abd al-Qadir. 'al-Ikhtilaf al-fuqaha' fi ijtihadathum wa turuq al-astifada minhu' [The Difference among the Jurists on Their Interpretations and Ways to Benefit from It], Lesson 4, al-Durus al-Hasaniyya [The Hasanid Lessons], Kingdom of Morocco, Wizarat al-Awqaf wa-al-Shu'un al-Islamiyya [Ministry of Endowments and Islamic Affairs], 14 Ramadan 1439 A.H./30 May 2018, www.habous.gov.ma/dourouss/1527-الدروس-الحسنية الدروس-الحسنية-2018/11140-عبد-القادر-الكتاني-اختلاف-الفقهاء-في-اجتهاداتهم-وطرق-الاستفادة-منه.html. Accessed 4 November 2018.

al-Maktaba al-'Arabiyya al-Kubra [The Great Arab Library]. *Al-Manar*, vol. 11, section 4, pp. 268–74. http://arabicmegalibrary.com/pages-8492-14-3571.html. Accessed 11 January 2017.

McCants, William. 'Islamic State Invokes Prophecy to Justify Its Claim to Khilafat'. Brookings Institute, 5 November 2014. www.brookings.edu/blog/markaz/2014/11/05/islamic-state-invokes-prophecy-to-justify-its-claim-to-khilafat/. Accessed 2 February 2015.

MEMRI. 'Saudi Professor of Islamic Law Abd al-Aziz Fawzan al-Fawzan Calls for "Positive Hatred" of Christians'. MEMRI TV, clip number 992. Middle East Media Research Institute, 16 December 2005. www.memri.org/tv/saudi-professor-islamic-law-abd-al-aziz-fawzan-al-fawzan-calls-positive-hatred-christians. Accessed 18 November 2017.

Myers, Lisa [and NBC Production Team]. 'More Evidence of Saudi Doubletalk?' *NBC News*, 26 April 2005. www.nbcnews.com/id/

7645118/ns/nbc_nightly_news_with_brian_williams-nbc_news_investi
gates/t/more-evidence-saudi-doubletalk/#.W1ked1UzaUk. Accessed 12
October 2017.

al-Qanat al-Hikma. 'Mufti al-Mamlaka al-Sa'udiyya 'Abd al 'Aziz Al al-
Shaykh yufti bi-wujub al-jihad fi Suriya madiyyan wa ma'nawiyyan'
[Mufti of the Kingdom of Saudi Arabia Pronounces on the Necessity of
Jihad Morally and Materially in Syria]. YouTube video, 9 March 2014.
www.youtube.com/watch?v=lvzOZEtvwJU. Accessed 26 July 2018.

Reliefweb. 'Islamic Solidarity Fund Projects Financing Approvals Total US
$249 million', 29 May 2017. https://reliefweb.int/report/occupied-pales
tinian-territory/islamic-solidarity-fund-projects-financing-approvals-
total-us. Accessed 5 February 2018.

Senanayake, Sumedha. 'Istanbul Conference Enflames Sectarian Tensions'.
Religioscope: www.religion.info, 23 December 2006. https://english.reli
gion.info/2006/12/23/iraq-istanbul-conference-enflames-sectarian-tensions/.
Accessed 9 January 2018.

Shariati, 'Ali. 'Mohammad Iqbal, A Manifestation of Self-reconstruction and
Reformation'. Dr Ali Shariati (website). www.shariati.com/english/iqbal
.html. Accessed 1 October 2017.

al-Shaykh, 'Abd al-'Aziz Al. 'Hal da'wa al-Shaykkh Ibn 'Abd al-Wahhab
da'wa takfiriyya?' [Was the Da'wa of Shaykh Ibn 'Abd al-Wahhab a
Takfiri Da'wa?]. *Riyasat al-'Amma li-idarat al-buhuth al-'ilmiyya
wa-al-iifta'* [General Presidency of Scholarly Research and *Ifta'*]. www
.alifta.net/Fatawa/FatawaChapters.aspx?languagename=ar&View=
Page&PageID=53&PageNo=1&BookID=6. Accessed 24 April 2018.

Solojuve1897. 'Shaykh Yusuf al-Qaradawi is asked about the aqeedah of al-
Azhar'. YouTube video, 30 November 2011. www.youtube.com/
watch?v=BG8PEU0Iqn8. Accessed 16 April 2017.

al-Sulayman, 'Abd al-Rahman. 'Arabic Translators International'. Online
forum, 17 October 2009. www.atinternational.org/forums/showthread
.php?t=7018. Accessed 14 November 2017.

Voice of Deoband. 'Turkey President Reciting Quran/Tayyip Erdogan Real
Sultan of Ummah'. YouTube video, 22 January 2017. www.youtube
.com/watch?v=EWOTxfdzKCg. Accessed 3 March 2018.

al-Zarqawi, Abu Musab. 'Zarqawi Letter', translated by Coalition Provisional Authority. U.S. Department of State, released online from
20 January 2001 to 20 January, 2009 at https://2001-2009.state.gov/
p/nea/rls/31694.htm.

Theses and Dissertations

Foody, Kathleen M. 'Thinking Islam: Islamic Scholars, Tradition, and the State in the Islamic Republic of Iran'. PhD dissertation, University of North Carolina, 2012.

Mavani, Hamid. 'Doctrine of Imamate in Twelver Shi'ism: Traditional, Theological, Philosophical and Mystical Perspectives'. PhD dissertation, McGill University, 2005.

Rezai, 'Ali Siyar. 'Velayat-e Faqih: Innovation or within Tradition'. Master's dissertation, Arizona State University, 2016.

Shafi, Perwez. 'Towards a General Theory of Islamic Revolution: The Problem of Legitimacy and the Transformation of the Contemporary Muslim Nation-State System'. PhD dissertation, Walden University, 1993.

Index